Holding On

Holding On

A STORY OF LOVE AND SURVIVAL

JO GAMBI

PORTRAIT

For more information on Rob and Jo Gambi visit
www.robandjogambi.com

Visit the Portrait website!

· ·

PORTRAIT

Portrait publishes a wide range of non-fiction, including
biography, history, science, music, popular culture and sport.

Visit our website to:

- read descriptions of our popular titles
- buy our books over the internet
- take advantage of our special offers
- enter our monthly competition
- learn more about your favourite Portrait authors

VISIT OUR WEBSITE AT: www.portraitbooks.com

Copyright © 2006 by Jo Gambi

First published in 2006 by Portrait
an imprint of Piatkus Books Ltd
5 Windmill Street
London W1T 2JA
e-mail: info@piatkus.co.uk

Reprinted 2006

The moral right of the author has been asserted

*A catalogue record for this book is
available from the British Library*

ISBN 0 7499 5083 8

Picture Credits:
Page 1 *bottom* G. Sergeant; **Page 13** *bottom left* B. Crouse
All other images are from the author's collection (Nikon cameras)

Set in Sabon by Phoenix Photosetting, Chatham, Kent
www.phoenixphotosetting.co.uk

Printed and bound in Great Britain by
MPG Books, Bodmin, Cornwall

For Rob . . .

Contents

THE SEVEN SUMMITS

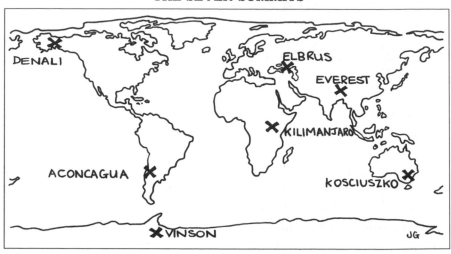

The Seven Summits and two Poles

Mountain	Height (m/ft)	Continent	Date
Denali (McKinley)	6,194 m / 20,320 ft	North America	12 June 2003
Kilimanjaro	5,895 m / 19,340 ft	Africa	30 July 2003
Vinson	4,897 m / 16,067 ft	Antarctica	15 December 2003
South Pole	90° south	Antarctica	29 December 2003
Aconcagua	6,959 m / 22,830 ft	South America	26 January 2004
Kosciuszko	2,228 m / 7,310 ft	Australia	7 March 2004
Everest	8,850 m / 29,035 ft	Asia	24 May 2004
Elbrus	5,642 m / 18,510 ft	Europe	20 July 2004
North Pole	90° north	Polar Ice cap	20 April 2005

Additional Summits 2003 to 2005

Cho Oyu (8,201m – Tibet), Mt. Shinn (4,660m – Antarctica), Cerro Fitz Gerald (5,600m – Argentina), Island Peak (6,189m – Nepal), Ama Dablam (6,897m – Nepal), Carstensz Pyramid (4,884m – Papua).

Acknowledgements

I would like to express my deep and heartfelt thanks to the following people . . .

To those who helped Rob through his cancer and on his journey back to health: Dr Bob Phillips, Rob's oncologist, for your tireless dedication to the cause. Thank you also Mr Meirion Thomas, Rob's surgeon, along with Fran Braxton, Marcella O'Brien, Eve O'Connor and all the other medical staff involved in his care at the Lister, Charing Cross, Cromwell and Hammersmith hospitals.

To those who helped Rob after he became ill in Nepal: Terry Moore and Carma for helping organise Rob's evacuation. The helicopter rescue pilot, for making repeated attempts to reach us in difficult conditions. Thank you for not giving up; it meant more to us than you'll ever know. All the hospital staff in Kathmandu and Bangkok, who helped stabilise and care for Rob while he awaited repatriation. Mr Thomas and those who treated Rob on his return to the UK.

To AMP and Henderson Global Investors: For providing continued global medical cover as part of Rob's sabbatical, without which things could have turned out so differently when Rob became ill in Nepal.

To our guides and friends we have climbed with over the years: For their friendship and experience. A special thank you to Nick Banks for the mountain skills and knowledge you passed on over the years, so much of which gave us the confidence to climb further afield.

To our expedition team leaders: Especially to Ryan Campbell and Clark Fyans (Mountain Trip) – thank you for believing in us; Russell Brice (Himalayan Experience) – thank you for giving us a chance; Luis Benitez (Adventure Consultants) – thank you for your enthusiasm and for being a comrade.

To our Sherpas and cook teams on Cho Oyu, Everest and Ama Dablam: With special thanks to Loppasang, Karsang, Kili Pemba, Nawang Drumdu, Lachu, KB, Chakra and Lhakpa – for your hard work, strength and humility. Thank you for enabling us to experience the wonders of your mountain home.

To all our friends that we have met while journeying in the mountains and Polar regions: I regret that there are not enough pages here to mention you all by name, but it has been a privilege to experience some beautiful corners of the planet alongside you. Never stop exploring!

To all those who generously donated to Cancer Research UK and the building of the Tibetan School as part of our Everest fundraising appeal: a very big thank you.

To those who have helped me with this book: Rob for being with me every step of the way – you have been awesome; Nigel Braggins for your unswerving patience, invaluable advice and design input, you have been a rock. For comments on the text, Mum and Dad, as always – you have been fantastic; my sister in law, Ros Hogbin and my editor Alan Brooke. Our family and friends, for their encouragement and help; especially my brother Tim Hogbin, Vix and Andy Maronge, Sarah McCulloch, Gray Levett and Gill Greenwood.

To our families and friends: Thank you for being a constant source of encouragement when Rob was ill and for your unending enthusiasm for our travels.

Last and most importantly: to Rob's parents – Tony and Maryse, and my parents – Geoff and Sylvia. Thank you for your unwavering love, support and prayers through all our trials and adventures.

And above all, to my dear husband Rob ... what can I say? Thank you for your love and for being you.

Climbing Terms

abseil (or rappel) – method of descending steep ground, sheer rock or ice by sliding down a rope using a friction device to control speed.

Acute Mountain Sickness – a range of symptoms caused by hypoxia (see **hypoxia**) which are due to the decreased atmospheric oxygen at altitude.

anchor – any method of attaching a rope to a mountain. This can be done by using a karabiner (clip) to hold the rope in combination with an anchoring device e.g. snow stake, ice screw, piton (metal peg), sling or nut (metal block jammed into rock cracks).

belay – a system whereby the climber is safeguarded on the rope by their climbing partner (the belayer), who is secured to the mountain by an anchor. In the event of the climber falling the belayer controls the rope using a friction brake (belay device).

Bergschrund – a large crevasse where the moving glacier or ice pulls away from the steeper ice of a mountain face.

col (or 'La' in Tibetan) – a depression or pass lying on a ridge usually between two peaks. Col is a Welsh word meaning saddle.

cornice – an overhanging mass of snow or ice on a mountain, formed by the wind as it blows snow off a ridge.

couloir – a steep gully in a mountainside, which may be filled with snow, ice or rock.

crampons – metal frames with downward and forward pointing spikes that are attached to the soles of the boot for climbing steep slopes or faces of ice or snow.

death zone – above 8,000m where thin air cannot support human life for more than a matter of hourse or at most days. Even above 5,500m life cannot be permanently sustained.

fixed rope (or fixed lines) – ropes fixed to the mountain by anchors that climbers clip into for safety on steep or exposed sections.

headwall – the steep slope of rock, snow or ice that forms the upper end of the valley or glacier.

hypoxia – a pathological condition in which the body is deprived of an adequate oxygen supply. At altitude climbers become hypoxic and can experience a range of symptoms including headaches, shortness of breath, fatigue, nausea, dizziness and reduced balance.

karabiner – a sprung metal clip used to hold a freely running rope, or to attach a rope to an anchor.

katabatic wind – the movement of cold air as it sinks and flows downwards off hills or glaciers.

leads – an expanse of open water (Arctic Ocean) that is revealed as wind or ocean currents cause the pack ice to break up.

mechanical ascender (or **jumar**) – a climbing tool used to ascend a rope, acting as a one way jamming device: freely sliding up the rope but locking when pulled downward. Used to climb steep/vertical ground once a fixed rope is in place.

nilas ice – a thin elastic rind of ice up to ten centimetres thick that easily bends on waves and swells under pressure. Dark nilas is up to five centimetres thick and is not safe to stand on. Light nilas is five to ten centimetres thick and can tolerate some loading.

pitch – a section of a climbing route, up to a rope length in extent

pressure ridge – an elongated pile of ice rubble (broken pack ice) up to several metres in height, which form as pressures from wind or ocean currents cause the ice to compress and break up.

serac – a pinnacle or block of ice formed as a mass of ice is pulled downwards by gravity and breaks apart.

sling – a loop of nylon tape, or rope used for many purposes in climbing e.g. hung over a rock spike to provide an anchor.

snow shoes – wide metal frames filled with a plastic or leather mesh, that are attached to the sole of boots and provide a broad platform to prevent the foot sinking into the snow.

snow stake – a metal stake approximately 50 cm long, driven into snow for use as an anchor when climbing.

spindrift – loose snow carried by the wind.

traces – two ropes that run from a waist or chest harness and attach to a sled or pulk.

whiteout – bad weather resulting in severely restricted or nil visibility.

Prologue

IN A REMOTE high valley of the Himalaya, our solitary tent stood at 4,300 metres. Daylight had long since drained from the sky and the towering sentinels of rock and ice loomed over us in the darkness. I felt utterly alone.

Crawling back into the tent, I lay next to Rob and prayed. There was nothing more I could do. It was 7.45 pm on Sunday, 6 October 2002 – 48 hours since Rob had become ill. In just two days he'd deteriorated significantly. Something was wrong with his intestines, but this was no ordinary affliction. His symptoms didn't add up. Rob was not the strong, capable husband I'd had just days ago.

The mountains of our dreams had become our waking nightmare. Swirling wreaths of cloud now entombed their once enticing rock towers and left us trapped. In our tiny canvas home, the minutes passed like hours. I listened to Rob's every groan.

'Are you OK, Honey?' I whispered in the blackness.

'Feel worse,' Rob mumbled from his sleeping bag.

'What can I do?'

'Just pray.' Returning to our silent worlds of fear and pain, I lay back on my sleeping bag. The ice crystals dropped onto my face, but I didn't notice them any more. There seemed little chance of Rob improving without medical intervention, but here, high in the mountains, there was nothing that could be done.

I tried to ignore my fears, but they crawled uninvited from the recesses of my mind to torment me. Rob's blood was already thick due to the rarefied air at high altitude but now it was thickening still further. He couldn't eat, he couldn't even drink, yet he was constantly vomiting. Critically dehydrated as he was, a fatal blood clot could form at any moment. If it lodged in his heart, brain or lungs, their function would be compromised in an instant. These thoughts hung in my mind like a death sentence.

This was only the first week of our first expedition and already we'd failed. How farcical that we had dreamed of the Seven Summits. We'd barely even started and it was all over. At 6,476 metres, Mera Peak – the highest trekking peak in Nepal – was merely intended to test us at altitude, but now it was testing Rob's very existence.

I'd met Rob seven years ago, we'd been married for six. Despite our love for the mountains, our busy careers had always prevented us attempting anything this high. But now we'd carved out time to be together and follow our dreams.

Just days ago we'd stood side by side, ready to face the high places together. Now our battle was redefined. The unseen enemy was at our door once again. But I knew Rob was a fighter, he would not allow difficulties to prevail. When he had faced cancer for a second time, just four years after we'd married, he had become more determined than ever to seize life. We weren't here by chance. This was the culmination of years of dreams, plans and training. Rob had made death wait before and I prayed he would do so again.

Lying in the stillness of the night, I longed for daylight – for with dawn would come hope. Hope that we could call for a helicopter. Hope that I could get Rob out of this seemingly godforsaken place. Hope that Rob would survive.

Holding
On

CHAPTER 1

Rendezvous

'Only those who risk going too far can possibly find out how far one can go.'

T.S. Eliot

'BYE GUYS – have a good weekend,' I called back over my shoulder. 'You too Jo, happy sailing!'

It was 5.45 pm on Friday, 17 June 1995. I was determined to leave the office early, keen to get to the south coast quickly to prepare for my sailing exam the next day. With the train strike I knew traffic was bound to be heavy.

Out through the heavy rotating doors, I jostled through the workers and tourists on Baker Street. Pondering the last meeting of the day I swiftly resolved to put Marks and Spencer out of my mind for the next 48 hours.

As usual I had no seat on the tube and with the hot weather I was left feeling dirty and sticky. But today was Friday so I didn't care. In no time at all I'd changed into my shorts and T-shirt at my Kensal Green bed-sit and was at the wheel of my little red Peugeot picking my way through the Friday traffic. I was heading towards my rendezvous outside the Hammersmith Palais nightclub.

The rendezvous was with a stranger called Rob Gambi. I hadn't met him before but he'd contacted me a few days earlier needing transport to the south coast. He'd lent his car to his parents for their travels in Europe but the train strike had left him stranded. I was supposedly looking out for someone with a holdall.

Thirty minutes later, despite gridlock outside the BBC at Shepherds Bush, I had driven the five miles to Hammersmith. Spotting a man who fitted the description, I landed my fist on the horn. He ran over and opened my passenger door.

'Hi – are you Rob?' I enquired, wanting to be sure I'd got the right 'man with holdall'.

'Yes. You must be Jo?'

'That's me. Hop in, better not stop here.'

Throwing his holdall in the back, he jumped in and we sped away, avoiding the attentions of a lurking traffic warden. 'Thanks for picking me up,' Rob started. A cheeky reply popped into my head, that I wasn't picking him up, I was merely providing transport, but I thought better of it.

The weekend went well and those of us sitting our day skipper exam passed successfully. Rob was staying on to do the intensive one-week course. Having said my goodbyes to the crew, I was pulling out of the marina car park when he raced over to me.

'Do you want to meet for a drink sometime in London?' he said leaning in through my passenger window.

Oh, here we go, I thought, trying to maintain a neutral face.

'Yeah – sure.'

'Great. Have you got a number?' he asked. I jotted it down, not wanting to be impolite. I didn't want to commit to anything resembling a date right now. He seemed harmless enough, though.

In the end the drink in London fell by the wayside, but I didn't escape that easily. My excuse of being on holiday in Chamonix was the perfect alibi. Or so I thought, until Rob announced that he too would coincidentally be in the French Alps, the very same week.

'Yeah – really,' he said. 'I'm visiting my parents in Lausanne, near Chamonix. I've got to collect my car.' Despite my suspicions, it sounded plausible as I knew he'd lent his parents the car while they were over from Australia. Nevertheless, I was feeling cautious. I'd only recently concluded a relationship.

'I don't know how it'll work for us to meet up. I'm actually climbing with a friend.'

'What are you going to climb?' Rob enquired.

'Hopefully the Matterhorn,' I said, imagining I would put him off further questions, even though I wasn't sure I'd be doing any such thing.

'Why don't I climb the Matterhorn with you?' he joked. But before I could respond he'd made another suggestion. 'Or . . . how about meeting up for just a walk?'

In spite of his persistence, I thought his suggestion was a good one. 'OK. Let's meet for a walk then,' I conceded, giving him details, albeit rather vague ones, of where I'd be staying.

*

A week later, full of summer holiday anticipation, I arrived at Geneva Airport with my friend Helen. For years both of our families had hiked together in the British hills and now Helen and I were venturing further afield to the European Alps. We yanked our rucksacks off the luggage conveyor and collected our ice axes from outsize baggage. The following morning we were up in the mountains above the valley of Chamonix doing what we loved, stomping up the hills, breathing in the clear mountain air and soaking up the views. We were itching to get climbing, but for the more serious stuff we were going with our guide Nick Banks.

The night before meeting Nick, Helen and I were in our hostel chomping through a hearty bowl of pasta when there was a knock at the door.

'Hey there – anyone at home?' I instantly recognised the Australian accent. Somehow Rob had managed to locate our hostel with uncanny ease despite my vague directions. Trying not to look too impressed by his initiative, I calmly invited him in and introduced him to Helen.

'Didn't want to interrupt your dinner, but how do you fancy meeting up for a walk tomorrow?' Rob asked.

'That would be great, but we'd planned to do some climbing with our guide.'

'No worries. Could I come climbing with you guys?'

I paused, somewhat surprised at such a direct request. 'I couldn't say. Given the type of climbing we're going to do, our guide may not want more than two of us on the rope. Why don't you come and ask him yourself tomorrow? We're meeting for coffee at nine in the Terrasse café.'

'Great, see you then.' Leaving us to our pasta Rob slipped out with a satisfied smile, though wondered what he was getting himself into.

The next morning was again crisp and clear as Helen and I set out to meet Nick and make plans for the next few days. Within minutes we were relaxing outside the café, sipping lattes and exchanging stories. Nick was a Kiwi, though he'd lived in north Wales for years. He was a well-known and respected guide and spent most of his summers working in the Alps. I admired Nick for his no-nonsense attitude and solid professionalism, and his safety record was second to none.

We discussed our ideas and agreed to climb some Chamonix peaks over the next few days. Just as we'd settled our plan Rob arrived.

'Nick, this is Rob – another Antipodean who's a long way from home.'

'All right mate, good to meet ya,' Nick said, reaching over to shake hands.

I'd only met Rob recently, so he was still an unknown quantity. I knew he was born in Australia and his parents were European, although they grew up in Egypt. I'd also found out that he worked in London as a fund manager, that he loved windsurfing – and that he'd had cancer recently. That was it. But despite barely knowing him, I couldn't ignore one fact – he was now in the middle of our planning meeting.

Settled with his croissant and coffee, Rob caught Nick's eye across the café table. 'So, do you think I could come climbing with you guys?'

'Ah.' Nick laughed and raised an eyebrow. 'Depends on whether the girls want you along, mate, and how much climbing you've done.' His blunt New Zealand style was refreshing. Smiling, I shrugged and nodded at Nick. I was happy either way but didn't want to make the decision. I hated saying no.

'Actually I haven't climbed before,' Rob announced quietly, studying Nick's face for his reaction.

'Never climbed?' Nick said scratching his head. Rob shook his head.

'So, you've never used crampons or an ice axe?'

'No.' Rob held his gaze.

'Harness?'

'No.'

'Have you ever done any hiking in the Alps then?' he asked with an incredulous smile.

'Not really,' said Rob, realising what was coming.

'Well then sorry mate, the answer is no, you can't come. But why don't you get a guide, buy some kit, do some routes, then you can come back and see me. How does that sound?'

I watched Rob's face intently. 'No worries,' he smiled. He was surprisingly pragmatic about Nick's refusal and seemed perfectly happy with the alternatives presented.

Off the hook, I sighed discreetly, no longer feeling responsible for this partial stranger gatecrashing our girlie holiday. Minutes later we'd said our goodbyes and disappeared into the bustling streets.

Nick, Helen and I were heading off to hike up to a mountain hut later that day. From there we planned to climb the Aiguille d'Argentière, a rocky snowcapped giant overlooking the Chamonix valley. We would make an alpine start, setting off around 2 am, while the snow pack was still frozen and stable, and climb through the night to summit just after dawn. Reflecting on the morning's conversations, I doubted that Rob would bother with Nick's suggestions. I guessed that the next time I would see him, if at all, would be back in the UK.

*

Just ten minutes after waving goodbye, Rob had found his way to Rue des Moulins. As a narrow cobbled walkway of cafés, restaurants and boutiques, it was crowded with hanging baskets that burst with myriad pinks and purples. This little corner of ancient Chamonix was home to the Bureau des Guides.

Stooping beneath the low door frame, Rob stepped inside. A scruffy chap with a face weathered beyond his years sidled over. '*Je peux vous aider?*' (can I help you?) he said, leaning on the chipped wooden front desk.

'Yes, I'd like to climb the Matterhorn,' said Rob, as if he was merely asking for a pound of tomatoes at the local market.

'Matterhorn, eh?'

'Yes, the Matterhorn,' Rob repeated.

'What climbing 'ave you done?' he enquired in a thick French accent.

'None.' Rob sensed again that his complete ignorance of climbing was something of a novelty; he was after all in the climbing Mecca of the Alps, if not the world. Alpinism was even considered to have been invented in Chamonix in 1760 when Horace Benedict de Saussure first offered a reward for summiting Mont Blanc, then a far more formidable task. Undeterred by his environment, Rob held his ground.

Another well-worn individual behind the desk peered up at him through his tousled hair, muttering '*un fou*' (madman). Rob pretended not to understand. Smiling at the man on the desk, he reiterated his request.

The man leant over the desk towards Rob. 'So . . .' He paused. 'You never climb but you like to climb Matterhorn . . . this week?'

'Yes.' Rob stuck to his guns.

'You never use crampons?'

'No.'

'Ice axe, 'arness?'

'Nothing.'

Suddenly the man pushed off the desk, clapping his hands together. 'OK, I tell you what we do. We give you a week stressing and straining to get fit, a bit of technical, a bit of climbing on rock, on steep ice, some cramponing, some ice axe. Then we take you up Matterhorn. OK. I 'ave just the guide for you. Philippe, he –'

'But,' interrupting him in full flow Rob confessed, 'I don't have any climbing boots, helmet, harness or an axe or –'

'Is no problem. You meet Philippe and you buy shop.' Rob took Philippe's number and headed for a phone booth, hoping it was merely the language barrier and not that he genuinely needed to buy the entire shop.

Moments later, Rob was in a booth and the phone was ringing.

'Is that Philippe?'

'*Oui*, 'allo.'

'My name is Rob –'

Before he could finish Philippe interrupted. 'Ah yes, you are Robert and you 'ave never climbed, is that true?' The conversation was beginning to have a familiar ring to it. 'And you 'ave no crampon, no 'arness, no ice axe, no boots, no 'elmet?'

'No, I need everything.' Rob said patiently, once again spelling out that he had done nothing, knew nothing and did not own one single piece of climbing kit.

'OK – *pas de problème*, Robert. We go, we buy and we fix. I meet you in 30 minute at Technicien du Sport shop.' And that was that.

Half an hour later in the shop Philippe kept thrusting all manner of climbing gear into Rob's hands. 'This is good, but I don't know if you like colour?' he said, waving some climbing trousers in the air. Next he handed Rob an ice axe. 'Is this good for length, Robert?'

'Dunno mate, you're the expert. I don't know one axe from another.' Inspecting the axe, Rob was thrilled to have his very own climbing weapon. Despite not knowing how to use it, he felt quite the mountaineer.

'Right,' said Philippe, 'you are ready for mountain!' Rob noticed a glint in his eye, but with all these new toys, there was no time to worry. Philippe had told him that tomorrow they were off to climb the Cosmique Arête, whatever that was.

*

The following day at 8.15 am, Nick, Helen and I topped out on the Aiguille d'Argentière. It had been a perfect clear night with enough moonlight to guide us most of the way without head torches. As we kicked our final steps into the snow of the summit ridge the panorama opened out before us, a carpet of white peaks jutting into the glowing dawn sky. Helen and I were mesmerised as we watched the sun's rays burst over the horizon. Looking back down to the valley, I wondered what Rob had eventually got up to. Would he have bothered with Nick's suggestion? Perhaps he was back in Lausanne with his parents.

*

At the same time, just a few valleys away, Rob and Philippe were riding the cable car up past the impressive cliffs of the Aiguille du Midi. But Rob's excitement had dissolved into terror as the cable car began to climb almost vertically.

Emerging from the lift at 3,842 metres, Philippe started nonchalantly to describe the route for their day ahead as if listing off directions in an A to Z. 'So Robert, today we climb Cosmique Arête, it is fantastic! You will like!'

Rob's wide eyes spun around wildly, scanning the horizon littered with impossibly high, jagged peaks. It was not at all obvious what Philippe was talking about, until he pointed upwards.

'What? Up that flipping thing there? You've got to be joking, mate,' blurted Rob.

'It is easy, Robert. I keep you safe on rope.'

'Right.' Rob's voice tailed off. Having seen what looked like a sheer drop of thousands of feet straight from the cable car station virtually all the way to the valley floor, he couldn't comprehend how they were even going to reach the base of the climb without killing themselves.

Within just 45 minutes, already breathless from the altitude, Rob was standing with Philippe at the base of the climb. 'This is good, Robert. Now we go up. You can follow, OK?'

'Uh-huh,' Rob replied, unconvinced.

'And Robert, don't climb with the hands, eh. Climb with the feet. OK?'

Rob nodded, muttering 'OK.' But everything was most definitely not OK. His thoughts were racing.

I had absolutely no idea what Philippe meant by 'don't climb with the hands'. It sounded like suicide, but I was in no mind to question details. All I felt was a sense of overwhelming dread. My spontaneous decision yesterday to take up a life-threatening extreme sport when I was approaching my forties, now felt somewhat deranged. In the comfort of the climbing shop, it had all seemed so harmless. Perhaps something like hill walking would have been a more sensible place to start. But it was too late now. I was here, and Philippe had just disappeared in some gully above me.

The rope trailed after Philippe, slithering like a snake along the base of the rock face. Rob was alone and an eerie silence fell around him as he waited for Philippe's signal. He was about to enter the vertical world.

Hours later, high on the arête, Rob clung motionless to the rock face as it peeled away beneath him. Thousands of feet below, the town of Chamonix nestled between the steep fir-clad valley walls. Rob's eyes darted left and right scanning the rock face for some imperfection, a small crack on which he could gain purchase. His eyes locked on an outcrop. That had to be his next handhold. Millimetre by millimetre his fingertips crawled up the cold granite. His face pressed into the hard unyielding rock. A grating sensation crept up his legs as his boots continued to lose traction on the sloping foothold. Out of time, he had to reach for the ledge. Sucking in his breath, he gave one final push.

But it was too little, too late. As he moved, his feet spun off their fragile perch, flinging his legs out into space. His head jerked into the rock face and a cracking sound reverberated as his helmet smashed into the rock. Slipping from his other handhold, Rob dropped away. With a last desperate attempt he threw his arm towards a ledge of rock. He missed and fell. The silence seemed to last for ever, even the breeze funnelling up the rock face was gone. Suddenly a whooshing noise pierced the silence. Rob's body was jerked upwards as his harness jammed like a vice around his waist. He swung, suspended by a single thin line, tight as a steel cable.

His chest thumped and his heart felt like it was pushing into his throat. Rob clenched the rope as if frozen to it, barely daring to breathe.

'Robert.' A voice echoed from the gully above. There was no-one to be seen and the blinding overhead sun made it impossible to make out anything as the cliff vanished skywards.

'Robert,' the voice came again, 'OK?'

'Philippe,' Rob shouted back, fighting for breath. 'I'm hanging.'

'OK, Robert. I 'ave you,' Philippe hollered. Rob's head fell forwards onto the rope.

'Robert, you must get back on the rock.'

Clearing his throat, Rob managed a strangled 'OK.' The chinstrap of the helmet dug into his throat and he wanted to rip it off, but not now. He had to get back onto the rock and Philippe couldn't help him with that. Clinging to the rope with one hand, Rob leant forward, his fingertips straining towards the ledge. Like a blind man his hand was reading the rock surface. He felt along a horizontal crack and jammed his fingers as deep as they would go. Hauling himself up he balanced precariously on a ledge, his helmet pressed hard into the wall. He shouted up to Philippe, 'I'm climbing.'

A distant 'OK' echoed off the walls and with that Rob once again began tentatively to ascend. Philippe had said they were nearly there, just a few more rope lengths to go, perhaps no more than 80 metres of vertical ascent. Rob was not going to be beaten now.

Fifty minutes later Philippe and Rob climbed over the viewing balcony platform of the Aiguille du Midi cable car station. They had finished with a dramatic and unusual entrance to the station as the climb wound its way straight up the rock face beneath the platform. It was 1.45 pm on 12 July 1995 and Rob had just climbed the famous Cosmique Arête. In so doing he had just completed the first ever rock climb of his life.

Clambering over the railings they hauled their rucksacks onto the platform and were immediately swamped by photographers, mainly Japanese, wildly snapping and chattering away while excitedly pointing in their direction. Two tiny Japanese women bustled forward waving their camera under Rob's chin. Still out of breath and thinking they wanted his services as a photographer, Rob reached for the camera.

'No, no. We have photo with you,' they demanded in stereo.

'Us?' But even as Rob laughed unbelievingly, the little ladies manoeuvred him and Philippe in front of the camera now held by a frail, wrinkled Japanese man. Smiles all round were followed by furious bowing and reversing away as the ladies left Rob and Philippe to relax after their efforts. Collapsing onto the platform, Rob felt ravenous but even with the smell of toasted cheese sandwiches and coffee drifting around, it was far too much effort to move again. Philippe patted Rob on his shoulder and they laughed as he examined his scratched, bleeding forearms.

'Unbelievable, mate. That was awesome. Can't believe what I've just done!'

'Very good first climb, Robert. We will make you ready for Matterhorn, *pas de problème.*'

'Hope the effort pays off . . . Will tomorrow be any easier?'

'Of course.' Phillipe said reassuringly

Somewhere between utter exhaustion and total euphoria, Rob stretched his legs on the warm wood of the deck and drifted away, recollecting his holidays in the Alps as a teenager.

I remember watching mountaineers from afar on precipitous ledges. I had total admiration for them but thought they were utter lunatics. I'd always had an intense fear of heights and I believed no-one could ever pay me enough to do something that crazy. Today, my feelings about climbers and climbing were unchanged, except now I was the crazy one, and, worse still, I was funding this madness out of my own pocket! There had to be an easier way to win a girl's interest, but now I was here I felt strangely hooked.

Rob had drifted into a deep peaceful sleep despite the hubbub around him. Philippe tapped his arm. 'Let's go, we need rest for tomorrow, ' he said, stubbing his cigarette out on the deck. In a tired daze Rob clambered to his feet, slinging his sack over his right shoulder and they headed for the cable car to the valley below.

*

The following day Nick, Helen and I had another early start and by 7 am we were enjoying views across France, Switzerland and Italy from the summit of Le Tour Noir, at 3,837 metres. As a rocky pinnacle at the head of the Argentière Glacier, its steep flanks were littered with shattered rocks, some the size of televisions, requiring delicate foot placements to avoid knocking debris onto the person below. Helen and I worked well together on this terrain and by sunrise Nick had christened us both 'twinkle toes'.

*

That very same morning Rob and Philippe were high above the valley floor again. Philippe was perched four metres above Rob on the other side of the bergschrund, a gaping crevasse, formed where the moving glacier is torn away from the ice wall of the steeper mountain flanks above.

'Come, Robert, I 'ave you.'

Rob stared into the bottomless chasm. It was the first crevasse he'd ever seen up close. Glancing at the seemingly insurmountable wall of ice between himself and Philippe, his gaze returned to the dark pit in front him. This was not turning out to be the relaxing wander in the alpine meadows he'd imagined two days ago. Inches from his feet, the ice quickly changed from a glistening blue into cold grey, abruptly receding into blackness as it plummeted away.

Rob raised his axes and took the plunge, launching out towards the ice face on the other side of the crevasse. He planted the axes firmly into the wall, his entire body pinned to the ice. One arm at a time he repeatedly swung his axes, hoping for the reassurance of a good hold. Ice shards clattered down onto his helmet. Though his lungs cried out for air he didn't dare breathe deeply for fear of disturbing his delicate holds. He craned his head down to check his foot position but suddenly averted his eyes, remembering the crevasse that gaped directly beneath him. He couldn't allow himself to see that right now.

'Robert. Keep climbing, *pas de problème*.'

Incredulous at Philippe's optimism, Rob muttered expletives under his breath in an attempt to channel his fear. His arms quivered, straining to stay attached to the ice. 'Hold me tight, Philippe,' he called and with three sharp intakes of breath started upwards, thrashing and kicking until he finally pulled himself over the upper edge of the bergschrund. There he crumpled in half, leaning onto his ice axe. The thin air made the effort of climbing even tougher and left him panting hard. 'Thought you said this climb would be easier than yesterday?' he said, trying to catch his breath.

'*Mais oui*. It is easier but a little more exposed.'

'More exposed – what's that?'

'When we get to rock ridge we have much air and big drop – but climbing is very good, good rock, you will see.' Rob wished he'd never asked.

It wasn't long before they'd left the steep snow and Rob felt the familiar grating of the rough granite digging into his forearms. They were perched high on the Petite Verte ridge, in places less than a boot's width wide. The airy ridge rose dramatically above the surrounding flanks of the mountain. As they crossed over to the other side Rob crouched low, trying to distract himself from the views below. The ground vanished all around for hundreds of feet, the disorienting sense of space and nothingness making him dizzy. Terrified by the exposure, feeling out of his depth, he could find no comfort anywhere. Everything inside him desperately wanted to cling to the rock and never move again. Fear gripped his stomach like a vice and voices inside his head battled for airtime – one telling him to go back before he got himself killed, the other cajoling him on. One manoeuvre at a time, Philippe and Rob continued slowly upwards.

Several harrowing hours later they were safely below the bergschrund once again. Rob had collapsed in a jubilant heap of rope and kit, revelling that he was alive and safely off the ridge.

'So, Philippe, is the Matterhorn more difficult than today?' Rob braced himself for the predictable answer.

'Yes. A little.' Knowing Philippe to be a master of understatement, this was not good news at all. 'You learn fast Robert but you 'ave time for Matterhorn – maybe next year eh?'

'Well, I do and I don't – maybe it'll be too late by then.' Rob mused resignedly.

*

At the head of the valley, not so far away Nick, Helen and I were now descending via a steeper but less friable route and we were making good progress. We could just see the Argentière mountain hut appearing from the rocky face that camouflaged it. Maybe another hour or so and we'd be there drinking tea and eating the hut guardian's apple pie. Just the thought of it gave me a spurt of energy. It was only 10.15 am but it was already hot work on the glacier with the blinding sun radiating off the ice in all directions. Even with my dark glasses, I was dazzled.

Finally, we trudged hot and sweaty up the steps of the hut, our metal climbing gear clanking as it swung from our harnesses. At last I could smell that apple pie. All that ever remained to be done at this stage was eat, walk to the valley and eat, shower and eat again – a fitting reward.

*

After the morning's work, Rob slowly gathered his gear and stuffed it haphazardly into his rucksack. Philippe was already back on his feet. Rubbing his hands together, he proposed a one-hour walk across the glacier up to a mountain hut for refreshments. In theory this didn't sound too stressful, but then neither had Philippe's description of anything else they'd done so far. Rob was wary, but the lure of refreshments so close seemed too tempting to ignore. 'Let's do it then, Philippe. I could murder a drink.'

The glacier was 'dry' due to the warmer summer temperatures leaving the ice grey and dirty, without its winter carpet of snow. Though less attractive to look at, this is considerably safer as the winter snows no longer hide the treacherous chasms beneath. Tramping through the tortured maze of ice ridges and crevasses Rob experienced a strange sensation. For the first time he was enjoying himself without being terrified.

At last, I wasn't clinging to vertical rock. Though surrounded by yawning crevasses, I could navigate safely around them. For the first time I was able to catch my breath and appreciate where I was. I was amazed at the towering serrated peaks that overshadowed our high valley and the tumbling masses of azure ice blocks on the glacier. The ice-chilled air flowing down the glacier was a welcome relief from the scorching sun. I was finally getting used to walking with crampons on my feet. On the glacier, my metal spikes had started to squeak in the different ice; it sounded as if I was walking on styrofoam. Hypnotised by Philippe's swishing rope and the chinking of my climbing gear, I momentarily forgot how tired I was.

As they neared the hut Rob thought again about the Matterhorn, frustrated that it was out of reach. But there was nothing he could do to change that in the few days that remained. He wondered if I would remember his declaration to climb the Matterhorn with me later that week and comforted himself that if he didn't see me again until the UK, maybe I would forget.

An hour and a half and several drinks later, Rob was beginning to feel human again as he and Philippe basked on the hut terrace. Clambering to his feet, Rob wandered off to find the facilities. Minutes later he returned across the terrace and stopped abruptly, unable to believe what he was seeing. He had spotted me, of all people, right there in front of him packing my rucksack. Seconds later I would have walked off that terrace and our paths would never have crossed.

CHAPTER 2

Roping Together

'Love is not about gazing at each other, but looking together in the same direction.'

Antoine de Saint-Exupery

'**J**o!' Rob shouted excitedly across the hut balcony. I spun around. 'How's it going?'

To my utter amazement, there was Rob. I was totally thrown. *What is he doing here? The only way to get here is across the glacier.*

'I'm here with Philippe, my guide,' Rob explained. 'Philippe, *vien ici, vien ici.*'

My head was spinning as I tried to absorb everything all at once. He'd never climbed before and now, a few days later – here he was, harnessed up, with his own guide. Attempting to remain as cool as possible, but failing, I exclaimed, 'Fantastic – wow, you're here!'

Philippe sauntered over, a roll-up cigarette hanging from the corner of his mouth. '*Bonjour, ça va?*' His cigarette bounced up and down as he spoke.

'*Ça va bien, merci,*' I replied shaking hands and feeling embarrassed about my terrible French accent compared to Rob's.

I turned back to Rob, noticing for the first time his toned physique. *Must be the climbing clothes*, I thought. Momentarily distracted by his smiling eyes, I caught myself, and started quizzing him. 'So, have you been climbing?' I hardly dared believe he had simply taken Nick's advice.

'Yep, just did the Petite Verte.'

'That's fantastic – how was it?' I suddenly realised that was the second time I had used the word 'fantastic' and I should probably tone it down.

'Absolutely scared the crap out of me!'

'Oh,' I said, surprised by his answer. 'But did you enjoy the views?' I blurted.

'Not really, spent most of the time holding on for dear life. Look at my arms.' Rob presented me with his forearms, a scratched and bloody sight.

'Did you fall?'

'Nope, just trying to hold on. What do ya reckon – think a climbing lesson would help?' he laughed.

I was amazed. 'Well done you for giving it a go. So are you coming down for a drink in the valley?' *Blast – now I've done it*, I thought. I had got carried away, but it was too late now. I hoped Nick and Helen wouldn't mind.

Just then I spotted the other two waiting for me on some rocks and excused myself. 'Look, I'd better go. Nick and Helen are waiting for me. We'll be in the café by the lift station. Cheerio.' With that I clumped off as fast as possible in my heavy plastic boots to catch up with the others.

Exiting the bottom of the téléphérique station in the valley below I did a double take. Rob and Philippe were already there. How could this be? They must have charged down the glacier and managed to get a cable car before us. I couldn't help but be impressed by Rob's commitment. Before we could even get our sacks off he had offered us all drinks and disappeared inside the café. Within minutes we were lost in the joy of ice creams, cold beers and comfy chairs.

'So are you still up for the Matterhorn then, Rob?' I asked.

'Maybe not this year,' Rob shrugged. I wasn't exactly surprised. Even though he had just managed two exposed alpine climbs, he'd still only started rock climbing yesterday. With Helen not keen and Rob's earlier enthusiasm abating, I reluctantly resolved to come back and try the Matterhorn the following year. My introduction to climbing had been almost as extreme as Rob's. At 18, taking part in Operation Raleigh community projects on Mount Kenya, I was given the opportunity to attempt its true climbing summit, Batian at 5,199 metres. Bad weather had forced us to back off just a few rope lengths below the summit, but the experience had whetted my appetite. A pilot light had gone on inside that was not going to be snuffed out. Having since climbed Mont Blanc – the highest peak in western Europe at 4,810 metres, the Matterhorn now had my attention.

As if detecting my disappointment, Rob said he'd still like to climb it at some stage. 'I just need to do a bit more climbing first. But why don't you take Philippe? I still have him booked for climbing the Matterhorn at the end of this week.'

'Really?' I couldn't believe what he had just suggested. It was the perfect opportunity. I knew Nick was already booked for the latter part of the week but I was fit and acclimatised, and the weather was stable. All I needed was two days.

Before I had a chance to answer, Rob suggested that we should all go to Zermatt. While Philippe and I climbed the Matterhorn, he and Helen would go for a hike. The idea seemed to meet with general approval and with that the plan was agreed.

*

Several days later, with the Matterhorn climbed we were back in Chamonix. Helen, Rob and I had just spent another day hiking, before Rob and I finished off with a spot of rafting on the Arve River before dinner. It had rained heavily throughout the previous night and the river was swollen and running fast. Frantically digging our paddles into the water, we rode the waves like a bucking bronco. Every few minutes we laughed with relief as we were ejected into another peaceful eddy. With animated shouts from the paddle team, I leant forward and excitedly grabbed Rob's arm. 'This is great, isn't it?'

But even as I scolded myself for being too familiar, he shouted back, 'Yeah, love it. Hopefully we'll get some bigger stuff before we're done!'

I was not so sure I actually wanted it too much bigger, but carried away in the fun of the moment I yelled, 'Yeah – bring it on.' I was intrigued that while Rob didn't like hanging on to a rock face, he clearly didn't mind being tossed around by angry water with the risk of being thrown out and pummelled on the rocks.

Back in the rafting store we peeled our wetsuits off and climbed back into our warm dry clothes. I was now feeling somewhat sheepish about having grabbed Rob's arm. Before we went rafting Rob had been talking about meeting up in London again, which had elicited a defensive response from me. I'd explained I didn't want to get involved with anyone. So if my subsequent actions had surprised me, Rob must have been really confused.

That night Helen, Rob and I were all staying in the Vagabond hostel. With another hearty bowl of pasta planned, Rob and I dashed outside to fetch bags of food from the car, just as the heavens opened. The street lights made everything glisten orange in the rain and within five seconds we were both drenched. Crashing into each other, we scrambled to put the lid of the car down before the boot got soaked. Laughing at how wet we were, Rob rested his hand on my arm. 'I feel wetter now than when we were rafting!'

As he said that he leant forwards. Our lips touched. My heart raced, and before I could engage my brain we had melted together with the rain streaming down our cheeks. Pulling away just a few inches we focused on each other's eyes. I was speechless, my mind almost steaming with the confusion of what I had just allowed myself to do. Rob studied my face intently. Somehow I had just experienced the most unnerving connection with him. Disoriented, my only defence was to move on quickly as if nothing had happened. I'd try and figure it out later, somewhere dry, with all the lights on. Without saying a word to each other, we grabbed the food bags and ran back to the hostel to dry off.

*

Several weeks later, Rob and I did eventually meet up in London. In fact, it turned out to be verging on a candlelit dinner. The weeks went by and as we saw more of each other, my determination not to get involved was fast disintegrating. We loved each other's company and felt totally relaxed together despite our different backgrounds. Rob was born in Australia, and had a Swiss mother and an Italian father, while I was plain old English. But we seemed to have a similar approach to life and found more and more in common as time went on. Although Rob had never climbed when we first met, within a few months he was enthusiastically planning weekends in the Alps and booking himself onto climbing courses. In addition, our shared beliefs bonded our growing friendship. Although from Roman Catholic and Anglican backgrounds, neither of us found God in the ceremonial aspects of the church. To us God was much bigger than our man-made religions.

My brothers, Andy and Tim, warmed to Rob, as did my parents. Their approval was important. In just a few months, we had gone from being strangers to close friends. But I was 26 and Rob was 37, and I still had lots of concerns. Would the age gap be a problem?

Would he disappear back to Australia in a few years? How was I going to meet his family and see where he'd come from? To complicate things further, I had been considering a career change, so how would this work? And then there was the fact that Rob had had cancer in his early thirties. It scared me to be getting involved with someone who had that history. Selfishly I wanted to protect myself from getting hurt.

I had so many questions filling my head and none of them had straightforward answers. But it was my mum who helped clarify things for me. She asked one day 'Do you love him, Jo?' and the answer that came in my heart, not my head, resolved all my unanswered questions.

It was nearly Christmas when Rob announced that we were going away for a few days over New Year. On New Year's Eve, after a romantic dinner out, we were on the hotel balcony overlooking the Grand Canal in Venice. Snow was falling, and it lay in a glistening carpet over the balcony. Revelling in the moment, I turned to see Rob writing in the snow, 'WILL YOU MARRY ME?' Without saying a word I bent down and mischievously wrote alongside, 'MAYBE . . .'

'Maybe!' Rob exclaimed. But I couldn't contain myself a moment longer and scrubbed out 'MAYBE' and wrote 'YES'.

'So, will you marry me?' Rob asked out loud.

'Yes, you know I will,' I said beaming and pulling him towards me. With hugs and kisses we held each other tightly under the balcony lights as snowflakes danced around us. Filled with nervous excitement, we had just made the biggest commitment of our lives. Back in our hotel room, surrounded by champagne, red roses and chocolates, we phoned our parents to announce the good news.

*

Nearly nine months later, on 7 September 1996, I walked down the aisle, arm in arm with my dad. My eyes were set on Rob, who was full of excited anticipation for our big day. As we said our vows, I struggled to absorb what I was saying. *'To have and to hold from this day forward, for better for worse, for richer for poorer, in sickness and in health . . .'* On such a happy, perfect day, it was impossible to comprehend the magnitude of what we were really promising. But we believed in our vows and wanted them to be real. We aspired to a lasting relationship like both our parents had, with well over 70 years of marriage between them. Supportive and loving, they had a richness and maturity in their lives together that we both respected and hoped for.

In the middle of the wedding service Derek, our church pastor, gave a talk. He said that like a navigational shipping buoy we would be tossed around by storms, but we'd survive, being well anchored together in our relationship and our shared faith. Surely that day he couldn't have imagined, any more than we did, what life held in store for us over the next couple of years.

Back in the UK after our honeymoon we were quickly immersed in London life. I'd given up my office job at Marks and Spencer to study physiotherapy and work as a volunteer at Hammersmith Hospital, while Rob was given a new post boosting the performance and morale of the equities team. After nine months of marriage, we found we were seeing less and less of each other and neither of us liked it. Nevertheless, our holidays were sacrosanct and we always spent them outdoors – sailing, windsurfing, skiing or climbing. Our breaks from the daily grind were not without their setbacks, though. Whether alone or with others, we seemed to be associated with a growing catalogue of disasters, ranging from friends who broke legs and tore muscles to foul weather and avalanches that regularly dogged us. Even at home we couldn't escape hospitals, especially when Rob sustained multiple leg fractures after being knocked off his bike while cycling to work.

In spite of our apparent bad luck, we continued to take every opportunity to improve our skills, both at sea and in the mountains. We often discussed taking time out from work to travel. We talked of sailing an ocean or climbing in the greater ranges of the Himalaya, Andes or Rockies and squirrelled away money at every opportunity for such an adventure.

*

In February of my final year of physiotherapy studies, we went on an ice-climbing course in Scotland. When we arrived, Rob was just recovering from a bout of flu and found it particularly hard going as we battled through horizontal sleet and gale force winds. Once back in London his health improved but as the weeks went by he never seemed quite right. His neck glands, the site of his previous cancer, remained swollen and painful for many weeks, so we decided to bring forward his regular check-up with his oncologist.

Rob had been seeing Dr Bob Phillips for check-ups ever since his first episode of cancer, seven years earlier. This time, in March 2000, Dr Phillips wasn't too concerned, but wanted to run some further tests as a safety check. A few days later Fran, Dr Phillips' secretary, telephoned. He wanted to see Rob again soon.

Greeting Rob with his usual warm handshake, Dr Phillips flicked through sheets of test results. 'Well, Rob,' he said looking up from the notes, 'there does seem to be something a little unusual about your blood results. You have a slightly raised ESR (erythrocyte sedimentation rate), so I want to run a few more tests if you don't mind.'

'No problem. But what do the results mean?' Rob asked, noticing the slight frown on Dr Phillips' face.

'Maybe nothing at this stage, Rob. These levels are often raised in the blood if you've been fighting infection, as you have with your recent flu.'

That night Rob told me what Dr Phillips had said. Though neither of us wanted to admit it, we were concerned that he wanted to run more tests. Shortly afterwards, when Rob had a CT scan of his chest, neck and abdomen, Dr Phillips confirmed that some of Rob's lymph nodes were enlarged, though it was still inconclusive and possibly just a reaction to Rob's episode of flu earlier in the year.

Dr Phillips was always upbeat, but he was both surprised and concerned at these results and wanted to keep a close eye on Rob. As the months went by, Rob was seemingly well, albeit with reduced energy levels but his ESR level continued to slowly increase. We did our best to lead a normal life, but the news of steadily worsening results was impossible to ignore.

Later that summer, I graduated and started work as a physiotherapist at University College London Hospital. I spent my first six months working in intensive care, the high dependency unit and on a gastrointestinal ward. I loved the variety of patients I treated and in spite of my reduced salary and inconveniences such as on-call duties, I was happy and fulfilled.

Rob remained generally well enough throughout that summer with

occasional swollen glands but no conclusive symptoms. But as the
weeks progressed Dr Phillips became concerned when Rob's blood
results started to show rising LDH levels (lactate dehydrogenase) – an
indicator of cell death and a tumour marker for lymphomas. Soon
after, in September, Rob started to develop some unusual but
distinctive symptoms. He had begun to lose weight, was having night
sweats and had a gnawing pain in his abdomen and back. Every night
the pain would wake him and painkillers didn't touch it. Alarm bells
were ringing in my head. If I had a patient with Rob's symptoms I
would refer them immediately elsewhere for tests. He was
experiencing some of the classic symptoms of cancer. I didn't want to
worry Rob with my thoughts, but I urged him to bring forward his
next appointment with Dr Phillips.

Rob's symptoms did indeed capture Dr Phillips' attention. All the
indications were that something uninvited was active in his system. By
October, after further tests and scans, Dr Phillips contacted Rob while
he was away on business. The results had come through.

'Evening, Rob. Sorry to bother you while you're away – I'd like to
discuss your results.'

'Thanks for calling, Bob. What did the scan show?'

'It looks like the disease in your abdominal lymph nodes is now
definitely progressive. We will need to do a biopsy as soon as possible.'

Rob's mind raced. 'Day surgery?'

'I'm afraid not, Rob. I've discussed it with the radiology staff and
they felt the nodes are so close to your spine that even a CT guided
biopsy would be too difficult. I've spoken with Mr Meirion Thomas.
He's an excellent surgeon, and he's agreed to do a laparotomy. The
approach will be through your abdomen. It'll be quite a large incision
but it'll be much safer.'

'Well, it's got to be done, so the next question is when?'

'As soon as you can get time off work. The sooner the better, so we
can find out what's going on.'

The scan showed that Rob had multiple enlarged nodes in his
abdomen, many of which had grown beyond the two centimetre
threshold diameter and were now fist sized. The plan was to remove
just enough for microscopy, to confirm the nature of the disease.
Leaving the rest would allow their shrinkage to be monitored during
treatment, if it was required. Rob would also need to have a bone

marrow sample taken from his pelvic bone, a procedure he hated with a passion.

It was near impossible for Rob to concentrate on work the following day. His mind ran over and over the previous night's conversation. Back in the office, he booked a fortnight's holiday off work, hoping he would be well enough to return without questions being asked.

*

His operation went smoothly and the day after his surgery I raced from work so I could help him get out of bed for the first time. Ironically, part of my day job at the time was to treat patients who, like Rob, had just had a laparotomy. A week later he was discharged home, but we were still waiting for the biopsy results. Time seemed to stand still as we waited, the uncertainty filling our thoughts every minute of every day. Finally we received the call. Dr Phillips wanted to see Rob.

'Well, Rob, I really didn't expect this,' he started. My heart sank. Thoughts flooded my mind as I tried to concentrate on exactly what he was saying. 'I'm sorry to say the biopsy results indicate that the nodes are malignant. We need to start a course of treatment right away.'

We were stunned. We had just been told Rob had cancer again.

'It's progressed into the next subtype of the cancer you had previously in your neck lymph nodes. We will need to give you an aggressive course of chemotherapy, plus radiotherapy to make sure we completely clear it.'

The enormity of what Dr Phillips was telling us seemed impossible to grasp. Though we'd suspected this for months, it didn't seem real now that we were being told. But it was all too real. Our world had been turned upside down.

Rob immediately wanted to try and get a handle on what Dr Phillips meant when he said 'aggressive' chemotherapy. 'So on a scale of one to ten, if ten is the most aggressive sort of treatment, how aggressive will mine be?' Rob asked.

'Probably around eight. We have to make sure we get it all.'

We continued with a barrage of questions. What are the odds of success for this treatment? When can treatment start? How long will it take? We both struggled to absorb all that Dr Phillips was saying and to quantify what Rob was dealing with.

It was a cold, damp day in October and as we left the Lister Hospital something of our joie de vivre had been taken away. We both felt weighed down with the reality of what lay ahead. Life had suddenly been put on hold.

CHAPTER 3

Making Death Wait

'If you are going through hell, keep going.'

Winston Churchill

'HEY, MUM.'

'Hello love. How are you both doing?'

'Not brilliant. We got the results of Rob's biopsy today.'

'Oh.' She paused. 'What did Dr Phillips say?'

'Rob's lymph nodes are malignant. Dr Phillips wants to treat it aggressively to make sure they get it all.'

'Oh, I'm so sorry, my love,' Mum said.

'I know,' I sighed. There was little more I could say.

'Have you told Rob's parents yet?'

'No, and Rob doesn't plan to. He doesn't want to worry them when they're in Australia. He'll tell them after his treatment.'

Just yesterday, Rob had been diagnosed with Hodgkin's disease for the second time. But it had now advanced a stage. Reed-Sternberg cells, one indicator of this particular lymphoma, had extensively infiltrated his abdominal lymph nodes. Life had turned an unwelcome corner for us. I was scared, suspended somewhere between shock and denial. Despite fearing it for months, I'd still felt strangely numb when Dr Phillips delivered the news. We tried to listen bravely as he explained the curability of this type of cancer, but even with the probability of a reasonable outcome, just discussing survival rates was chilling. With the uncertainty of waiting over, we had to embrace a different fear, one of how Rob would cope with chemotherapy. Despite bracing himself for this news, it still didn't seem real for him.

It couldn't be happening again. I'd only just got back on the road to health and fitness after my broken leg. But deep down I had sensed this moment coming. At least now I could do something about it

25

instead of waiting for my sentence to be announced. I was expecting the worst from the chemotherapy, and I secretly hoped I'd be pleasantly surprised. But there was no escaping my position. I was looking down the barrel of several months of slow poisoning.

Feeling our time had been stolen, we stopped planning ahead, cancelled our holiday for the following spring and put our social engagements on hold. All that counted now was getting through the next few months. The furthest we could see was the end of Rob's treatment. With our dreams swiftly realigned, we just hoped for a normal life once again. We were now engaged with the unseen enemy and it had our full attention.

The plan was for 12 weekly doses of chemotherapy followed by a stem cell harvest and then four weeks of radiotherapy. Rob had to start his chemotherapy as soon as possible, that December. It was an unwelcome Christmas present, but he wanted to get it over and done with. With the diagnosis confirmed, I scoured books, medical journals, the internet, even the *British National Formulary* – a book used by pharmacists and medics – for every available opinion about the latest treatment protocols, nutrition, exercise and complementary health for cancer patients. Studying the drugs Rob would be taking, I grappled privately with the never-ending lists of potential side effects. During my lunch breaks at work I would head to the oncology wards to read their pamphlets. There was little I could do to lessen the blow of chemotherapy for Rob, but I hoped a better understanding might help us both prepare for the months ahead.

Before chemotherapy could commence, various tests and errands had to be run. Rob's GP gave him multiple vaccinations to protect his immune system. A cardiologist carried out a study of Rob's heart because one of the drugs might potentially damage his heart muscle and stop it functioning effectively. By establishing the condition of his heart before starting, they could monitor it more accurately as his treatment progressed.

Another necessary but unpleasant task that Rob needed to carry out was a visit to the fertility clinic. Dr Phillips suggested Rob had some of his sperm cryogenically preserved. The chemotherapy would make him temporarily infertile and might even permanently damage the testicles. Although the sperm would be taken while he had cancer, it would be better than nothing.

On Thursday, 21 December Rob arrived at the hospital for his first dose of chemotherapy. Time had stood still as we waited for his treatment to start. Knowing the cancer was eating away inside him, maybe even spreading through his lymphatic system to his organs, was agonising. His lungs, liver and bone marrow were particularly at risk.

The first morning was filled with a barrage of paperwork, blood tests and appointments. Rob met Marcella and Eve, the two senior oncology nurses who would be overseeing the administration of his chemotherapy. Dressed in their starched pink uniforms and white plastic aprons, their quiet efficiency belied a passion to see life prevail.

Finally, at 10.15 am Eve and Marcella reappeared pushing trolleys. Rob's toxic cocktail had arrived. Handling them reverently with gloved hands, they secured the bags on their drip stands; should the chemicals leak they would burn a hole in their skin immediately. These clear fluids would march through Rob's system, seeking out the traitors. Rob's defence would be his healthy cells, and though battle weary, as long as they did not surrender, there would be an end in sight. Eve carefully and precisely slid the needles into Rob's veins. Any leakage into his surrounding tissues could do untold damage. The invasion was about to begin.

I raced from work to be with Rob as soon as possible. I wished I could take Thursdays off to be with him during his chemotherapy. The red stone exterior of the Lister Hospital was now familiar, but this time I'd be visiting him on the sixth floor, oncology. I padded down the corridor, its carpeted floor muting the trolleys that rattled with medical equipment. The atmosphere was strangely calm, almost serene. It was like entering a war zone hospital. But these were private inner wars between the good and diseased cells, between the human spirit and death itself.

Finding Rob's name on the wall, I gently pushed open the door.

'Hello, you must be Jo. I'm Eve.' A nurse said pulling her latex glove off and shaking my hand with a firm grip.

'Hi. Pleased to meet you, Eve.'

'Did you have a good day at the hospital?' she asked me. Clearly Rob had been talking about my job.

'Yes, fine thanks. Just too many patients and not enough time, you know how it is.'

'Sure I do.' She smiled knowingly back at me. 'Everything has gone well today though.'

'Has he been behaving?' I asked, flashing Rob a cheeky smile.

'So, far so good. I'll leave you two for a while. Call me if you need anything, Rob.'

Despite being familiar with treating patients with lines, wires and monitors everywhere, it was still a shock to see Rob surrounded by drip stands. His bed was scattered with newspapers, documents and cables. He'd been distracting himself for most of the day, on the phone to work and watching the markets from his laptop.

Leaning over the drip lines I kissed him.

'So, Honey, how's it going?' I asked, pulling up a chair beside his bed.

'Not too bad although I feel really itchy, as if I've got ants crawling under my skin. I just want to get pumped with this toxic juice and get out of here, quick smart.'

I squeezed his hand and gave an understanding nod. 'The drip bags look nearly finished,' I noted, hoping there weren't any more to come.

'Yeah – can't say I'm looking forward to three months of this.'

The nurses had offered Rob the option of staying in hospital overnight but he was keen to get home. The drugs had made him dizzy, so I offered to drive, but by the time we'd got to the car Rob insisted he was OK. I was going to have to learn not to be overly protective.

The effects of Rob's first chemo dose were mild. His mouth was sore, he had some acid reflux and a curiously itchy face, but he was able to enjoy the turkey and Christmas celebrations at my parents' house and felt relatively unaffected. However, instead of New Year's resolutions, that year we drew up spreadsheets to manage his cocktail of drugs. In order to minimise the side effects of the chemotherapy, he had to take over 120 tablets every week. Keeping track of them was a logistical nightmare; they all had to be taken at certain times of day and in specific combinations.

Having started chemotherapy over the Christmas holiday period, Rob wanted to inform his team at work of the situation in early January. They already suspected something was wrong. He had been looking unwell and losing weight, and had been increasingly preoccupied in the preceding months. In spite of this, a hush fell over the room as he relayed the details.

'Morning everyone, thanks for coming at short notice. I need to update you on a personal matter. I've been diagnosed with cancer and I need to have three months of weekly chemo. So I'll be away on Thursdays and probably other days too as time goes on.'

'Is there anything we can do?' one of the team asked.

'The best way to help me will be business as usual. When I'm not physically here, I'll always be available on the phone.' He paused. 'And just so you know, I will also be shaving my head soon. In case you hadn't noticed, the little I have is fast disappearing!'

*

Every week Dr Phillips meticulously assessed Rob and checked his results before giving approval for his chemotherapy dose. When the appointments were early, I'd join Rob before going to work.

'So how are you this morning, Jo?' Dr Phillips beamed at me. He was always positive and had an infectious enthusiasm for life. His desire to see people well and happy was so overarching that he often seemed as concerned about me as he was about Rob.

'Good, thanks, I just can't keep up with Rob or his voracious appetite at the moment,' I joked. The truth was, Rob was so wired by the steroids that he was permanently famished and had become an insomniac. As the London office closed for the day, he'd get on the phone to Sydney and start all over again. I'd become so tired trying to look after him and keep up with his erratic sleep habits that I'd gone down with a cold.

'Sounds like we need to adjust your steroid dose, Rob,' Dr Phillips noted. He had previously suggested Rob should avoid people with coughs and colds as his immune system became weakened. Now I, of all people, had one. I knew a minor ailment could develop into something far more serious and my job only served to increase my fear. Not only had I just seen one of my cancer patients pass away as a result of pnemonia but every day I also had to treat patients with grisly chest infections. Though our time together was more important than ever, we found ourselves keeping our distance for fear that I would pass something on.

For the first few weeks the steroids gave me a real boost. Dr Phillips had said it wouldn't last but I wanted to use my extra energy to get all my ducks lined up. I drew up a will and sorted my life insurance. Even though Jo urged me not to worry about those things, it helped me deal with the cancer. It was my way of staying in control, whatever happened.

By 18 January 2001, Rob's pre-treatment blood test results were not good. His white blood cell count had fallen below the baseline and Dr Phillips didn't want to continue treatment while his immune system was so compromised. It was only his fourth week and Rob was frustrated to be falling behind schedule so soon. The entire process was going to be a tortuous balancing act.

Even though Rob wasn't to be treated that week, Marcella and Eve were tireless in their care. They called him at home to see how he was doing and to check he was drinking enough water. Some of the chemicals could damage the bladder and the build up of uric acid could lead to gout, so it was good to flush them out.

By now Rob's hair had become thin and patchy and he'd asked me to shave the remnants. On completion of his new look, he bore a remarkable resemblance to a Tibetan monk, so we messed around dressing him up in bed sheets and taking photos. But generally there wasn't much to laugh at. The less pleasant aspects of hair loss were soon to follow; his eyelashes dropped out, leaving his eyes dry and irritable.

The following week Rob's blood test was more positive, and he was able to resume treatment. But the side effects were beginning to make themselves felt. Chemotherapy aims to interrupt the fast growth cycle of the cancer cells. This means any healthy cells with a fast turnover, like those lining Rob's mouth, were vulnerable. His mouth now felt eaten away and his gums would bleed with no provocation. Other symptoms continued to develop too – discoloured and wrinkled nails, cuts that refused to heal, strange blisters on his hands and feet, a sore throat, runny nose and a phlegmy cough – but Rob generally tried to ignore his expanding list of ailments.

Every week Dr Phillips would ask about any new or unusual symptoms. One side effect that particularly concerned him was the tingling and numbness that had developed in Rob's hands and feet.

One of the drugs was causing peripheral neuropathy and damaging the nerve endings in his fingers and toes. To minimise the damage, Rob's drug regime was changed immediately but it still took six months to regain sensation.

By mid February Rob was over halfway through his chemotherapy treatment, his frame visibly shrinking as his muscles wasted. The chemo had suppressed his appetite and he simply couldn't eat enough to combat the effects of the drugs. Cooking was one of the few things I could do to help, but to him everything tasted of metal. The light exercise programme that I had written out for him in the early days had also fallen by the wayside. He was permanently exhausted and I packed the weights away out of sight.

With the cumulative effects of treatment, he also spent less time at the office or even working from home. His team at work were fully supportive but still Rob forced himself to perform. I often repeated Dr Phillip's words of advice: 'Don't push yourself, allow your body to rest, it's fighting hard.'

We lived by Rob's chemo schedule and with my own hospital work and on-call duties, I spent most of my waking hours in one hospital or another. Our moods followed Rob's blood results. Every week he charted them and plotted graphs to watch the trend. Just as he'd always watched the financial markets like a hawk, his own performance index now had his attention. Marcella and Eve came to predict Rob's questions. 'When you get a chance can I have a print-out of my bloods?' he would ask.

'Already done. There you go,' Eve said, efficiently whipping a bundle of papers from her pocket.

'Thanks. So how are things going at home this week?' Rob enjoyed his talks with the nurses, especially when he felt able to help or shed new light on a situation. Even at work, this aspect of his job as a manager always brought him satisfaction. The nature of Rob's treatment was very personal and the nurses knew it. Cancer makes you vulnerable, you can't avoid it when you face such a challenge to your very existence. Knowing it was a vulnerable time for Rob, the nurses made themselves vulnerable too. By the end of his treatment there wasn't much they didn't talk about.

The nurses became distressed as it became harder to site the needles. Rob's veins were collapsing under the assault of the toxic chemicals, his arms were a colourful array of bruises and scabs. The drugs were so corrosive that they'd left brown burn lines up his arms. Yet, despite the growing list of unpleasant side effects, he could keep striking doses off in his diary. With each passing week he was one step nearer the end.

Rob treated the whole thing as a military operation. He imagined the chemotherapy drugs as the ultimate military force – the aircraft carriers, jets, land troops and special forces – which would annihilate the cancer. Some days he would tell me with such conviction 'we're going to blast the crap out of it', that I was convinced any cancer cell would be running for cover.

Despite his mental resolve, his physical deterioration became more and more apparent as time passed. I hated having to watch him dwindle. Even going up the stairs would leave him fatigued and breathless. The suppression of his red blood cell production had made him anaemic. The drugs systematically ravaged his body. But there was no alternative. Despite all this, I sometimes felt Rob coped better than me. 'Don't you sometimes ask why – why me?' I asked him.

'Not really. I've lived healthily, there's nothing I could have done differently. *Que sera, sera.*'

But sometimes I wanted a reason to help rationalise the cancer away. I wondered if this was a lesson, something God was trying to teach us. Perhaps patience, perhaps trust. Either way, I had to resolve not to be dragged down by it.

As Rob's health deteriorated our lives were stripped to the core. We stopped arguing – nothing was important enough to argue about. We learnt to love each other in a new way. What we had once seen as problems now paled into insignificance. Our lives assumed a more balanced perspective. What mattered was to be alive, to love and be loved. Every day we prayed for health and happiness. This simplicity was precious, something we didn't ever want to lose.

Social events became increasingly awkward and were frequently cancelled. Many of our friends and their children were battling with winter colds and Rob couldn't risk exposure to them. Then, on the rare occasion that everyone was healthy, Rob was often too exhausted to make an appearance. Even with all the caring and supportive phone calls and cards from family and friends, we still felt isolated.

I fought every day with the fact that I could not improve how Rob felt. The fridge was permanently brimming with broccoli, kale, free range chicken, tofu, and all kinds of fruits, but often all Rob could face was noodle soup from the local Japanese restaurant. Insipid as it was, it was the one thing he enjoyed. Even with all domestic tasks attended to and everything from foot massages to favourite DVDs, it all proved superficial. The poisons had to run their course.

Towards the end of Rob's chemotherapy, I no longer arrived at the hospital to find him on the phone to work colleagues. Instead he was asleep as his intravenous lines dripped silently away. In a permanent state of exhaustion, his recovery between treatments was now negligible. He was bald, pale and wasted with dark rings under his eyes. He seemed to have shrunk within his own skin. He looked older, artificially weathered by the flow of drugs through his veins. On his tenth dose, I crept into his room and sat at the end of his bed while he slept. When he woke he felt groggy and weak.

'Hi, Honey, how are you doing?' I asked, stroking his head.

'I feel like I'm cooking from the inside with acid in my veins. I'm just one big chemical experiment.'

'Not long now' I encouraged him. 'You're doing great.'

Rob's working week had changed dramatically by now. The cumulative effect of his treatment had weakened him so much that the two-hour commute to and from work was too much. Even one day a week had become a struggle and he relinquished that too. When I arrived home after work, though he had been home all day, he was still shattered and went to bed immediately after dinner.

I spent long dark evenings alone with my thoughts. Seated at my desk, I tried to distract myself with some physiotherapy journal or other, but my concentration was abysmal. Instead I went round in circles asking questions and finding no answers. Why had the first five years of our marriage been a catalogue of injury and illness? I knew cancer would always be a risk for Rob, but why so soon? What would our future hold if we were like this in our prime years? Would we be able to have children? Was I going to have to spend my future alone?

Normally I talked to Rob about everything, but I wanted to be strong for him. Despite burying my feelings, from time to time I couldn't stop a deep gnawing sadness. I didn't want to lose Rob, not now, not so prematurely. I just wanted a normal life where we could have a family and grow old together. At times I felt that life was slipping through my hands. Yet, as I wrestled with these thoughts, I did eventually find peace. Deep inside I knew the answers all along. Neither Rob's life nor mine were ours to hold. Our lives were a gift and we had to take each day as it was given.

When I went to bed, if Rob so much as twitched, I would wake. Sometimes he had nightmares and woke up sweating and disoriented. He always apologised for waking me but I'd get him some water and medicine to settle his stomach. At other times, I'd just watch him and pray until he fell asleep again.

On 15 March 2001 Rob had his last dose of chemotherapy. Despite his catalogue of side effects, the worst phase of his treatment was behind him. We met with Dr Phillips in his office.

'Well done, Rob, you've handled the treatment well but I want you to have a break before your stem cell harvesting and radiotherapy. Your body needs a chance to recover.'

We'd been temporarily let out of the treatment prison and were free from the hospital for a few weeks. It felt wonderful. I'd been saving up my annual leave at work for this very moment. We now planned to take three weeks off over Easter so Rob would have plenty of time to recover. However, persuading my boss to grant an extra few days above the usual fortnight wasn't easy.

Eventually, I was granted the three weeks and when Easter arrived, we stayed with our friends Simon and Louise, who'd just had a baby boy. Rob loved holding Fergus' tiny body in his arms and joked about their matching bald heads. Even though he still had bad days, every week he clawed his way back to feeling a little stronger and a little more normal.

The next phase of treatment was stem cell harvesting. It was an insurance policy. If the cancer came back Rob would be able to have his own stem cells transplanted. But before they harvested his cells, they had to ensure they were completely free of any active cancerous cells. To do this Rob needed one final high dose of chemotherapy.

It took 24 hours of continuous infusion to load him up with enough of the drug. It was fed into a central line in his upper chest, running directly into a large vein feeding his heart. This dose couldn't be delivered to his arms, partly because the veins were already damaged but mainly because the slower blood flow wouldn't carry the drug away fast enough before the toxins damaged Rob's tissues.

I arrived at hospital, this time Charing Cross, to see how he was doing. He was asleep with a selection of newspapers sprawled over his bed. Stroking his hand I whispered, 'It's only me.'

'Hi Bella.' He stirred. 'Thanks for coming.' I gave him a kiss and pulled the chair over.

'Yet another scar on my chest,' he smiled, pointing at the line. His chest was fast becoming a montage of medical history, with tattoos from previous radiotherapy, the nine-inch abdominal scar from his recent operation and now this hole made by a central line.

Days after the infusion, a scan confirmed there were no longer any metabolically active cancer cells. Rob could now start two weeks of growth factor injections which would stimulate production of healthy white stem cells. These would then be harvested and separated for storage and the rest of his blood returned to him. To save him going to hospital every day we were allowed to do the injections ourselves at home. We tried them in numerous locations but in the end Rob preferred the injections in his abdomen. Within days the growth factor was taking effect and he'd started to sprout new hair on his head, chest, arms and legs. Sadly this was short lived. Just 14 days later, with the injections finished, the effects wore off, as did the hair on Rob's head.

The less pleasant side effects of the growth factor were the strong pains in Rob's spine as his bone marrow was forced to over-produce. I wired him up to a pain relief machine which he had used when he first had back pain from the cancer the previous year. The electrical impulses helped block the pain messages at his spinal cord before they reached the brain. With the machine on the highest setting, I couldn't touch the electrodes without feeling as though I'd just touched an electric fence, but for Rob it was nothing more than a mild distraction.

Thankfully the next and final phase of treatment, radiotherapy, was a known quantity. Rob was at last on the home straight. Though he felt tired and lethargic, it was nothing compared to the ravaging effects of the chemotherapy. Aside from his radiotherapy appointments he even resumed life in the office once more. The four weeks of radiotherapy passed without event, their only lasting mark being a large rectangle of darkened skin on his lower back.

On 15 June 2001 Rob had his last treatment. Eighteen months

since he had first felt unwell, he was still weak and vulnerable to infection. But finally the shadow of cancer had begun to recede.

*

Bob Phillips stood up from his desk with a beaming smile. Walking over to Rob he put his arm round his shoulder. 'Well done, young man. Your treatment is finished and I'm pleased with the results of your last scan.'

'Great! Thanks for everything Bob . . . so what's the likelihood of it coming back a third time?'

'Well, everything is looking good right now, but we need to keep a close eye on things over the next few years. You are definitely in remission but it's impossible to say it won't come back.'

Sitting next to Rob, though I was ecstatic and relieved at the results of the last scan, I was silently disappointed. I'd been looking forward to closing the book on this part of our lives, but somehow we would have to live with it open. No-one was going to tell Rob he was completely cured. They had eliminated the signs of active disease and brought it under control. That was all they could do.

We now faced a choice, to live under the shadow of cancer or just live. Life was not going to be perfect. Privately, I had hoped for guarantees but there were none. No-one was going to tell me Rob and I would have a long life together. But for now, Rob had his health back. It was something neither of us would ever take for granted.

By July 2001 Dr Phillips was happy for Rob to visit Australia, as long as we kept an eye out for bruising and bleeding or signs of infection. Rob was keen to tell his parents but he wanted to tell them face to face, so they could see he was OK. Once over the initial shock of the news, they understood Rob's reasons for not telling them but made him promise never to hide anything like that again. It was wonderful to spend time with them and a relief for both of us to be able to talk about it. It had been a long 18 months keeping up brave faces from the other side of the world.

Back in the UK Rob continued with his regular hospital check-ups and within weeks he was itching to get back to the gym. Unfortunately, by September his enthusiasm had backfired and, with his immune system still weak, he had developed shingles. Shortly afterwards several toe nails had become ingrown and needed minor surgery, just another kickback from chemotherapy. Despite such temporary setbacks, life was beginning to feel normal once more. But it wasn't the same. We both sensed we were at a threshold.

We talked about our dreams, hopes and desires. We still wanted a family in the future, although Dr Phillips had advised us to wait three years until the chemicals were fully out of Rob's system. But more than anything, we simply wanted to have some quality time together. Long before Rob became sick we had started saving to take a break so we could go travelling, but our dreams had long since been filed away. Now, we were daring to dream once more. We were still fascinated by the greater ranges and we realised our dreams would stay dreams if we didn't take action to convert them into reality. Before long, unlikely as it seemed, we even found ourselves discussing how we'd train for a Himalayan peak.

We began to talk about travelling to the seven continents and climbing the highest mountain on each of them – the Seven Summits. Of course, this included Everest, which was out of our reach, but the rest intrigued us.

As the months rolled by and this idea came more sharply into focus, so did the enormity of such an undertaking and the commitment that would be required. The Seven Summits, in order of height on their respective continents, are Everest (Asia), Aconcagua (South America), Denali (North America), Kilimanjaro (Africa), Elbrus (Europe), Vinson (Antarctica) and Kosciuszko (Australia). We had first heard about the Seven Summits when Rob read a book by Dick Bass, an American businessman, who in 1985 became the first person to climb all seven. At the time, it was a closely contested race between Bass and a professional Canadian climber, Pat Morrow. But when Bass beat him by a matter of months, Morrow found another summit to include in the seven and claimed a different 'first'. Since then there has been much debate, with no clear conclusion. Notwithstanding all that, Bass' vision and legacy remain and the Seven Summits were put on the climbing map for good.

Initially we vacillated between continuing with our jobs, allowing life to go on much as before, and taking time off. Our friends quizzed us about our plan. How would we get back into our jobs if we took a year out? How would we pay the mortgage while we were away? How was Rob going to cope with climbing after his illness? We didn't have all the answers but we did know that our familiar jobs and life in London were not the security blanket we'd subconsciously imagined. Our time together had become our priority. The challenge to make such a radical change in our lifestyle seemed enormous but neither of us wanted to live with regrets.

Our thoughts finally crystallised after a conversation with Dr Phillips. Rob was keener than ever to quantify his chances of staying healthy and kept pushing for answers. 'Yes, but what's the risk?' he pressed. He wanted numbers, something concrete to deal with.

'There's a 50% chance of recurrence in the first three years, but it will drop off after that.'

'Is there anything I can do to minimise that?'

'Not really, Rob. Just keep doing what you've always done, stay fit and healthy and minimise stress, though I appreciate that can be difficult in your line of work.' Sitting there in Dr Phillips' office, we both knew our questions had been answered.

*

Leaving work was a landmark for Rob. After more than 20 years in the financial business, he was leaving part of himself behind. With bright opportunities beckoning it was hard to step off the career ladder but Rob comforted himself with his favourite quote: 'Who on their death bed ever wishes they had spent more time at the office?'

It was 8.35 am on a Wednesday morning in March 2002 when Rob finally handed in his resignation.

I heaved a sigh of relief. I'd finally done it. Not only had I resigned but after 22 years, I was about to stop work. As I told my bosses, Roger and Ian, the most amazing feeling swept over me. An almost palpable weight lifted off my shoulders. I felt like I was levitating above the seat in Ian's office and had to look at my feet to check I was still grounded.

With Rob's leaving date set, we started to plan the coming months. Attempting the Seven Summits, or at least six of them, was going to be a tall order. We'd need several months of fitness training, followed by a trekking trip to the Himalaya to test ourselves at high altitude. To do this we decided to climb Mera and Island Peaks, both above

6,000 metres, in Nepal that September. Being in the Everest region, there was the added attraction of seeing Everest 'in the flesh' for the first time. We had read that on a clear day she was visible from Mera Peak base camp.

After Nepal we planned a steady build up of expeditions. First we intended to travel to Antarctica to attempt Vinson – the highest mountain on the Antarctic continent – as well as a few neighbouring peaks. We envisaged that surviving the mind-numbing temperatures and operating in such a remote location would teach us about basic survival and push our limits further. We then planned to attempt an unclimbed peak with our guiding friend Nick Banks. It was called Cerro Aguillera, situated on the remote Cordillera Sarmiento off the wild, weather-pounded coast of southern Chile. This wasn't one of the Seven Summits, but we had plans to attempt many different climbs and adventures on our travels around the world. Ultimately the Seven Summits gave our travelling a focus and a reason to visit each continent. Everest though, remained a fanciful notion. The farthest we could stretch our minds was Denali, the highest mountain in North America. It was allegedly the second hardest of the Seven Summits after Everest, and we planned to attempt it the following spring.

By the end of April 2002, we were both unemployed. I had stopped teaching Pilates and had resigned from my physiotherapy posts at UCL Hospital and the London Welsh Rugby Club. It wasn't an ideal time to be stopping my career, but it seemed there would never be a perfect time to leave. The following month, a touching tribute was paid to Rob at his leaving party. There were also plenty of jokes about his inability to relax on a beach and suggestions for him to try it one day.

With both of us free from the ties of work, we were supposed to be hitting the open road, but the first thing I hit was the operating table. I'd had chronic sinusitis for over a year and my ENT consultant told me I needed surgery to correct the underlying causes. Several weeks after surgery I was finally feeling a little more robust but was still a long way from the fighting form needed for our forthcoming adventures. However, by the end of May, we'd stored all our belongings in warehouses, let our house and sold the car. There was no going back.

Our first trip was a week on the Isle of Skye, but I spent it in bed while Rob languished out of breath behind our friends as they strolled up the Scottish fells. Even they were surprised at the mismatch between our ambitious plans for Himalayan peaks and our virtually non-existent levels of fitness. Nonetheless they were wonderfully supportive and my good friend and bridesmaid Mags sent us off with some encouraging words from Psalm 121 in the Bible: *'The Lord will watch over your coming and going both now and for ever more.'*

After Skye we spent two weeks sailing off the south coast. It was the last time we were to sail on our faithful little boat before we sold her to help pay for our travels. By mid June of 2002, we finally headed out to the Greek island of Lefkas to start our training in earnest. For the next three months we planned to do nothing but build up our strength and stamina for our first Himalayan mountain in September.

Initially our bodies protested. We both felt weak and feeble and the slightest exertion left us collapsed in a heap. But as the weeks went by, we grew fitter and within four weeks our efforts were beginning to pay off. We would start at 6 am with a 40- to 60-kilometre cycle ride, continue with weight training and finish with a few hours of windsurfing. Finally our bodies stopped complaining, our energy levels increased and our aches and pains settled down.

Our next training destination was the Alps for six weeks of hiking and climbing. It was exciting to have felt healthy for several weeks and by the end of September we were fit, strong and ready for bigger mountains. We finally dared to believe that, maybe, our dreams and plans were not so far fetched after all.

CHAPTER 4

Broken Inside

'What doesn't kill you makes you stronger.'
Friedrich Nietzsche

IN EARLY OCTOBER, the day before flying to Nepal, I developed a sinus infection. Even hauling our kit around Heathrow Airport left me breathing hard and wondering how I'd cope at altitude.

Nev and Terry, both ex-RAF, were heading up our expedition and slowly rounded up the team at check in. I became acquainted with our new team mates from behind a face scarf; everyone needed healthy lungs to perform up high.

We arrived at Kathmandu's Tribhuvan International Airport the following evening and boarded a rickety bus. The sultry air was thick with dust and fumes and the streets were a chaotic circus. Motorbikes carried whole families with babies on the handlebars. Rickshaws overflowed and push bikes were laden with entire market stalls. We lurched across a dilapidated bridge over a rancid green river, choked with refuse. Upstream, black spirals of smoke rose from stone platforms where bodies were being cremated. After 45 minutes of dodging and weaving we escaped the mêlée and arrived at the Summit Hotel, an oasis of calm on the outskirts of Kathmandu.

By 7 am the next morning we were picking our way through bustling hordes of locals, trekkers and officious airport staff at the domestic terminal of Tribhuvan Airport. While our queue to enter the terminal zigzagged its way across the car park, monkeys swung from nearby electricity pylons, clearly unaware of the risks of such entertainment. Having braved the eccentricities of airport security, we were soon flying through towers of frothing cumulus in a noisy twin-propeller aircraft. Far below, we could see an emerald patchwork of terraces which followed every curve and bend of the terrain like the contours on a map; and tiny settlements were perched on every

41

available ridge. Peering through the clouds we glimpsed the higher peaks towering above the lush, forested foothills. The foothills were higher than most mountains in the European Alps, yet appeared like molehills compared to the snowcapped giants that reared up behind them.

We were due to land on the hair-raising runway in Lukla. Our pilot pointed the nose of our plane down so steeply that we were almost hanging in our seat belts. As we approached, we could see that the runway ended abruptly in a 30-foot stone wall, behind which the mountain reared up. I said a hasty prayer for the brakes. Many planes had come to grief on this runway – or rather just off it – but thankfully our pilot's skill was equal to the task.

The village of Lukla lies deep inside the great Khumbu valley region. Perched at 2,880 metres above a dramatic forested cliff, it is famous as the Himalayan village from which most Everest expeditions start – the place where great Himalayan climbers have trodden, from Hillary and Tensing to Messner and Bonnington. It is also the home territory of the Sherpa people – gentle in spirit but physically tough and uniquely able to live in this high kingdom of rarefied air.

Lukla was little more than a colourful street lined with shops and guesthouses. As we picked our way through yaks being herded along the street, we began to feel like the pied piper as a giggling throng of children ran after us shouting 'Bop, bop!'. They wanted balloons, unsurprisingly not an item on our kit list, so biros had to suffice. At the far end of Lukla, an ornate archway hung over the track as it snaked its way into the steep valley beyond. Days away along that track and many kilometres above where we stood was Everest base camp and beyond that Everest herself, or as the locals call her 'Sagarmatha' – the Goddess of the Sky. We felt drawn like a magnet just to set eyes on her frightening slopes. But we were here to climb Mera and Island Peaks. Anywhere else in the world they would be giants in their own right, yet here in the heart of the Himalaya, they were lost in a garden of giants.

Heading away from the Khumbu, we set out for the Hinku valley, and after an eight-hour trek arrived in the small village of Puijan. With my cold, the thinner, drier air left me wheezing as if I had just run a marathon, but the dramatic views more than compensated for this. The plunging forest-clad valleys were laced with waterfalls that evaporated into myriad rainbows as they erupted over the gorge cliffs far below.

Setting off the following day we had our first glimpse of a serious Himalayan giant, Cho Oyu at 8,201 metres. Even though she was over 30 kilometres away, she dwarfed everything around. For the first time, I was beginning to appreciate the magnitude of an 8,000-metre peak. Who were we to even think of climbing something that high?

I pushed such thoughts to the back of my mind as we continued up the side of the valley. Even the giant ferns were dwarfed by the high tree canopy. Trailing mosses and colourful lichens decorated anything that stood still and the screech of exotic birds echoed as the morning mist rose like steam from the deep ravines. I half expected to feel an earth-shaking thud, as if we had strayed into some prehistoric land and were being eyed up for dinner. However, our fiercest enemies were far smaller . . . leeches. Creatures of great cunning, they would drop out of trees on to us, burrow through our clothes and, in their relentless search for blood, even crawl into people's mouths as they slept.

*

On our third day, before setting out from Pangom village, we visited the local monastery, perched on the ridge top, to receive a blessing from the monks. Colourful prayer flags garnished the terracotta-painted walls and fluttered in the morning breeze. Taking our shoes off at the entrance, we quietly filed into the central prayer room. It was thick with incense and a pungent smell of burning yak butter. Even with the vibrant painted décor in gold, reds and blues, the small windows banished virtually all daylight, and the candles did little to add illumination.

As we settled down onto some rugs, a 30-foot statue of a Buddha with its head pressed against the ceiling and a menacing wide-eyed stare appeared out of the gloom. At its feet, sacred objects were crammed into every nook and cranny. Finally the special moment I'd been waiting for arrived, as the four monks began to chant. But having imagined that their music would be wonderfully ethereal, I was surprised when it turned out to be a series of discordant *ums* and *yuns*, interspersed every now and again with ear-jangling cymbals, bells, trumpets and the occasional bang of a drum. After an hour we were all beginning to fidget and Carma, our head Sherpa, whispered, 'They stop playing when you pay donation.' With this new revelation, we gratefully left our donations, bowed and stepped back into the fresh air and sunlight. In the end, it felt more peaceful and spiritual outside, where monks quietly worked the soil and the wind danced through the colourful prayer flags.

Later that morning as we progressed up the muddy jungle trail, a mass of twisted roots – all that visibly held the hillside together – provided vital handholds to help us climb. In places the trail was so steep that it was virtually a wall of vegetation. I felt less safe here than when we were rock climbing, and found myself repeatedly telling Rob to watch his footing.

After several hours on the trail, the mist cleared momentarily and we were treated to our first view of Mera Peak, all 6,476 metres of her. Everyone was taken aback. Even from a considerable distance Mera dominated the skyline and her slopes seemed impenetrable. Dramatic cliffs of rock and ice flanked her southern side like the ramparts of a giant fortress, creating a seemingly impossible gulf between us and the summit. Though we were now above 3,000 metres, we were still ensconced in the jungle of the valley. Up there, it was too high and hostile for anything to survive. It was easy to understand why the Sherpa people consider the mountains to be the throne room of the gods and not for mere mortals to tread. Seconds later Mera had been swallowed up again, as if she were a figment of our imagination.

On the fifth day of our trek, after days of ascent and descent, our overall height gain was negligible, but it was enough to leave the leeches and jungle behind. As we climbed into a zone of cooler air at around 3,500 metres, the forest canopy gave way to alpine firs revealing stunning views of the Hinku valley. Unlike any valley we'd ever seen, it was so big that several Scottish valleys would fit into it, with room to spare. We were already at an altitude nearly three times the height of Ben Nevis and we'd not even reached base camp. But today for the first time, it felt as if we were really making progress towards the mountains. My cold was on the mend, Rob had escaped it and we were having fewer headaches than most of the team. Our months of training and pre-acclimatisation in the Alps were finally paying off. Things were going well.

By dusk we had set up camp on delightfully flat ground a few metres from the crumbling edge of a giant river bed. The river itself was a broad, seething mass of uncrossable water, but even so it was dwarfed by the depression in which it sat. A few years ago a natural dam of glacial moraine higher up the valley had burst, allowing millions of tonnes of water to devastate everything in its path below. It had ripped the valley floor away and rolled boulders the size of trucks down it like bowls in an alley. The depression it left in its wake was ten metres deep and 100 metres wide. Thankfully, the sheer inaccessibility of the upper Hinku valley had put locals off living there and this alone meant that no-one had died as a result of this dramatic natural event.

That night, Rob went to bed before dinner complaining of stomach cramps and nausea.

'It's just the usual holiday tummy gripes,' I said.

'I'm not imagining it, you know', Rob replied hearing my tone.

'Well then you'd better take these,' I said passing him some antacid tablets.

By 6 am the next day, Saturday, 5 October, I was shuffling round in the tent and had my gear packed.

'Morning, Honey, rise and shine, we're really getting into the mountains today.'

Rob muttered from inside his bag and rolled over.

'How's your tummy?' I asked, hoping his cramps would have settled by now.

'Not good, felt sick all night.'

'Well, at least you haven't been sick,' I pointed out, as if to confirm that there wasn't a major problem.

'Look, I feel crap, OK,' Rob replied curtly. I felt deflated listening to his response. We'd had more than our fair share of problems and ailments. This couldn't be something else.

With camp dismantled once more, the team set out for Tagnag at 4,300 metres, where we would have a rest day before moving up to base camp. It was the most picturesque day of the trek so far, as we walked through carpets of alpine flowers with breathtaking 360° views of Kusum Kangaru, Mera and Kyashar Peaks. I was itching to use my camera but my excitement had to go straight back in its box. Rob had started vomiting and, worryingly, it was projectile. Arriving at Tagnag, the porters helped me erect our tent quickly and I bundled Rob inside with his mat and sleeping bag.

Once our cook had the stoves going I was able to fill my water bottle with hot water so Rob could hold it against his abdomen. I hoped it would relieve his cramps. Leaving him to rest I chatted with Nev and Terry. They reassured me Rob's condition was pretty common and should settle in the next 24 or 48 hours. A day of rest should see him on the mend.

Tagnag was a small temporary settlement used by locals in the warmer months. It seemed to exist largely for teams like ours that would buy dinners of potatoes, cabbage and yak meat on their way to higher places. At 4,300 metres, nearly the height of Mont Blanc, it was a harsh existence. Even in the warmer months Tagnag could be battered by weather that would make a Scottish storm seem mild.

The next day, after a night of vomiting, Rob was worse and neither of us had slept well. Unable to bear the metallic taste of the boiled water, Rob was becoming seriously dehydrated. Nev and Terry continued to reassure me, but we all agreed that he should start a course of antibiotics. Unfortunately the act of swallowing the tablet with some water merely triggered another vomiting episode. Seeing that Rob was exhausted, I made him comfy and left him to sleep. As I set out for a brief walk with the rest of the team, I could only hope it was a short-term stomach bug and that he was just a bit more susceptible than the rest of us.

We scrambled up to the huge breach in the moraine wall where the dam break had occurred. Behind the wall a turquoise lake filled the valley. Beyond its glistening waters, I could see the valley ahead as it wrapped around the lower flanks of Mera, and I could also make out the route that our team would take tomorrow. But the longer I stared the more cut off I felt. There was no way Rob could go higher in his current state. If anything he should descend, but right now he was too ill and just needed to rest. I hated feeling that the mountain was slipping away from us, yet I felt selfish for being disappointed and guilty for ever doubting that Rob was really ill. Turning away from Mera, something deep inside me knew I would have to let it go. I looked down towards our tents, now nothing more than specks with dark clouds ominously filling the valley beyond them. It was time to get back to camp.

Back at our tent Rob had filled the wash bowl with several more litres of vomit, now no more than dark green bile.

'Oh my love, how are you?' He was on all fours when I unzipped the tent.

'The cramps in my stomach are killing me. There's no position I can find to stop them and they're getting stronger.' But it was his fluid loss that played on my mind and it was being compounded by the thin, dry air. I needed to find a way for him to keep fluids down.

'Honey, I'm afraid you need to try an anti-nausea suppository to see if it will stop you vomiting.' Rob hung his head at my suggestion. I had tried to sound confident but this was my last option. It had to work.

Waiting for the suppository to take effect, I went through a series of checks. Listening to his tummy, I couldn't hear any bowel sounds. His abdomen was swollen and extremely tender with a sharp pain down his left side. His pulse and respiratory rate were elevated, but that was to be expected at this altitude.

I thumbed through my *Medicine for Mountaineering* book. His signs and symptoms didn't fit with an acute gastrointestinal infection, but they did fit something. As I read on a knot developed in my stomach and I silently prayed. *Please God, don't let it be this.*

'What do you think?' Rob asked, noticing me pause on one page.

'Not exactly sure,' I said hoping he wouldn't probe further. I wished I could reassure him but now I didn't know what to say.

'All I can tell you is it doesn't feel right.' Rob looked me in the eye, searching for some reassurance.

'I know, Honey, just try and rest and stay comfortable. I'm going for a chat with Vince. I'll be back in a minute.' Vince was a member of our team who happened to be a nurse. I didn't want to tell Rob what I was thinking, especially when I felt so unsure. We walked out of earshot of the tent.

'How is he, Jo?' asked Vince.

'Not good at all. His cramps are stronger and more frequent and he's losing so much fluid every time he vomits. His symptoms don't seem to fit with a normal stomach bug and he hasn't had diarrhoea once.'

'I've been reading the same book you've got Jo and I have my suspicions.' Vince paused. 'There's a chance he may have an obstructed intestine.' My heart sank. I'd had the same thoughts too, but that wasn't what I wanted to hear. 'Is that what you really think?' I questioned, hoping he'd waver.

'Well ... it could be a number of things but I do think it's a possibility.'

The words from the book kept going round and round in my mind: 'For intestinal obstruction – immediate evacuation is imperative since surgery is almost always necessary.'

'Thanks for talking Vince. I'm going to speak with Nev and Terry. I think we need to get Rob out.'

Nev and Terry agreed. Rob had to be evacuated. He was not improving as they'd expected. Nev planned to move higher up the mountain the following day with the rest of the team but Terry and Carma, our head Sherpa, would stay until a helicopter could reach us.

As if something was conspiring against us, Nev then told me that we had no way of contacting anyone for help because a Sherpa had gone ahead of the team to base camp with the emergency satellite phone. Furthermore it was now too late for anyone to go and retrieve it. I was livid inside. What was the point of an emergency phone halfway up the mountain? But there was no point discussing that now. All we could do was dispatch a porter to base camp at first light tomorrow. They'd move much faster than us and would be able to return to Tagnag with the phone the same day.

As we walked back to our tent, the irony of our situation seemed cruel. Just one day before, I'd been revelling in where we were, the remoteness and stark beauty of our surroundings. Yet now we were trapped in this graveyard of rock and ice. With night fast approaching, temperatures had dropped well below freezing again. Staying in the dark tent alone was miserable for Rob, so I waited till the last moment to leave him for dinner, making sure he had his head torch and the empty sick bowl to hand.

*

Forty-eight hours since Rob had started feeling unwell, even the weather had turned foul and by 10 pm snow was falling heavily. Huge slabs slid off our tent walls every time I climbed in and out to empty Rob's sick bowl. By 5 am the first signs of daylight were visible in our tent and it was Rob's third day of being unwell. I was shattered but awake. I looked again at my medicine book, but my eyes kept coming back to the same four words: 'Immediate evacuation is imperative'.

Moreover, Dr Phillips' advice was ringing in my ears. 'At the first sign of any problems, start Rob on antibiotics. His immune system may still be vulnerable.' Yet Rob hadn't managed to hold down any antibiotics. I deliberated for another hour before concluding it was his dehydration that was critical. Even rinsing his mouth with water to make him more comfortable was better than nothing, if that was all he could tolerate.

Rob was now dehydrating on numerous levels, all of which would be making his blood dangerously thick. His body was furiously producing more red blood cells every day in an attempt to extract more oxygen from the rarefied air. Even though he'd eaten nothing and drunk negligible amounts for days, his body kept on producing litres of bile which it promptly got rid of, draining his body of critical fluid. This was further exacerbated by the desiccating atmosphere that stole vital moisture from his lungs with every breath.

Nothing was working in Rob's favour. Even being curled up in a foetal position for days on end was allowing his circulation to stagnate. He was now in grave danger of a thrombosis – a clot that could lodge in his brain, heart or lungs and in minutes lead to a fatal stroke, heart attack or pulmonary embolism. I was scared for him but when I talked to him I tried to sound as calm and reassuring as possible. I needed him to believe everything was going to be all right.

Suddenly it dawned on me, there was something else I could do. Just as I used to try and get patients moving after an operation, I decided to encourage Rob to walk around the tent a few times to get his circulation moving. He was reluctant to move but trusted it would help. Outside it was a bitter morning with a fresh blanket of snow on the ground, so we waited another hour till the sun had crept over the surrounding peaks to warm our tent. I tied Rob's boots for him. The last time I'd done his laces up was two years ago after his abdominal operation and before that when he had a broken leg. As I helped him stand he felt faint and remained hunched over. Even being upright aggravated his pain.

By the time I'd got Rob back into his sleeping bag I'd missed breakfast with the team. They were putting their rucksacks on and getting ready to move to base camp above 5,000 metres. They wished us well as they left, confident we'd catch them up, but I knew inside we'd not be seeing them again.

It was early afternoon when the porter came puffing and panting back into camp carrying the precious black plastic case. '*Dhanyabaad, dhanyabaad*,' (thank you) I said shaking his hand with both of mine and wishing my Nepali wasn't so limited. With the arrival of communications our situation had dramatically improved. Within minutes Carma spoke with the helicopter base and after some seemingly heated haggling, the conversation came to an end.

'They try come now, but they say weather no good in valley.'

'Thanks, Carma. How long will it be?' I wanted to be able to tell Rob when the helicopter was coming.

'Maybe one hour. But this difficult place. Very high for helicopter. Helicopter too heavy so take co-pilot to Lukla first. Maybe two hours.' That meant the helicopter would arrive at around 4 pm. Another day was evaporating in front of me and there was nothing I could do.

Crawling back inside our tent I updated Rob on what was happening. 'I don't feel good about this,' he said, still holding his arms around his stomach.

'We're going to get you sorted, Rob. Please don't worry. Just stay warm and tell me if you need anything.'

'Is what I've got treatable?' Rob's fear was palpable and I hated hearing him even ask me such a question.

'Of course it's treatable,' I said as calmly and confidently as I could. 'Just not here. That's why we're getting you out to a hospital.'

It was 4.30 pm when I heard the first sound of the helicopter rotors, thudding away down the valley. I scrambled out of the tent yanking my packed rucksack out behind me. Terry and Carma were outside too. We all stared into the distance. Although it was clear above our heads, there was a thick blanket of cloud down the valley that broke just below our elevation. Holding my breath, I strained to hear the pitch of the helicopter. It seemed to be getting closer, but the seconds continued to tick by and it didn't emerge from the clouds below. Carma turned to me.

'Too much cloud, not safe for helicopter.'

'Really?' I said, hoping Carma was wrong, but even as he spoke the rotor noise changed. It was getting fainter, and he was right. It was not coming.

Time was rolling on and we had nearly lost another day. We made another call and they agreed to try again in an hour. Relieved that I now had some better news to tell Rob, I returned to the tent to find him fast asleep. Wanting him to rest as much as possible, I stayed outside, watching and waiting.

The next hour seemed endless. Then, at 5.50 pm, I heard the helicopter again. The beating rotors sounded tantalisingly near. But no sooner had my hopes been lifted, than they were dashed once again. The sound changed. The helicopter had turned around. Our chances of evacuation were over, swallowed up by the advancing clouds. The dampness of the evening air chilled me to the core. The sun had long disappeared, sinking behind the giant unnamed peaks that flanked our valley. I'd forgotten to dress properly and suddenly became aware I was shivering and had numb hands and feet. I had to break the news to Rob but I didn't know what I was going to say this time. I knew he'd be crushed at the thought of another long night in this desolate place and in such pain.

Reluctantly I turned towards our solitary tent. Looking down the valley it seemed an age ago that Rob had become ill. But after just three days without food, unable to keep even water down, he was desperately weak and critically dehydrated.

Rob lay on his side curled up in a foetal position, surrounded by a heap of clothes, torches and various items of medical kit. When he looked up at me his eyes were dark and sunken. He seemed to have aged in the same way he had from chemotherapy. His face was pasty and grey, the skin on his hands papery and wrinkled. Having packed my gear away in readiness for being rescued, I reluctantly started to unpack again. I tried to put off the bad news. 'How are you doing, Honey?'

'Same . . . Was that the helicopter again?'

'Yeah – well it was, but they had to turn back again. Weather wasn't good enough.' Desperate to offer some encouragement, I added, 'They'll try first thing tomorrow if the weather clears.'

'You're joking,' Rob said and fell silent. I shook my head.

'And what if the weather doesn't clear?' he pressed.

'The porters will have to carry you over Zatr La Pass. It's a short cut. They could get you to Lukla in two days.' Rob didn't respond. With the pass reaching to 5,000 metres, the extra altitude could be fatal in his current condition. Let alone the difficulties of spending two days in a porter's basket. We both knew it wasn't a realistic option and silently prayed it wouldn't come to that.

I had a strong sense of foreboding. I knew then that if it came to being carried out in a basket, I wouldn't make it. I didn't know what was wrong with me, Jo was doing her best, but without the helicopter we were stuffed. Something inside me knew for certain that if the helicopter didn't come within the next 24 or 48 hours – I'd be dead. I was scared for my life.

Silently I withdrew from the tent and took Rob's sick bowl away to empty. The thick clouds had brought darkness earlier than usual so I took my head torch. Having emptied the contents of the bowl behind a rock, I bashed at a nearby icy runnel with a stone before eventually breaking through to the stream trickling underneath. Rinsing the bowl I washed my hands in the icy water and padded back.

Crawling into our tent after dinner with my head torch off, I shuffled into my sleeping bag as quietly as I could. Rob was asleep. In the stillness and without a breath of wind outside, I could even hear the snowflakes landing on the tent. I was exhausted, yet my mind wouldn't stop and my thoughts spiralled into a vortex of despair. *Why is it Rob again? Why not me? Why do disaster and illness keep following us?* Tears ran down my cheeks and I clasped my fingers round my lips, I didn't want to wake Rob. My head throbbed from not drinking enough. I groped in the dark for my bottle, swigging back some silty water. I had to look after myself better, I couldn't afford to get ill. As the night wore on the silence was only broken by some distant rumblings of avalanche or ice fall. I wondered how the rest of the team were and hoped they were camped in a protected location.

It was now 3.30 am on Tuesday, 8 October, and Rob had just been sick again. Pulling on my boots and down jacket, I manoeuvred out of the tent to empty his bowl. Although I still received a faceful of snow as I pushed the tent flap out of the way, I suddenly realised it had finally stopped snowing. I clicked my head torch off so I could see the sky. It was almost too good to be true. It was clearing and I could just make out stars as they flickered through openings in the clouds.

Although bitterly cold, it was a still and peaceful night. 'Please help us, Lord. Bring the helicopter tomorrow,' I whispered.

Having set my alarm for 5.45 am so I could be up for first light, I eventually drifted off to sleep sometime after 4 am. I was startled awake by crashing noises, and discovered our tent was shaking wildly as if caught in some maelstrom. 'Jo, Jo.' Carma was bashing our tent. It was 6.20 am and I'd overslept. In a panic I furiously stuffed my sleeping bag away, rolled up my mat and yanked my boots on. Before I'd even finished tying my laces I could hear the familiar sound of rotors. The helicopter was coming.

'Rob, sorry, you've got to get up, the heli's coming. Quick as you can.'

Terry ran over to us. 'Are you both ready?' he asked.

'Not quite. Can you give Rob a hand while I finish packing his stuff?' Rob was thrown out into the freezing air and Terry helped him over to the stone wall so he could sit down. Even beneath all his layers Rob's outline looked wasted. The angles of his shoulders made his fleece sit on him as if he were a coat hanger, his trousers just hung from his waist.

'Terry, give this to Rob,' I shouted, throwing his down jacket out of the door. A minute later I clambered out dragging our rucksacks behind. Suddenly I stopped and whipped around in the direction of the helicopter. The rotor sound had changed. 'What's happening, Terry?' I called out, sensing the obvious answer but desperately hoping he'd have a different explanation.

'Looks like they had to abort again.' Even as he spoke the rotors had faded away. They'd turned back to Lukla, and looking down the valley I could see why. A huge bank of fog was blocking their approach. Although we were clear of it, the fog had effectively made us unreachable.

'Please come back,' I said under my breath, 'please.'

Forty-five minutes later, the helicopter tried and failed once more. With each attempt, it became increasingly difficult to reassure Rob. His voice sounded weak. 'I don't think I'm going to make it if I don't get out this morning.'

'Honey, the heli will come, we're going to get you out of here,' I said, squeezing his hand tight but feeling desperately scared inside.

Rob's intuition was often right but this time I needed him to be wrong. Even though we kept piling extra clothes on him, he continued to shiver violently. He had no reserves to keep warm. With no news as to when the helicopter would try again, we had to get him somewhere warmer. Our tent had been dismantled so we took him to the hut and wrapped him up in Terry's sleeping bag.

Eventually, at 8.15 am I heard the familiar sound of helicopter rotors again, but this time it was different. I could see the helicopter. It had made it through a temporary clearing in the fog. Our chance to escape was finally here. Running as fast as I could back to the hut, I burst in through the door. 'The heli's coming, Rob,' I gasped catching my breath. 'We need to go.' We had to move fast. The helicopter wouldn't be able to wait for us and the pilot might decide to turn around at any second.

'Are you sure it's coming?' Rob whispered, his throat so parched that his voice was low and gravelly.

'Yes, I've seen it. Let's go.' Helping him off the bench, I pulled his right arm around my shoulder. 'Lean on me, Honey.' I grabbed his waist and winced to feel his bony pelvis. His stance was stooped and he moved like an old man. Carma came running over and took Rob's other side and we began to move much faster. Rob's toes clipped every protruding rock even though we tried to guide him and each time he lurched forwards, we buckled to take the strain.

'Nearly there, Rob,' I puffed. The altitude made everything doubly hard and it was all Rob could do just to stay upright. Terry waved madly, signalling us to stay low as we approached the helicopter. The deafening sound of the rotors now overhead was music to my ears. 'A few more steps, you're doing great,' I shouted. The rotor wash blasted down on us but it filled me with a new lease of life. I finally felt sure we were going to get the medical help Rob so badly needed.

Shovelling Rob up into the seat, I climbed up next to him in the helicopter and secured our seat belts. The rotor tune increased in pitch and within seconds our tiny vibrating cabin began to lift off. I reached over and squeezed Rob's hand tightly. His head was bowed and he didn't move. Glancing down, the people on the ground were soon mere dots and we were sweeping down the valley towards civilisation. We'd escaped the jaws of the mountain.

CHAPTER 5

The Long Way Home

'In the middle of every difficulty lies opportunity.'
Albert Einstein

By 9 AM WE had landed in Kathmandu. Rob was efficiently delivered to a nearby hospital. Its foyer was bustling with waiting relatives and bored onlookers, all keen to catch sight of the sick tourist. As the nurses set to work, their attempts to get intravenous lines flowing repeatedly failed due to Rob's thickened blood. Eventually they succeeded and Rob was rigged up with multiple infusions of antibiotics, general fluids and sugars.

I sank exhausted into the chair beside his bed, happy to see the fluids hydrating him at last. Soon after, with a barium Xray, ultrasound scan and blood tests underway, a nurse asked Rob for faecal and urine samples and handed him two 35mm film canisters. Quite apart from any obvious difficulties relating to container size, this was impossible. Rob had nothing to give.

Hours later I convinced the nurses to put down their cigarettes and find Rob's results. Inspecting the scan report, five words caught my attention. 'Diagnosis: total gastric outlet obstruction'. Despite suspecting an obstruction, it was still a shock to see it in writing. Just then a doctor arrived, thankfully with a good command of English.

'You are very lucky to be alive, Sir. I really don't know how because your blood is so thick. Our tests show your intestines are totally obstructed just below your stomach. We need to have a look inside to identify the cause. It may be cancer.' His last four words hit us like a gunshot. We had never suspected that this could be cancer again, and though we both tried to ignore the doctor's words, a seed of anxiety had been sown. Could Rob really be that unlucky?

With the Emergency area nothing more than an extension of the front foyer, I arranged to have Rob relocated. The second-floor corridor smelt disconcertingly of petrol and I hoped the no smoking policy was more tightly enforced than I'd seen downstairs. Wheeling Rob into the room, we were greeted by stained bed sheets and a warm cloud of sun-dried pigeon excrement blowing through the window grate. My temporary excitement at the private bathroom soon vanished when I discovered the toilet didn't flush and the single tap spewed water so brown you wouldn't even use it on the garden.

Later that day, having left Rob in order to phone our insurance company, I returned to find him looking pale and frightened with the nurses forcefully trying to shove a tube up his nose. It was a nasogastric tube designed to pass through the nose to the stomach and intended to drain Rob's bile and stop his cramps and vomiting. But it was crude and looked more like a garden hosepipe than a piece of medical equipment. I held Rob's hand and tried not to look alarmed.

'They can't get it in, I keep on gagging' he said and moments later erupted with bile spraying both nurses and myself. He was utterly distraught and I was furious to discover they had not even bothered with a local anaesthetic.

As I finished helping Rob remove his dirty, sick-covered trekking clothes, a porter wheeled a trolley bed in.

'Home,' he said pointing to Rob who immediately looked bewildered.

'What do you mean, home?' I said.

'Go home,' he repeated. After unsuccessful sign language, I ushered him back outside. I tried to prevent further intrusions but failed as a constant stream of bored visiting relatives wandered in, as if Rob were an attraction at the local zoo.

After a fitful night's sleep on the cockroach-infested concrete floor beside Rob's bed, I was woken at 6 am by two cleaners. Sloshing a filthy bucket of grey water across the floor, one of them started to shake Rob's drip bags violently. Rob was barely awake,

'What the hell are they doing?' he muttered.

'Nurse's job,' I said gently prising the drip bag out of her hand and hanging it back up.

That morning Dr Patel, the Chief Medical Director of the hospital visited Rob.

'Your husband will need surgery, Mrs Gambi.'

'Can we fly back to the UK for that?' With my question Dr Patel's face changed, as if I'd personally offended him, but he quickly broke out into a reassuring smile.

'Yes I believe he can fly and I understand why you want to get home, but he can have surgery here if you wish. I would be very happy to operate on a foreign person, we don't often have that opportunity.' I was flattered that he wanted to operate on Rob but his comments made me nervous. Even if the operation were a success, Rob's rehabilitation and weaning him back onto food would be fraught with difficulty. I had been unable to find any kitchens and the so-called 'canteen' amounted to little more than a squalid kiosk on the far side of the car park. All it sold were greasy samosas that lay on a grimy formica shelf and were covered in flies.

Before Dr Patel left, he skilfully inserted a nasogastric tube for Rob and asked the nurses to record Rob's urine and bile outputs. However, this was soon thwarted by cleaners who repeatedly emptied his bags without measuring them. Managing to circumvent them, I acquired my own measuring jug, keeping records in my diary, but accurate measurements were still impossible. With no stopper caps available, Rob's bile bag continually leaked onto his bed sheets, until a nurse eventually closed it by stuffing it with my sweet wrappers retrieved from the bin.

Later that day, two other nurses arrived, announcing they were to 'give enema'. Knowing the obstruction was near Rob's stomach, it seemed inconceivable that a rectal infusion of fluid would reach along 25 feet of intestines. Added to which, there was no evidence as yet that the obstruction was even inside the intestine itself. But whatever my opinion, it was Rob's panicked face and their equipment – a filthy bowl of scummy yellow liquid with a perished rubber hose and some rusty scissors sitting in it – that made me put my foot down.

'No enema. Your equipment isn't sterile.'

'We give enema,' the nurse repeated.

'No! No enema. I want to see doctor.' I scowled, at which the nurses scurried away.

'*I need to get out of here quickly!!!!*' Rob wrote in my diary. He had now lost his voice from inflammation caused by the large bore tube running down his throat. Moments later two young doctors arrived with wrapped sterile enema equipment and Rob reluctantly consented.

Contacting our insurance company again, I handed the phone to Dr Patel. He spoke resolutely.

'Mr Gambi has had a totally obstructed intestine for six days now and I don't expect it to resolve naturally. He needs surgery and he is keen to have that in the UK. I am happy for him to fly with a medical escort . . .'. The insurance company medics disagreed. As far as they were concerned, Rob didn't need surgery but confusingly, they believed he was too unwell to fly. It was stalemate but we had to persist.

'How do you feel about staying there, Mrs Gambi?' the insurance company nurse asked me.

'Not good. He needs to come home,' I paused for a second, 'but it's a *fait accompli* at your end, isn't it?'

'Yes, I'm afraid so,' the nurse replied. But I knew that without their consent I had no way of getting Rob home for surgery and begged her to reconsider. She promised to call back in 30 minutes. Four hours came and went and I received no phone call. Every hour I left messages and empty promises were made to call me back. Then just before midnight after the 24-hour Emergency team changed shift, they lost Rob's records and I had to start all over again.

In search of support from the UK, I solicited further medical opinion from the expedition company doctor plus Dr Phillips and Rob's previous surgeon, Mr Thomas. They all agreed with Dr Patel's assessment. Rob needed surgery, was fit to fly with a medical escort and should be repatriated immediately. Both the expedition company doctor and operations director offered to liase with the insurance company on our behalf but even they couldn't make progress. We were stuck, and that was that.

Dr Patel's warnings were now running amok in my imagination. He'd cautioned me that leaving Rob's intestine totally obstructed could be fatal. Without surgery to resolve it, he warned, Rob's bowel could strangulate or perforate, causing gangrene or septicaemia – blood poisoning that could kill him within hours. I felt desperate hearing his words. I had imagined that once we had escaped from the mountains, Rob's situation would dramatically improve. Yet now, it seemed we had simply exchanged one battle for another.

Several days later, having spoken with countless staff from the 24-hour Emergency team, nothing had been resolved. I returned to find the morning shift of nurses terrorising Rob once again with their forceful tactics. Not only was Rob's blood still thick and clogging the lines, but his veins were also collapsing, a throw back to his chemotherapy.

'No please, don't hit, it's painful. Please be gentle,' I said, resting my hand on the nurse's arm. Rob had written me another note *'new needles'* and pointed at a fresh unpunctured part of his arm.

Another day passed and I continued my calls to our insurers. Unable to conceal my frustration, I told them that in the very least they were reneging on promises to return calls, and that was totally unacceptable.

'Well what would you like me to do about it, Mrs Gambi?'

'I just want to move things forward.'

'Well no-one is available to talk with you now,' she replied curtly as if I were wasting her time.

'Well when will they be available?' I pressed but she didn't know.

'Look, I'm really concerned about my husband. He needs surgery and the conditions here are far from perfect. . .'

'Well Mrs Gambi, those are the conditions you should expect if you select that type of travel destination.'

I was incensed. 'Hang on a minute, we paid for insurance cover in Nepal, so what's that got to do with it? And what if he gets gangrene or blood poisoning? That could kill him in hours.'

'We'll deal with that if it happens.' With her last comment, I gave up and asked for someone to call me as soon as they were free.

Half an hour later, though days after we'd arrived, I received my first call from the 24-hour team.

'So, Mrs Gambi, what can we do for you?' he said as if I was about to order a takeaway pizza. At this point the penny finally dropped. It seemed they were all incapable of treating this situation as an international medical rescue, despite that being their sole reason for existing. The international part of it seemed too difficult, the medical part seemed irrelevant and the rescue part too expensive. So all in all, they'd have been better trying to sell used cars. Nevertheless, I had to try but I was quickly interrupted.

'So can you tell me what happened to your husband in November 2000?'

'Why are you asking me that, when you clearly have Rob's medical history there in front of you?' He ignored my question and continued 'We can't authorise any action until we have consent for accessing Robert's medical records.' I attempted to nip his line of thinking in the bud and explained that Rob's oncologist and the expedition doctor had already agreed to write letters verifying his obstruction was unpredictable, so our claims could be supported. But this was about more than just claims. What were they trying to do? Wriggle out of everything while he was still critically ill? Refuse emergency care? Refuse repatriation? I was at my wits' end.

'Of course you can have his previous medical records, but please can we simultaneously deal with my husband's medical situation?'

'I'm afraid your verbal consent isn't good enough, Robert needs to sign a document.'

'How?' I said fizzing inside but trying to stay calm.

'I'll fax it immediately.' Three hours later, I was still waiting. Once again, it seemed we were trapped. I had no way of overcoming the insurance company's stalling tactics, but I could not and would not give up.

Back in Rob's room the nurses were busy again. He held a message up *'Everytime you go, they come and attack me. What's happening now?'* I felt terrible, but knew I had to come clean. Things were fast spiralling out of control.

'I'm waiting for a fax that you need to sign.'

'But what about surgery and getting out of here?'

'I'm trying,' I replied.

'TELL THEM TO PULL THEIR FINGER OUT AND DO THEIR BLOODY JOB!!!' This time Rob had scribbled so hard that he had ripped through several pages. *'Maybe it's cheaper to fly bodies home – preferred financial outcome?!'*

'Don't say things like that!' I chided him but he was already furiously writing something else. He had just remembered another insurance company from his previous job that might still cover him. I raced to the phone. Moments later I was back and promptly burst into tears. *'What's wrong?'*

'ACE insurance . . . They're so nice, they actually care about what's happening to you.'

'Come here' he wrote. I threaded myself carefully through his intravenous lines and we held each other tightly. Feeling his bony rib

cage, I realised it was the first time we'd hugged since it had all started.

'I think they might be able to help us, Honey', I smiled wiping my eyes.

Within half an hour Dr Patel and the ACE insurance medics had spoken and made a decision. Rob was to be medivac'd immediately by air ambulance and transferred to the Bumrungrad Hospital in Bangkok. It would be a better place for him to await repatriation.

At 3.30 pm the next day one of the hospital staff burst through the door.

'Plane landed Miss, plane here!' Thirty minutes later a team of smartly dressed medical staff swept into Rob's room with holdalls of equipment and a stretcher trolley. Aware of time pressures, they hurriedly took observations, collected Rob's medical notes and fitted a new bile bag along with an assortment of wires and sensors. In no time at all Rob was plugged into a monitor, transferred to the stretcher trolley, strapped in and whisked out of the door.

Having arrived at Kathmandu's Tribuhvan Airport, there was only an hour and a half of daylight left before our flight would be grounded for the night. The minutes ticked by as Rob's ambulance waited beside the runway and I battled to persuade officials that boarding passes weren't necessary for a private air ambulance. After an hour had passed, in desperation, I threw caution to the wind. I grabbed back our passports from five squabbling security guards, gesticulated at my watch and shouted 'What is so complicated about allowing a sick person to leave your country?' It had the desired effect. Seconds later I was fast tracked through Departures with an escort.

When we finally reached the Bumrungrad Hospital in Bangkok at 2 am, I could have cried. The Accident & Emergency department was a scene of efficiency and cleanliness and Rob's new room was overwhelming. It not only had curtains and clean white sheets but also a bathroom with a proper toilet, a shower and two bottles of mineral water.

Five consultants including a gastroenterologist, oncologist, surgeon and intensive care specialist visited Rob that night and the round of tests began again. Rob's intestine was still obstructed and opinion remained that surgery was necessary. What alarmed us more was the radiologist's assessment. He had identified abnormal changes in Rob's stomach lining, cited them as potentially cancerous and recommended a gastroscopy and stomach biopsy. Had Dr Patel been right about cancer after all?

Having been on a momentary high in our new and more promising surroundings, we were plunged back into despair. It was nearly two weeks since Rob had become seriously ill and had been unable to eat or drink. Despite the best efforts of medical staff, his veins continued to refuse any intravenous nutrition, we were still thousands of miles from home, he needed surgery, and now this?

Rob was scribbling again and with a deep sigh thrust his note towards me.

'That's it, I'm finished!'

'Finished what?' I asked. He scrawled three more words. *'Finished with mountains.'*

I studied Rob's gaunt face and weary eyes. He was deadly serious.

That night as I lay in the dark beside Rob's bed, I wrestled with my thoughts and cried to God. *Why has Rob's life been threatened twice in two years? Why have you allowed this to happen?* I felt like a boxer, pummelled until senseless, crushed and unable to bounce back.

The following day, the news came that we had been waiting for. Along with Rob's medical escort, we were flying home that night.

*

Nearly four weeks after we had left the UK full of anticipation for our first Himalayan climb, we arrived at London Heathrow. Thanking our Thai doctor we said our goodbyes and were greeted by an ambulance and paramedics. Within two hours Rob had been admitted to the Lister Hospital and his surgery had been confirmed for the following morning. At last, we were home from our little trek in the Himalaya.

Sunday, 20 October 2002 was overcast and damp but inside the brightly lit Lister Hospital, Rob was recovering from his operation the previous day. 'Well, Mr Gambi, your operation was successful,' said Mr Thomas as he walked over to Rob's bed. 'I had to remove two very thick bands of scar tissue that had wrapped themselves around your jejunum. However, I'm pleased to say that despite being totally obstructed for several weeks your intestines weren't damaged. You are extremely fortunate, Robert.'

Mr Thomas suspected that the scar tissue had been caused by a combination of Rob's previous operation and his radiotherapy. He had no explanation for why it had wrapped itself around Rob's intestines or the timing of it, but he assured Rob that he'd carried out two thorough inspections inside his abdomen and there was no further scar tissue to be found.

Dr Phillips also came to see Rob immediately after his operation and reassured him this was not a recurrence of his cancer. After nearly three weeks without food and weighing just 59 kilos, ten kilos lighter than normal, Rob was slowly able to start eating again. After a week he was discharged from hospital with the advice that he should be able to return to strenuous activities within two to three months. It was now just a matter of recuperating at home. By now, 'home' existed more as a figment of our imaginations, but friends and family all generously offered spare rooms. We moved in with my parents where, much to Rob's delight, my mother pandered to his every culinary whim.

In spite of the heavy financial penalties associated with cancelling our Antarctic expedition, our sense of relief remained strong and I was continually grateful for Rob's restored health. Against the odds, he was once again making a comeback. I had no other explanation, but that someone had been watching over us.

*

In December 2002, we visited Rob's parents in Australia for a few weeks. Once again, they were greatly relieved to see Rob on the mend. Much to Rob's delight, his mother picked up where mine had left off as she set about feeding him up with her irresistible cuisine. By January 2003, though Rob had largely recovered from his operation, we continued to avoid any discussions about the future. In the months since Rob's surgery my sinusitis had been troubling me again and I had started to develop asthma. My consultant prescribed steroid sprays but it was his suggestion that I should spend some time in the mountains that caught my attention. It sounded almost too good to be true. The lack of allergens in mountain air would make it the best place to recover. Nevertheless, I decided not to raise the subject of mountains until Rob did. If that wasn't for a long time or maybe never, I'd just have to deal with that but I secretly hoped he'd come around.

Two days later Rob made an announcement. 'I think we should start training to climb Denali.'

I couldn't believe my ears. 'Are you joking?'

'Not at all. That's what I think we should do. If we don't do it now, we never will. I'm not going to be beaten that easily.' Trying to keep calm, I was bursting with excitement. Part of me had died that day in hospital when he announced he was finished with mountains. But now, the embers of our dreams were being fanned into flame.

Owing to Denali's location near the Arctic Circle, its high altitude and the need to carry heavy loads, it is a formidable task for even the fittest and toughest of climbers. With the initial euphoria of our decision behind us, the reality of the challenge ahead became overwhelming. With time lost we were now unable to have a steady build up of increasingly difficult expeditions. We would have to adjust our minds to getting back on track, but under different circumstances. The season for climbing Denali started in May, which gave us four months to transform our bodies into lean, fit, pack-carrying machines. As with any sport, the best way to train for it is to do it, and we planned to head for the mountains. Rob's surgeon, however, didn't want him disappearing on a remote expedition for several months, so we found a pleasant compromise – a ski resort. We'd be in the mountains but we'd have access to a Western hospital, should we need it.

Initially Rob's sliced and stitched abdominal muscles protested at having to exercise but after a few weeks they settled down. By March 2003, despite other minor health setbacks, we had slowly worked our way back to the start line. For the next two months we pounded around the hills of Whistler in Canada with heavy backpacks. We ran, skied, lifted weights and trained till we hurt. Our bodies groaned and creaked, pleading with us to stop but eventually they began to respond and even asked for more. We clawed our way back to fitness, until at last our little exercise chart showed some respectable figures. After two months Rob was carrying 35 kilos, half his body weight, without so much as a grimace.

On 19 May 2003, exactly seven months since Rob's surgery, we were finally on our way to Alaska to climb Denali – 'The High One'. We were nervous about setting out again, and a nagging fear was resurrected in our minds. When would the next disaster occur? Preparation had felt safe, going was dangerous. That was when things fell apart. But we couldn't let history limit the future. If we kept on trying, sooner or later things would surely go our way.

CHAPTER 6

Return to High Places

'A journey of a thousand miles begins with a single step.'
Chinese proverb

Our taxi pulled up outside the Inlet Bed and Breakfast in Anchorage, Alaska.

'People get killed on that mountain, you know,' called the driver in his American drawl as we piled our luggage on the pavement. 'Y'all have a safe time.'

'Thanks, we'll try,' I called.

The following day as we stood at the cash desk in the local climbing shop, I was suddenly aware of a large presence behind me. 'You must be Rob and Jo.' I swung around to find myself staring at someone's chest. Overshadowing me was a scruffy-haired, unshaven giant.

'Hi. And you are . . . ?' I said, craning my neck.

'I'm Ryan and this is Clark – we're going to be your guides on Denali.' Bumping into our guides was fortuitous as we had plenty of unanswered kit questions. Showing them our large 80-litre rucksacks, they just laughed.

'Oh no, that's just a baby rucksack. You guys are gonna need a daddy rucksack for this mountain,' Ryan beamed knowingly.

That night we met the rest of our team. Rob was thrilled to discover that of the 11 members, seven had medical training of some sort. As well as myself, Art was a paramedic, Jeff was a fireman and Juliet a doctor, in addition to which Ryan, Clark and their assistant Bill also had medical experience. 'I'm relieved there's such a comprehensive medical team on standby!' Rob whispered.

'You're not going to need it, Honey!' I whispered back, hoping I sounded more confident than I felt. We both knew nothing could be taken for granted.

As we swapped stories and information, we were relieved initially to discover we weren't the only ones on our first major expedition, but were surprised to discover we had considerably more technical climbing experience than most. But even as our spirits had risen they sank again when Jim, another team member, showed us gruesome photos of the shredded, raw heel blisters that had caused him to fail only three days into his Denali expedition the previous year.

Everyone had different opinions about climbing kit and it seemed that only trial and error would reveal what was right for us. Hopefully this process would avoid a catastrophe like frostbite due to inadequate gloves, though a hernia from carrying half the climbing shop seemed more likely. We were not totally without direction, though, and our guides put a foot down at some luxury items, including my fourth pair of underpants. One thing I refused to trim back, however, was my sizeable medical kit that would allow for most eventualities apart from brain surgery. In spite of my new rucksack being so large that I could fit inside, it was soon overflowing and depressingly well over half my body weight.

For weeks before we'd arrived in Alaska, I'd tossed and turned every night as my mind was flooded with unanswered questions. Were we ready? Was attempting the second hardest of the Seven Summits for our first expedition foolish? How would we cope with the infamous headwall – the 1,000-foot wall of ice and the crux of the climb. Then there was the extreme cold, the altitude and the load carrying. Would Rob get ill again and if he did, how would we cope in such a remote location?

Rob had been equally plagued by his own fears about our forthcoming climb.

Extreme anxiety summed up my feelings about Denali. Everything we knew about the mountain told us we would need incredible strength and endurance. Would I have enough in the tank? I'd never been above 4,800 metres before. Would I perform with the loads at altitude? Above all I didn't want to screw things up for us again.

We were a bundle of nervous anticipation. Some friends had joked we should be seeking out therapy rather than such climbs but this was our dream, and together we wanted to make it happen.

Denali is not to be underestimated. As the highest point near the Arctic Circle, rising abruptly from near sea level, Denali creates her own weather. She is regularly and swiftly engulfed by unrelenting storms that roll in from the Gulf of Alaska and the Bering Sea and transform her into an icy graveyard. She demanded the utmost respect and cruelly punished those who didn't give it.

It was 23 May when we set off to Talkeetna, from where we would fly to base camp. We'd been advised to put on some extra weight because we'd lose so much on the trip, so for our final binge we stocked up at Wal-Mart and ate non-stop, all the way to Talkeetna. With our National Park Service registration and briefing behind us, we loaded up several single-propeller, four-seater planes and taxied off down the runway. Once we were airborne, all four of us sat in stunned silence as the vista opened up. The tundra plains were garnished with exquisite patterns of winding rivers, patchwork forests and glistening lakes. But it was the intimidating hulk of Denali that held our attention. She towered for six vertical kilometres above the plains, one of the greatest vertical height gains anywhere in the world. We had never laid eyes on a mountain of such grandeur or enormity. Even from afar, her ice-encased flanks dazzled us in the morning sun.

Eventually Rob broke the silence over the radio mic. 'You've got to be joking.'

'Yeah, maybe we should have quit while we were ahead!' I retorted. Thankfully our pilot was a little less fazed by the surroundings. He skilfully manoeuvred the plane between two jagged peaks, its wing tips appearing to be just metres from the imposing rock walls. Seconds later he casually announced 'Hey folks, that was One Shot Pass,' sending ripples of relief around our tiny cabin.

Eventually base camp came into sight, an array of brightly coloured tents just visible as dots nestling beneath Mount Frances. A few minutes later, hammering and shaking, our little plane bounced along the ice, landing safely at 2,100 metres on the south-east fork of the Kahiltna Glacier. It seemed hard to believe that this sprawling giant was just one of an estimated 100,000 glaciers in Alaska alone.

Moments earlier from the air Mount Hunter had been dwarfed alongside Denali – now she reared up in front of us. For thousands of feet sheer ice cliffs vanished skywards and giant ice blocks, known as seracs, hung poised in gravity-defying positions. If they were to collapse, they would wreak devastation on all in their path.

Then turning our gaze to Denali, we stood motionless, stunned at the sheer magnitude of the mountain. Seeing us spellbound, Ryan shouted jovially, 'Some guys see Denali and get straight back on the plane.' It was clear to see why. My head was still buzzing with discouraging statistics from our National Park briefing. Knowing that only 50% were successful on Denali meant that Rob and I only had a 25% chance of summiting together. The odds didn't look good.

We set to work building camp and quickly discovered erecting tents was the easy part. Other tasks, like building walls and digging a mess tent pit, took hours. We were particularly careful to keep our crampons and ice axes away from the tents. Ryan had reminded us how, in strong winds, one small rip could instantly become a massive tear. His words were sobering: 'That's how tents are lost and people die. So no mistakes, guys.' We quickly became dehydrated after our efforts. Altitude is a harsh master. The lack of oxygen and dry air punish you if you don't stay hydrated with at least five litres of fluids a day. From now on, everything we did, or didn't do, would have immediate consequences.

Base camp was reported to have a 'proper' toilet, so with camp built I tramped off to investigate the facilities. A short walk beyond the tents brought me to a small plywood stand with a hole in the middle. Parking myself on it, I felt conspicuous in the extreme. Squatting behind a rock or bush is one thing but to brazenly sit outside on a toilet for all to see felt downright ridiculous, not to mention highly embarrassing. Within moments, though, I had been distracted from my plight by the views of Mount Foraker in front of me. It became the most uplifting bathroom experience I'd ever had. Rob also appreciated the magnificence of this toilet and noted that if it wasn't for the risk of sustaining frostbitten crown jewels from the vicious updraft, it would be the perfect place for a good book.

We were up at 4.30 am the next day. The plan was to do as much work as possible before it became too hot, though at −15°C that was hard to imagine. At a latitude of 63° north, Denali is just 3° from the Arctic Circle. At this time of year the sun only dipped below the horizon between 11 pm and 3 am and even then, it never got dark. Dusk merged imperceptibly with dawn and despite the gnawing cold, the endless daylight gave an inviting feel to the morning.

By 7 am, with our chest and seat harnesses in place, our sleds rigged and rucksacks strapped on, we were ready to take a load of supplies to camp one. Ryan walked over to us.

'Rob and Jo, I want you two to be on different rope teams.'

Rob and I flashed a glance at each other. This was definitely not part of our plan.

'Fine, because . . . ?' I asked Ryan quizzically.

'Because I want to spread the experience evenly over the three rope teams. So I'd like Rob on Ed and Jack's rope and Jo, you'll be with Art and Juliet.'

Seeing our faces, he reassured us we'd see more of each other at break times with this set-up. The rope teams would have to maintain tension during breaks because of the crevasse risk but our teams would pull alongside each other, putting Rob and me close enough to talk. It sounded logical but even so I didn't like having Rob taken from under my nose.

'OK gang, let's haul some ass,' shouted Ryan and our three rope teams slowly filed out of camp.

Even as I took my first steps, my petite 5 foot 4 inch frame creaked with the load, and these were probably the most effortless steps of the entire expedition. We had so much equipment to carry that we would move it up to each camp in two loads. Effectively, we would be climbing Denali twice. The first load was to cache spare food, fuel, clothes and personal items like camera films and toilet rolls. The second was to move camp, carrying tents, sleeping bags, stoves, spare food and fuel plus our medical kit, toiletries, diary and cameras. Despite having trained with 30-kilo packs, I remained confused for most of the day as to why my pack felt so cripplingly heavy.

Our route went steadily down Heartbreak Hill on the south-east fork of the Kahiltna, then turned north onto the main glacier. For centuries the Kahiltna Glacier has carried millions of tonnes of ice from Denali's slopes and at an impressive 72 kilometres, it is the longest glacier not only in the Denali National Park but in the entire Alaska Range. We walked for four hours following this prehistoric mass to reach camp one. It was only ten kilometres in distance, yet our loads weighed us down like beasts of burden. Unexpectedly, even at 2,500 metres, the altitude made a noticeable difference and we crawled up the Kahiltna at a tortoise-like pace.

On reaching camp one, we found it was a flat area on the glacier at the bottom of Ski Hill. The name might conjure up the image of a pleasant ski resort slope, but this was far from it. This wind-crusted slope, strewn with ice lumps, had crevasses big enough to swallow up your local sports centre and still leave room for more. Often a thin veneer of snow hid these chasms, waiting for an unsuspecting climber to tread in the wrong place and vanish. Denali was littered with deceptive names, like Motorcycle Hill, where no motorbike could ever go; Squirrel Point, where no squirrel in its right mind would be found; and Football Field where people unfortunately tended to die rather than play football. Windy Corner, however, was apparently no joke.

Having buried our food cache deep at camp one we positioned our crampons on top, their points facing upwards to deter mountain ravens. The chill of the morning had given way to the searing sun. We had been shaking with cold before we left base camp but were now melting as the suns rays blasted back off the glacier.

'Are you drinking enough, Rob?' I asked as we tied back into our respective rope teams.

'I've had a litre already.'

'Try and finish both litres before we get back to base camp.' My nervousness about Rob's health made me want to monitor everything. Given the sizzling beach-like temperatures, I would have felt more comfortable in a bikini. But unlike a tropical paradise, the temperatures plummeted to freezing in the shade and exposed flesh was ravaged by the high levels of ultraviolet radiation that penetrated the thinner air.

Back at base camp, at the end of our first day, Rob and I were both exhausted and elated to have survived. But getting to camp one again on the second day wasn't so simple. The weather had changed dramatically overnight, bringing a bitter wind with heavy snows and atrocious visibility. As we reached the bottom of Heartbreak Hill the ground levelled out giving us no points of reference. Staring out into the whiteness was disorienting and we felt as if we were walking inside a ping-pong ball. Unable to detect obstacles until we hit them, everyone continually tripped over lumps of ice and snow.

After continuing for some time into the void ahead, though our visibility was virtually zero I sensed the terrain was different from the previous day. It seemed subtly more undulating, indicating more

MAP OF DENALI

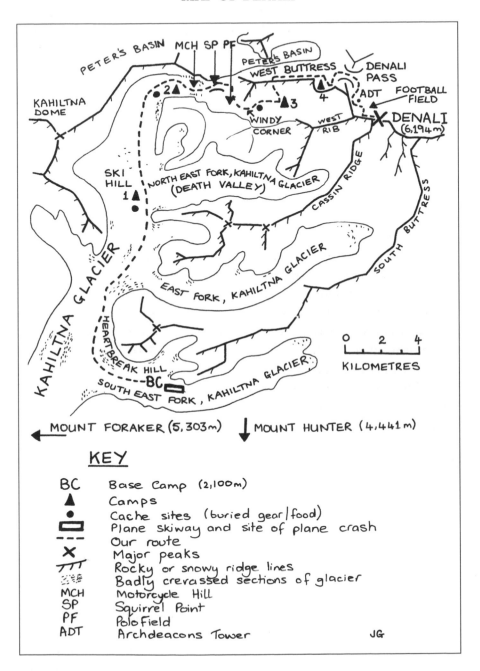

KEY

BC	Base Camp (2,100m)
▲	Camps
●	Cache sites (buried gear/food)
◻	Plane skiway and site of plane crash
- - -	Our route
✕	Major peaks
𝖳𝖳𝖳	Rocky or snowy ridge lines
⠿	Badly crevassed sections of glacier
MCH	Motorcycle Hill
SP	Squirrel Point
PF	Polo Field
ADT	Archdeacons Tower

JG

glacial movement and the presence of potential crevasses. Feeling concerned, I shared my thoughts with Rob as his rope team rested parallel with ours for a break. 'Well, your sense of direction has always been pretty good,' Rob acknowledged, but I felt awkward questioning our route and kept my thoughts to myself.

Some time later, my worst fears were confirmed. We had arrived in a cul-de-sac, surrounded by crevasses with nothing more than impossibly fragile-looking snow bridges to cross on. Ryan shouted at us all to stop where we were. 'OK guys, listen up.' He had to shout to make himself heard over the wind. 'I want you to keep the ropes tight, there's a load of big mother slots around here. We have no choice, we've gotta go back, it's too dangerous to find a way through here.' Turning around, we discovered our footprints had already vanished.

Three and a half hours later we had picked our way back to the bottom of Heartbreak Hill and were ready to start again. As the day rolled on we were disconcerted to find ourselves passing other teams who had given up finding camp one and put tents up where they were. But Ryan was determined to find camp one, where he knew it was safe ground. To save time Bill and Clark disappeared into the whiteness to reconnoitre while we all huddled on the ground like huskies, curled up in the blowing snow. Rob's team had stopped some way off and we weren't close enough to communicate. I watched him for a long time until he looked over at me. Reassured by even the smallest of nods, I returned to my private world inside my hood. After 45 minutes my right side was disappearing in drifting snow and felt numb from the wind. Bill and Clark had returned but they'd been unable to find camp one.

Having resolved to push on, all three rope teams crawled back into action again. This time we moved slowly and in parallel like a police search team. Everyone peered into the white gloom for the slightest hint of camp one. With the minutes ticking by and feeling hypnotised by the maddening whiteness, I suddenly stopped dead in my tracks. I had spotted an almost imperceptible chink in the white. I shouted excitedly to Clark, Ryan and Bill, 'I think I can see grey dots, can anyone else see them?' It went silent as everyone stopped and stared. 'Can you see them?' I called again, wondering if I was simply imagining them. Still there came no reply. Then finally Ryan hollered back, 'Awesome job, Jo, it's other tents at camp one!'

I was elated to have found it. Despite my fatigue, I discovered a new lease of energy. After an epic 11 hours the team pulled into camp, heaving jubilant sighs of relief.

The weather was equally abysmal the following day, giving us nothing to do other than ponder life, snack and dig snow away from our tents. With time to reflect I realised Rob and I weren't spending as much time together as I'd hoped. Being on different rope teams by day and feeling too cold or tired to chat while building camp only left us time in our tent. Having Juliet, Rob and myself squashed into a two-man tent wasn't particularly conducive either, but Juliet was an excellent tent buddy and we spent countless hours swapping medical stories and putting the world to rights.

Toilets and bowel habits became a focal point of conversation. Nobody enjoyed going to the loo in freezing conditions or in public, yet it was a must every day. We used biodegradable plastic bags, staked open with bamboo wands, all of which could be deposited in a crevasse before we moved camp. Of course, the use of a bag required deft control of one's sphincters for the purposes of separation. For this reason alone, even with our plastic pee funnels, Juliet and I envied the men. Privacy was also highly valued but having constructed a wall to shield us from our own team, we had foolishly neglected to protect it from others. As I was busy relieving myself a team of six Germans seemed to think that chatting just metres away from our bag would enhance my bathroom experience. And much to my dismay they even attempted to strike up conversation with me while I was unable to escape.

The next day was gloriously clear but as we scrambled out of the tent we heard the ominous rumblings of avalanches. In just 20 minutes, three huge sections of the mountainside had collapsed into the aptly named Death Valley that led off the Kahiltna. Tidal waves of billowing snow blasted into the sky and fanned across the valley floor. Thankfully the few brave climbers that had gone that way were hastily retreating towards our camp and would live to see another day.

We set out for our next cache location, just below camp two, using only rucksacks, as the sleds would have generated too much resistance in the deep snow. An hour later, my right buttock was protesting at my load and a burning pain was boring down my leg. Despite treating sciatica before, I had never experienced it and as I'd always suspected, it was deeply unpleasant. I couldn't even take my own advice to stop the aggravating activity.

Thankfully, a distraction was provided in the form of an impressive-looking bearded mountaineer who had just skied past. With fixed bars, instead of rope, between him and his sled to prevent his calves getting bashed on the downhill run, he was clearly well prepared. However, his skills were less honed in the department of reading terrain and controlling speed. Stopping in our tracks, we all watched in disbelief as he headed straight down Ski Hill. In no time at all he reached terminal velocity and exploded in spectacular style, sending skis, sled, rucksack, poles and clothes flying everywhere. We were relieved to see him land on firm ground. Not being on a rope, if he had fallen into a deep crevasse it would have meant certain death.

Every break we had was a godsend, but getting up afterwards was another matter. Having to maintain rope tension prevented us helping each other with our sacks. Rob invariably beat me to it and then patiently watched me from afar to check I was OK.

When we left camp in the mornings, I was able to help Jo put her sack on, but not during the day. I felt terrible having to watch her struggle. She called it her 'beached whale moment' as she performed a series of precisely choreographed manoeuvres to get back on her feet. Regular false starts left her buried face down under her rucksack, which thankfully she found amusing – most of the time.

After another gruelling day, we pulled back into camp. Untying my rope, I trudged over to Rob. We exchanged a brief kiss. 'Hi Honey, good day at the office?' I joked, feeling I'd barely seen him all day.

The next day we moved to camp two at 3,400 metres, just above our last cache site. Having named my sled 'Dolce', which means 'sweetness' in Italian, after my sister-in-law's dog, I had hoped it would behave. But by late morning the angle of the slope made my sled repeatedly race past me sideways, pulling me off my feet. It would then flip over, preventing forward progress. After the tenth time I was so incensed that I renamed it 'the Witch'. To make matters worse, hours of heavy breathing had left my throat parched and sandpapery and I was now out of water.

I wasn't alone in my battles, though, and the entire team was relieved to finally reach the elusive camp two. Arriving felt like entering a magical kingdom as sparkling ice crystals now filled the air like fairy dust. But my sense of wonder was short lived as I noticed the menacing seracs poised above, and started to work out the fall line for every ice block. Ryan was equally concerned with our situation on the ground. 'OK, guys, nobody is to go outside our marker wands for anything, there could be crevasses. We'll build camp right here.'

As soon as we'd dumped our kit, Jim, Clark, Jeff, Ryan and I set about digging tent platforms while the others sorted kit. Rob had developed a headache, so once the tents were up he rested inside while I disappeared to give some female design guidance for the toilet pit. Returning to our tent I found Rob still languishing with a headache.

'Have you had any headache tablets or water since we arrived?'

'Not yet.'

'Rob!' I exclaimed. 'You're not going to feel better unless you do something about it and you know you should be drinking.'

'I know you're right, Bella, I'm sorry.'

'Don't apologise to me, you've just got to stay on top of things.' I was frustrated and on edge. Any sign of Rob being ill, even a harmless headache, made me feel nervous and irritable and I still had to ask him if everything else felt OK. He knew what I was thinking and had the same thoughts.

Every time I even breathed harder I worried I was about to run out of energy. Even a simple headache made me wonder if that was the beginning of the end. Was I getting ill again? I felt paranoid about becoming run down and susceptible to illness. Some members of the team had questionable standards of personal hygiene. Just yesterday someone had not bothered to open the toilet sack, just defecating on top, leaving Jo, the next in line, to clear up. How would my immune system cope if I caught something? I desperately didn't want to get ill again.

After all my digging I too had developed a headache but I wasn't going to stop while there was work to be done, I was determined to do my fair share. Seeing Rob was cold, I pulled his down jacket and pants out before heading off to help Bill chisel out the mess tent steps.

The mess tent was a grand name for a deep snow hole that would accommodate our whole team and was covered with a lightweight tarpaulin. It was a never-ending task while in camp to prevent the steps disintegrating into a lethal 45° ice slide. Weary and struggling with the altitude, I had started to resent the burden of trying to look after Rob as well. Thankfully, hacking the ice was perfect therapy and I was soon back on an even keel and perhaps even more helpfully, too tired to talk.

Having had a so-called 'rest day' which entailed a four-hour hike to collect our cache that was buried just below camp two, our next task was to ferry a load to cache just below camp three. The temperature was still well below freezing, but felt warmer due to a layer of cloud trapping some of the Earth's heat. With the steepening terrain of Motorcycle Hill and Squirrel Point it was time to switch from snowshoes to crampons. We had reached an altitude where we would need to employ different techniques to keep going. We used the rest step method – a slow form of walking that involves locking the knee of the straight leg to allow the muscles a momentary rest while the other foot moves forwards. Although appearing very similar to normal walking, it is incredibly energy efficient, and with the increasingly rarefied air it would make all the difference between making forward progress and none at all. Pressure breathing was an equally critical technique. By pursing our lips as we exhaled we could generate small amounts of back pressure sufficient to marginally increase the amount of oxygen diffusing into our lungs.

At the top of Motorcycle Hill I noticed everyone in front gingerly stepping around an area that bore deep footprints. Alarmingly, on closer inspection the footprints had no bottom. Someone had punched right through a snow bridge to a gaping black hole beneath. The black chambers of the crevasses beneath us were like cathedrals. One bad foot placement would be like dropping through the dome of St Paul's. Knowing Alaska's glaciers could be 1,500 metres deep, we kept the ropes tight and tried to move more quickly.

Our steps required concentration as we neared Squirrel Point. The wind had scoured the snow leaving polished blue ice. Even our sharp crampons struggled to bite into this surface and with the altitude sapping my energy, I had no strength to bang my feet down harder. To our left the slope peeled away for thousands of feet into a dark rift, with nothing more than a small rocky outcrop separating us from its shadowy depths. The worry of exposure ate away at Rob's energy reserves, and I knew his imagination would be running wild; he would already have calculated how the outcrop would stop a fall, preventing him from being ejected off the cliff.

After Squirrel Point we traversed Polo Field, yet another misnomer. Even on this relatively level terrain we couldn't drop our guard. Like Russian roulette, our number could come up at any time, if the ground collapsed or rocks fell from above.

An hour later, our rope team rounded Windy Corner to find that Rob's team had stopped just in front. Peering ahead I was shocked to discover Rob had fallen into a crevasse. Despite stepping in exactly the same place as everyone else, he had pierced the thin snow bridge and was now wedged. With nothing but the thin air of the chasm beneath his right foot, his left crampon points had caught in his trousers and his rucksack was pinning him down. I resisted the urge to dash over and help. There was nothing I could do. The worst thing would be to get anywhere near him and further stress the fragile bridge. Not even his rope team could move to assist him; it was critical to keep the rope tight. With me willing him on, Rob fought for some minutes to extricate himself, moving as gently as he could. Finally he emerged, unscathed apart from ripped trousers, a crampon gash in his right thigh and shaken confidence.

Shortly afterwards we arrived at our cache location just above 4,000 metres. As soon as it was safe to untie, I went straight over to Rob and inspected his bleeding thigh.

'I'll have to patch you up when we get back to camp two.'

'I'm more worried about my fingers. They're totally numb, Jo,' Rob said, showing me his white fingertips. Mine were numb too, but worryingly he was getting the same sensation of pins and needles that he'd had during chemotherapy. Even with two pairs of thick gloves his damaged nerves were protesting. Together we rubbed and massaged his fingers during the few minutes we had to rest.

As we headed back, it was not long before the fickle weather was changing yet again. By the time we'd reached Squirrel Point, inches of snow had accumulated, making the hidden snow bridges even more treacherous. Fatigued, hungry and cold, we returned to camp two.

The following morning, after a fitful night's sleep and some vivid dreams courtesy of the altitude, I rolled over to find my frozen pee bottle inches from my face. I had annoyingly forgotten to sleep with it and would now have to carry it full to camp three. I quickly shoved it inside my cosy down-filled sleeping bag, along with my water bottles, spare clothes, head torch, boot liners, gloves and batteries. Bruises from lying on objects were now the norm but I didn't want frostnip too, so I wriggled until it slid past my feet into the mêlée of kit. My second discovery was an even more pressing issue – our tent walls had begun to collapse under the snow. I reluctantly left my bag and shuffled to the door. I had barely unzipped the outer fly two inches when my face was blasted as a mini tornado of snow funnelled through. I rezipped quickly, having learnt the valuable lesson that sometimes it's appropriate to wear goggles, even inside a tent. We had no choice but to get out and dig. It took 45 minutes for Juliet, Rob and me to get dressed and dig enough snow out of our vestibule just to be able to leave. Once we'd caught our breath, we set to work on the boys' tent where Jeff, Art and Jim were blissfully unaware that they were about to vanish beneath an ever-growing drift.

Back in the shelter of our tent, I was secretly relieved the weather would prevent us climbing. We all spent the morning on general maintenance and bodily repairs and my trusted nappy rash cream was shared around liberally to soothe our dry, cracked faces and hands. By late morning the sky had cleared, but higher up the gale force winds still roared, tearing snow plumes from the ridge above. We knew Windy Corner would be living up to its name. Yet despite these telltale signs, the mere arrival of some blue sky had been enough to persuade one team to leave camp. Perhaps confronting the rawness of the elements seemed a real adventure to them, but it seemed a remarkable squandering of energy. When they poked their heads above the parapet of Motorcycle Hill, the raging blast prevented any forward movement and finally convinced them of the difficulties they faced. Hours later and utterly fatigued, they straggled back into camp, several members having pointlessly sustained frostbite.

Thankfully the winds died down overnight but the following morning we were left with bitingly cold air temperatures in the wake of the storm. Tears formed in our eyes and instantly froze on our lashes. We left camp two masked and goggled up looking like bandits, without a centimetre of exposed flesh. In the breeze at the top of Motorcycle Hill, my two pairs of gloves, one of them rated to –20°C, were failing me miserably and the icy wind bit at my raw fingertips. With my laboured breathing I felt claustrophobic behind the mask. I ripped it off in a gasping fit, only to realise that my nose would not tolerate being exposed. The cold cut into my skin. Back behind my mask again, my lungs continued to heave, sucking desperately for more oxygen.

In some dim recess of my mind, it felt as if I were watching myself from above. I observed my pained movements with curiosity. *So this is what altitude is really like.* Altitude ravages your body for every last morsel of energy and power. Every fibre and sinew is left empty. Only the electrical impulses of my will and determination kept me moving. As my pack relentlessly ground my skeleton down, only one useful thought ran over and over in my head – *just one more step, right, just one more step, left* . . .

As we neared Squirrel Point the wind funnelled down the shallow gully blowing golden spindrift in ghostly eddies around our feet, a wondrous effect made possible only by the low sun and bitter wind. Mesmerised by its spell I was compelled to capture it on film, though this inevitably meant removing an outer glove from my already numb hand. It was such an ethereal sight that I couldn't pass it by. I hoped Rob would see beyond the freezing wind to appreciate the moment too. Just then, as if sensing my thoughts, he turned around and gave me a thumbs-up. I smiled at him behind my mask, happy to see he was OK.

Dog tired from six hours hauling our packs in mind-numbing temperatures, we arrived at camp three to face hours of shovelling, digging and sawing ice blocks in order to establish camp. The urge to erect our tent and collapse in an exhausted coma was overwhelming but without walls a storm could tear our canvas homes up as if they were made of tissue paper. Work at our new altitude of 4,400 metres was slow; any effort left us buckled over, gasping for air.

Lazing in our sleeping bags till 9 am the following morning felt absolutely decadent, but there was sound logic in our sloth. When the sun arrived, the temperature in our tent would shoot from –10°C to +15°C in as many minutes, an extremely civilised way to start the day. Ryan, Clark and Bill treated us to crispy bacon, bagels and French toast. Lugging the extra food was suddenly worth the effort and ten days into the expedition, our breakfast was a deeply moving experience for everyone, chefs included.

The next day, with only a short back carry to collect our cache from 400 metres below camp three, we had enough time and energy to absorb the wonders of our location. At sundown, Rob and I stood at the edge of camp soaking up the sublime views, shivering in spite of our down jackets, as the last vestige of warmth seeped from the low red sun. Mount Foraker and Mount Hunter gleamed like pink diamonds and although they dwarfed their surrounding peaks, they paled alongside Denali's giant flanks.

The following day we were to tackle the much-discussed headwall for the first time. As the most prolonged and steep section of the entire West Buttress route, it was the point at which many people failed. This would be our first significant test and though no-one said it, we all wondered who, if anyone, would be the first to crack. Denali's proportions are staggering and even after 12 hard days, we were only halfway up the mountain. It was now that the work really started. From here on the wind, temperatures and the rarefied atmosphere would become our enemies, threatening to extinguish our strength for the summit.

After the previous day's lie-in, we were back to early starts but with our increased elevation at camp four and the commensurate drop in temperatures, we had the luxury of sleeping until 6.30 am. It was simply too cold to get up sooner, although based on that reasoning, I could quite happily have stayed in bed all day. Despite lying in it was still −11°C in the tent and −20°C outside.

Cache days were generally easier than moving camp because we didn't have to dismantle everything, but it still took at least two hours for the team to get ready. 'Are we all dialled in?' Ryan shouted as we struggled into our harnesses, over-boots and crampons. Even with gloves on, our hands had lost all dexterity and refused to work. Everything took ten times as long as it should. My chest pockets were bursting with goggles, mask, handwarmers, snacks, suncream, balaklava and camera. I couldn't see my waist harness and bending over to fasten my crampons was a struggle.

After an hour and a half we'd crawled up the steep-angled snow field and reached the bergschrund. Like all crevasses that divide a steep ice wall from a lower-angled slope, it looked like a gaping set of

Rob in his element as he kicks back on summer holidays in the Greek Islands.

At home on the sea, as I help to deliver a friend's yacht from Southampton to the Algarve in Portugal.

On our special day, 7 September 1996, having just tied the knot at Holy Trinity, Hazelmere, UK.

Me climbing the Immaculate Wall in Echo Valley – one of the most impressive mountainous limestone regions in the Costa Blanca, Spain.

Months after a bike accident in May 1998, Rob enjoys some hillwalking in the Lake District after exchanging his full leg plaster for a half cast.

Rob abseils off the Riffelhorn, high above Zermatt in July 1999.

Ice climbing on Aonach Mór (Scotland) in February 2000. Months later Rob's health deteriorated, before being diagnosed with cancer for the second time.

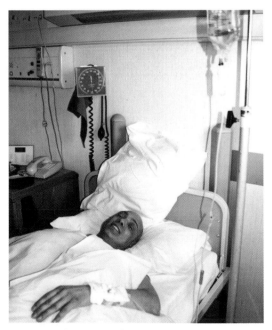

Brave smiles ... Rob in his fourth week of chemotherapy, eight more to go.

July 2001, two months after finishing his chemotherapy, a happy Rob has a meal with his family on a visit home to Australia.

At the top of a multi-pitch rock climb in Switzerland. After several months of training in the Mediterranean and Alps, we are ready for our first expedition.

One week into our first expedition, high in the Himalaya, Rob becomes critically ill with an obstructed intestine. The helicopter slips through a break in the bad weather, just in time to evacuate Rob.

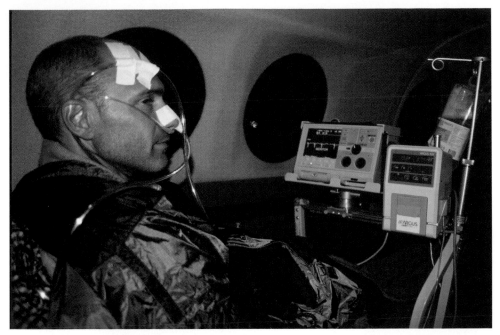

Rob waits for takeoff in the air ambulance at Delhi airport, en route from Kathmandu to Bangkok.

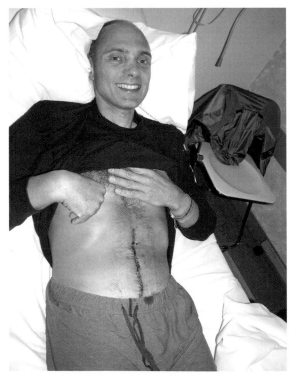

Rob shows off his new 'zipper'. After three weeks of being unable to eat or receive full intravenous feeding, he is ecstatic to hear the news that he can start eating again.

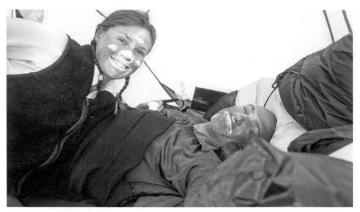

Stormbound at camp three on Denali, with lashings of nappy rash cream to help soothe our cracked lips and chapped faces.

My last steps along Denali's final summit ridge with the distant Alaskan tundra visible six vertical kilometres below.

Putting several difficult years behind us, Rob and I are jubilant to reach our first summit – Denali, on 12 June 2003.

Our ride from Denali base camp back to civilization evaporates as we watch our plane crash-land. The plane's nose and bent prop need digging out as its tail is hauled down with ropes.

After a starlit climb up through the steep western breach of the crater rim, we arrive on Africa's rooftop – Kilimanjaro (Uhuru Peak), 30 July 2003.

Local Tibetan nomads load their yaks with barrels of food, climbing gear and their personal belongings, ready for the 22 kilometre journey to advanced base camp on Cho Oyu.

Russell Brice briefs our team on how to use the hyperbaric Gamow bag in the event of life-threatening altitude sickness. Prayer flags decorate our glacier campsite after the previous day's puja ceremony.

Dawn breaks as we enter the death zone for the first time, and Cho Oyu's colossal shadow stretches across the Tibetan and Nepalese Himalaya.

jaws beckoning anyone who should be unlucky enough to fall from the ice cliff. Our next task was to cross this forbidding chasm in order to start the real climb. It was a little unnerving that the top of the headwall was still hidden from sight and all we could see was a wall of ice rising for 1,000 feet above our heads.

Up above, Rob had already made it over the bergschrund. With his pathological dislike of heights, the exposure on the headwall would be testing his nerves. But I felt proud to see him looking so strong and sure-footed.

For the first time on Denali I felt good. Today was a different day. I was confident about my rope work and climbing technique, so much so that I was even able to help Ed and Jack. We had read so much about the headwall and now we were finally on it, dispelling its myth. It was incredibly steep and excruciatingly hard work for my legs and lungs, but for the first time I knew I could do it. I was 'in the zone'.

The steep ice climb was rigged with a system of fixed ropes, starting at the bergschrund and attached to the mountain by occasional snow stakes. We would clip into these while remaining tied in our rope teams. Co-ordinating our mobile rope while clipping in and out of the fixed one required a system of perfect teamwork. Just one sudden, unexpected move by another team member could jerk us off our feet, starting a chain reaction of falls and sending the entire team down like dominoes. Of course, the fixed lines were there to stop falls but no-one was keen to test them.

As I reached my first changeover point I shouted, 'Anchor'. The rest of the team stopped while I transferred both my mechanical ascender (a locking device for climbing the rope) and my karabiner (a safety clip) to the next fixed rope. Once I was ready to move I shouted 'go' and in unison, our rope team cranked back into action. An inattentive moment at the changeover anchors would be a one-way ticket straight back to camp three. No-one could afford to lose their concentration. As we laboured up the headwall the team calls of 'anchor' became more than just a safety precaution, bringing precious seconds of respite from the pain of our oppressive loads and strangled lungs. With several teams pulling on the same ropes it took all my concentration just to stay upright and avoid being jerked off my feet.

My calves were as taut as steel wire from the torture of kicking into blue ice and holding the weight of my entire body and rucksack on my toes. But resting was not an option. It was impossible to sit or even to change body position and the team had to move as a unit. My mind felt deafened by the pain signals that screamed from my body. I began to wonder if I had finally met my match.

I fought for every step, willing myself on. The blue ice reared up in front of me just inches from my face. As if in a trance, I studied the crampon holes made by those above. They hadn't pierced far, the ice was too hard. I had to be careful, every step, every move. Strange images drifted into my mind as it tried to compute my pain. I pictured myself climbing a ladder with an armchair strapped to my back and a pillow over my face. Just keep moving I told myself, don't stop.

Many hours after leaving camp three, our three rope teams had collapsed in an exhausted but happy heap. We had all finally scaled the infamous headwall and were now at nearly 5,000 metres, on top of the West Buttress.

'Congratulations, Honey,' I said, patting Rob's leg. We were now above the height of Mont Blanc, Rob's previous personal best altitude, and not far from mine, on Chacaltaya at 5,400 metres in the Andes.

'We're not even at high camp yet,' Rob reminded me wearily.

'We'll get there. One step at a time.' This had become our favourite motto, whether it was getting Rob back to full health, regaining our fitness or now, climbing Denali. It was too much to try and contemplate the whole mountain, but broken down into the next day, the next hour, or often just the next step it became less daunting and stopped us giving up.

After burying our cache of food and fuel, we wearily descended back down the fixed lines toward camp three. Suddenly Juliet, who was in front of me, lost her footing. As she slipped, I lunged onto the ice, digging my axe in. It was the first time I'd ever used my ice axe in anger. While relieved that it worked, I was unnerved when it happened again soon after. If I failed to hold her and was pulled off too, it would just leave Clark to stop both of us falling.

By the time we were off the fixed lines my head felt like I was having a frontal lobotomy, minus the anaesthetic. The term 'headache' just didn't do justice to the dementing pain. I felt I was going crazy and the slightest of tugs on the rope made me scream in my head. Despite having drunk all my water in an attempt to curb the effects of altitude and dehydration, I had dramatically lost the battle. Back at camp three I took a double dose of painkillers and lay motionless in the tent, unable to think let alone sleep with my pounding head. I spent the night in a hazy state of pain, longing for my headache to leave me in peace. Thankfully Rob and Juliet had somehow escaped the headaches this time and did their best to make me comfortable.

The following day was our first official rest day, but perversely the sheer excitement made me want to get up earlier than normal. I'd woken with gnawing hunger pangs in my belly as a result of missing dinner. Disappearing into the depths of my sleeping bag, I polished off a bag of pretzels, cookies, fruit gums and a bar of chocolate, barely pausing for breath. With time on our hands during the morning, Rob, Jeff and Clark tried their luck at snow skating before we attempted to build igloos and carve snow sculptures. We even played a few rounds of Frisbee, but given we still couldn't walk without becoming breathless, it made for a very slow game.

By midday the weather was beginning to deteriorate once again and the entire team was recruited to build a much bigger wall around our mess tent which was about to become airborne. Jeff and I quickly set to work with a shovel and ice saw and the rest of the team soon joined in. While some of us cut and shovelled snow blocks, others collected and dragged them, while the rest built the wall. Jeff and I developed a system of sawing and digging and before long had a satisfyingly efficient production line up and running. After 15 minutes I went back to our tent for a drink and a rest.

Rob followed me to the tent. 'You aren't allowing anyone else to do the work, Jo.'

'What?' I said, confused by his comment. 'But no-one has asked me for the saw, and there's plenty of other tools and jobs, so what's the problem?'

Within minutes our exchanges had descended into a series of energy-wasting miscommunications, aggravated by our fatigue and anxiety for the climb ahead. Rob was concerned about his energy levels and ability to perform up high, and had pulled back from the work. With my desire to do my fair share and ensure we were pulling our weight, I was working extra hard. Rob didn't want me to burn out but I had reacted badly to his comments. Upset from our conversation, I marched off towards the mess tent.

'What's up, kiddo?' Ryan said, spotting I was upset. I explained our discussion.

'You just carry on. We really appreciate your work and wish some of the others would be more proactive.' Seeing I needed time alone, Ryan found me the perfect job of chinking the wall – a fiddly but satisfying task of packing every hole to minimise the wind erosion. As I chinked away, Juliet wandered over and gave me a hug. She didn't know what Rob and I had just been arguing about but I appreciated her concern.

*

By 6 June, we had been on Denali for two weeks and the barometer had plummeted once again. Trapped in camp with heavy snow and howling winds, there were now other dangers to contend with. Avalanches and serac falls had caused earthquake-like tremors in camp all morning and chunks of concrete blue ice the size of cars crashed down uncomfortably close. We were caught in our third storm of the expedition and everyone knew these storms were eating away at our precious reserves of energy, food and fuel. Sheltering from the raging elements in our tent, Juliet, Rob and I occupied ourselves for hours, thawing our wet wipes, untangling matted hair and patching up faces and hands. All this while discussing politics and global warming, which at −10°C didn't seem to be occurring inside our tent. Overnight the winds continued to shake the tent with such ferocity that sleeping on a train platform would have guaranteed a more peaceful night's sleep. At 6 am, we woke to the sound of Clark and Bill digging us out. Unbeknown to us, we had been slowly suffocating under a blanket of snow.

With the storm unabating and avalanches thundering around us, we finally began to air our private fears about summiting. Our expedition had an expiry date and once the food and fuel ran out we could go no further. We still needed to move to camp four, our final and highest camp. But even there, we'd have to wait for a weather window to make our summit bid. With every day that passed the summit was slipping further from our reach.

CHAPTER 7

Breaking the Spell

'There are only two ways to live your life. One is as though nothing is a miracle. The other is as though everything is a miracle.'

Albert Einstein

I WOKE UP refreshed after my first decent night's sleep since we'd arrived at camp three. For once I hadn't felt permanently suffocated and at last I had acclimatised to sleeping at 4,400 metres. After six stormbound days, we'd woken to a glorious morning outside. We had finally been granted the break we needed to move to high camp. With numb fingers and clumsy gloves, we dismantled our tent slowly. I even managed to carelessly attach my lips to a frozen tent pole as I attempted to defrost the join with my breath.

As we ate our porridge, the atmosphere in the mess tent was subdued. Yesterday we had heard the shocking news that a plane had crashed en route to base camp. Tragically everyone had been killed – the pilot, a guide and a father and son climbing team. Ryan and Clark had just lost two good friends.

By 8.30 am camp three was buzzing with impatient climbers who, like us, had been itching to move for nearly a week. Ryan's team had already left and Bill and Clark were champing at the bit. Having helped each other get our rucksacks on I passed Rob the rope and his thick outer gloves.

Ninety minutes later, we were ready to start back up the fixed lines and were waiting on a small platform below the bergschrund. Above us, Ryan swam vertically through deep snow as he broke trail and dug to find the lines. Tension was mounting as other teams grew impatient. An American guide, no more than my height, complained that Ryan was taking too long. 'Ryan is six foot four,' Clark pointed out. 'Have you seen how deep the snow is up there?' Over the next five minutes the mutterings amongst teams morphed into high altitude road rage, albeit in low volume and slow motion, as no-one had the energy for anything else.

Finally it was our rope team's turn and Clark started moving up the fixed lines. Since our last crossing, the bergschrund had opened up, leaving a gaping hole with disintegrating sides. The far side was several feet higher, necessitating a lunge up onto an unconsolidated wall of powdery snow that offered no purchase to axes or crampons. Waiting until the rope became tight I threw myself across, only just overcoming the downward pull of my rucksack. Moments later it was Juliet's turn but she didn't make it and was left hanging on the rope tied to my harness. Shaking with the strain, I willed my crampon points deeper into the ice until she clawed her way out.

Just as Art, the last on our rope team, cleared the bergschrund, the headwall gave a shudder. Ripping my hood back I looked up, fearing an avalanche above. I realised there was no escape, we were all attached to both the mountain and each other. The thought flashed through my mind that appreciating the beauty of an avalanche, instead of panicking, would be a far more profitable way to spend my last few seconds. Thankfully, it was merely the headwall ice shifting beneath us.

No more than 30 minutes after we started up the fixed lines, the weather had deteriorated significantly. Hours later, at the top of the headwall, gale force winds were whipping snow ferociously across the ridge. Tired from his efforts in the lead, Ryan decided to let the small, complaining guide and his team go ahead and break trail. One hour later, we were still waiting at the base of Washburn's Thumb, a large rocky prominence on the West Buttress, regretting having let the smaller guide go first. With no means of communicating, we knew nothing except that the team above were stuck on the lines and not moving. We had no choice but to wait. Huddling together as best we could against the raging elements, we tucked ourselves deep inside our down jackets. Stuffed full of soft goose feathers, these allowed us to survive conditions well outside the normal scope of human existence. Sealing every possible hole, I concentrated on keeping warmer air from being blown away. Rob had positioned himself to shield me from the full force of the wind.

'Nice spot for a picnic, hey!' I shouted to Rob and Juliet.

'Yeah, shame we didn't bring the wine hamper,' Rob joined in. Even standing right next to me, his words were barely audible over the wind and were whipped away, almost before they'd left his mouth.

'I'm sure it's brightening up a little,' Juliet shouted back, waving her arm towards the sky. That little phrase had become a standing joke in our tent as we'd weathered the storms of the last few weeks.

As time rolled by, I became tired of stamping my feet to stay warm and crouched down between my rucksack and a rock. The thermostat in my hypothalamus had now taken charge and triggered my muscles to shiver, but even this automatic reaction was barely adequate, generating only the equivalent heat of walking. Needing an external boost I cracked open another pair of hand warmers in an attempt to thaw my frozen fingertips. My temperature gauge only read −10°C but with the howling wind, the temperature felt much colder, nearer −35°C. After another hour, my shivering had converted to uncontrollable waves of violent shaking, my hands and feet felt like ice blocks and no amount of rubbing or shaking restored any warmth. Trying to jealously guard what little warmth I had left, I didn't want to move an inch but I needed to tell Rob how I felt. Twisting towards him I shouted over the wind, 'Rob, I'm getting too cold.'

'Hang in there Jo, wiggle your fingers and toes. I'll talk to Clark, see what the plan is.'

Like a hamster in a ball of straw I disappeared back inside my down jacket. The cold had me in its grip. I knew I needed to do something but I was already feeling lethargic.

It worried me hearing Jo say this. She rarely complained. I knew she'd been in hospital before with hypothermia after a storm trapped her on an exposed ski chair lift for hours. If she couldn't move and generate heat, she didn't have the reserves to stay warm, at least not for this long. She'd even stopped taking photos a while ago, a sure sign that she was battening down the hatches. I could see her shivering even with all her down gear on but there was nothing more I could do, we were both wearing everything we had. We would have to move soon, even if it meant going down.

I always loved pushing the limits, but I had no interest in taking unnecessary risks. People die in the mountains for a variety of reasons but being caught in a storm often ranks high among the contributing factors. The longer we waited, the more likely we were to have a problem. Much as I didn't want to go down, as we'd be forfeiting the summit, I wasn't prepared to sacrifice my fingers and toes or deteriorate into a numbed state of hypothermia.

Yet as the minutes ticked by I became increasingly sleepy and felt less and less concerned about our position. Even though I'd decided I needed to go down, I wasn't doing anything about it. Aroused from my icy haze, I was suddenly aware of someone shaking my arm. It was Rob.

'Come on, Jo. You've got to get up. The lines have cleared, we're going.'

'Going where? Up or down?' I replied, feeling drugged by the cold.

'Up. I'll help you get your sack back on.' I felt brittle from the cold, as if my rucksack would snap me in half. After hours of exposure to the worst of the storm, we started to climb again and deep inside I was relieved, most of all that we were going up and not down.

The blizzard conditions prevented us appreciating the true exposure of our position but my brain was not so easily fooled. With the snow ridge only a boot's width wide in places and the wind now blasting upwards, from below my feet, it meant only one thing – there were sheer drops below.

Dropping left we traversed just below the ridge line. Our progress was excruciatingly slow as we battled against the winds with our heavy sacks in the rarefied air. As I meticulously placed my feet where Clark's had been, to my horror the ground suddenly collapsed. Letting out a shriek, I was falling into Peter's Basin – a remote and cut off valley 1,000 metres below. Just one thought was in my mind. *Am I about to pull my three roped team mates off with me?* Clark was out of sight. I hadn't seen him clip into a snow stake. If Art had already unclipped us from the back stake, none of us would be attached to the mountain.

Plunging down I bounced into a deep bed of powdery snow that caked the face below. Swinging on my harness, I was almost as amazed as I was shocked. I had come to a stop after only ten feet. Coughing on the snow I'd inhaled, I was now on my back, head down and legs above with my rucksack pulling me towards the depths. All I could remember about Peter's Basin was that several unrecovered corpses still lay somewhere in the white abyss beneath me.

'Clark, are you clipped?' I shouted.

'We're OK. Are you all right, Jo?'

'Yeah,' I shouted back, feeling far from all right and shaking like a leaf. Stranded like a beetle on its back, I fought to right myself. Eventually scrabbling onto all fours, I lunged above with my axe, but the snow was too fluffy to grip. As I pushed up with my legs the unconsolidated snow acted like quicksand. The more I pushed, the more I sank. Stopping to reassess, I started to dig until I'd cleared a metre of powder and my axe twanged on a rock. Manoeuvring myself onto the rock for better purchase, I crawled and dug my way back up to the ridge. It turned out that miraculously, seconds before I fell, Clark had just clipped in. The timing of my fall couldn't have been more frighteningly perfect.

I was grateful to Juliet and Art who'd patiently waited for me to get sorted, but there was now a large hole, around which they'd have to negotiate. 'Sorry guys,' I shouted, but the wind instantly carried my words away. Seeing I was on my feet again Clark, who was now rested, set off at what felt like lightning speed. Even with one step every three seconds it was too fast and my heart broke into chest-crushing palpitations as I tried to keep up. I had no breath to ask him to slow down or the energy to stop, and the rope just jerked me along. Disoriented from my brief excursion into Peter's Basin, I struggled to remember if Rob's rope team was behind or in front. If he was behind I wanted to warn him about the hole, but there was no way to communicate. Looking in both directions, I couldn't see his team. I prayed he'd see it and his team would be clipped in.

It was 5.45 pm when we rolled into high camp at 5,200 metres. After a cruel nine hours labouring through the storm the fickle skies had cleared once again. I dropped my sack next to Rob's and we collapsed into each other's arms, laughing with joy and fatigue, overwhelmed that we'd made it.

'Congratulations, guys.' I looked up to see the friendly beam of John Evans, a friend from north Wales also making a summit attempt. An ex-para rescuer, he was now a ranger for the Denali National Park and he'd saved us three tent spaces with ready-built walls.

'You're a star,' I said, giving him a weary hug. After our epic day none of our team was in a fit state for three hours of wall building. Even putting the tents up, and repairing the walls demanded more

energy than we had. With camp set, we were too tired to eat and Rob
had collapsed halfway into his sleeping bag.

'Come on, Honey,' I said rubbing his back, 'you'll get cold. Get
inside.' Rob groaned some unintelligible words and shuffled further
inside. Within minutes Juliet, he and I had all drifted into an
exhausted sleep.

The following day six of us crammed into Ryan's three-man tent.
With no mess tent, we had reduced our team accommodation to three
tents, two of which were used to cook in. With a pile of legs and
sleeping bags in the middle we had just enough space beneath the
sagging ceiling for our jugs of steaming food. Nobody could move but
it was wonderfully cosy, making Juliet, Rob and me reluctant to
return to our own frosty, albeit spacious tent. With the increased
altitude, our appetites were suppressed and having once loved maple
syrup flavoured porridge, all I could stomach for breakfast was
reconstituted mashed potato.

The skies continued to deposit vast quantities of snow on us
throughout the day, every inch that fell increasing the danger of
avalanches and decreasing our opportunity to summit. To make
acclimatisation at high camp even harder, the low barometric pressure
of the frontal system had simulated a gain in altitude, even as we sat
in our tent. Just maintaining ourselves kept us busy all day. By the
time we had dressed, dug the tent out, shaken it, shovelled snow out
of the toilet bag, restaked it to avoid impalement during use,
undressed and had a snack, drink and lie down, we were ready to start
all over again. Everything took so much longer and required much
more effort. Even our intellects had been dulled by the altitude as was
evident in our conversations about favourite pet names, telemarketing
and porridge ingredients. Brad Washburn's research that at our
altitude, mental capacity is reduced by roughly 50% seemed to be
accurate. As we awaited fine weather, Juliet and I even resorted to
high-altitude domestic duties in an attempt to rectify Rob's 'corner of
shame' which had now expanded to engulf the entire tent.

I hated night times with a passion. I never seemed to sleep as well
as Juliet and Rob, but sandwiched between them there was nothing I
could do and nowhere to go. Rob's face was just inches from mine and
I found his periodic breathing – reputedly a common problem at
altitude – remarkably distracting. His breathing would gradually slow

and eventually stop altogether before starting up 15 seconds later with furious gasping. I was familiar with this phenomenon from hospital, known as Cheyne Stokes breathing, but it was normally a sign that someone was dying. So it took discipline to lie there and just listen.

The next day the warm sunshine flooding our tent fooled us until we examined the sky. Sitting directly above was a massive lenticular cloud. Stunningly beautiful to look at yet treacherous to be caught up in, it hovered silently above us like some UFO. The beauty of the lens-shaped cloud cap was deceptive though, and while high camp remained sunny and still, roaring winds encased the summit above and a storm pummelled the mountain below. We were trapped as if in the eye of the storm. Glistening gold in the morning sun, wild streamers of snow snaked off into the atmosphere from the Denali Pass. It was a fantastical sight and deceptively alluring.

Wrapped up, our team gathered outside, enthralled by the weather phenomenon we were witnessing. To be so near a lenticular cloud, yet untouched by the destructive power of the wind that carried it, was thrilling. The blue skies had lured one overly ambitious team to go for the summit. We watched them from afar as they risked inching up towards Denali Pass across a slope that had already been avalanching. Hours later, although they had made it to the pass, they were quickly beaten into submission and blasted back to high camp by the savage winds.

More heavy snow arrived that afternoon, along with forecasts of further bad weather. Having been hampered all the way up Denali by poor weather we had eaten more rations than expected, leaving us only five days' worth for high camp. With our third night looming fast and no improvement of the weather in sight, spirits sank low.

All night the wind pounded high camp and our fly sheet snapped furiously, making it impossible to sleep. By morning the barometric pressure had dropped yet again. The barometer quickly became the target of our disappointment, suffering repeated abuse for never delivering good news. In a moment of frustration I sat on it, hoping either to crush it or increase the pressure, I didn't care which. Although it was no longer snowing, the wind created snow drifts high against our tents. Digging it away felt like trying to keep up with the supermarket conveyor belt while packing your shopping. No matter how fast we dug it away, we couldn't keep up.

Initially the weather delay had been good news, giving us time to acclimatise, but now we were wasting away. Our bodies were unable to recover at this altitude and if we didn't summit soon we would run out of supplies. Killing more time, we went to Ryan's tent for an extreme coffee morning. There was no hot water and no coffee, but we did have warm water and some biscuits. Conversation focused obsessively on snack rationing, our favourite foods and domestic comforts. 'There are three things I'm really missing – my wife, the toilet, and the dog,' said Art wistfully. 'But it's a close run thing between the wife and the toilet,' he finished with a glint in his eye.

Our mood continued to fluctuate as we tried to stay upbeat, though our odds of summiting were now virtually nil. On the fourth evening at high camp we crammed into Ryan's tent once again, this time for the announcement we'd been dreading. 'Sorry, guys and gals, we're out of food tomorrow and the weather's still looking bad, so we'll have to go down. No summit this time.' Everyone's head was down, lost in their own thoughts. 'I know this isn't what you want to hear. You've given it everything to get here and in harder conditions than normal, but that's the deal. If she's not going to play ball – we can't fight her. Sorry, guys.' Our hearts sank. Ryan's words were no surprise but still came as a huge blow.

For the first time Rob and I were ready and in position and now it was Mother Nature who wasn't inviting us further. We'd imagined we were prepared for this moment, as if the days of waiting would have made our disappointment easier to deal with. Ryan continued to talk but Rob's thoughts and mine were elsewhere. Could we really be so unlucky? It was over a year since we'd left work and despite all our efforts, we'd failed to complete one successful expedition. Holding the summit loosely was a noble principle. But now we were so near we felt we were being robbed, though in reality it was never really ours.

Back in our tent we tried our best to pick ourselves up and focus on the positives. Rob felt a massive sense of accomplishment at having made it this far without a medical mishap and I felt a deep sense of relief. Just being at high camp was higher than we'd ever been together. It was a victory over our past, but conflicting emotions grated deep inside us. It had been our dream to reach the summit. Having to wait another year just to repeat this back-breaking climb was soul destroying. We knew it was the journey that counted, yet right now the destination seemed so important.

After our fourth night the pressure had dropped still further to 511 millibars. We didn't even bother to look outside. We had spent 20 days getting into position and today we would go down. To add insult to injury, I had unexpectedly started my period. In my state of altitude-induced amnesia I'd forgotten to take my contraceptive pill. It wasn't that I'd anticipated lots of romantic camping moments, but I was using the pill to avoid my period. It was a calculated risk on my part. The combined effects of the pill and altitude significantly increase the risk of thrombosis, and high-altitude medics deem 6,000 metres to be the maximum safe limit. Given that I'd only be above that height on summit day, I felt it was a calculated risk worth taking. But now my cunning plan had backfired.

Suddenly Ryan's voice boomed across camp. 'Rise and shine. The summit's a go, team! We're heading out in a few hours.'

We couldn't believe our ears. Scrabbling to look outside, we were stunned to discover a crystal clear morning. I didn't know if I was ecstatic or upset. Having waited so long for this moment, it seemed to have arrived at the worst possible time. But faced with our one and only opportunity there was not a minute to lose. Within seconds our inertia of the last few days had evaporated and our tent became a hive of activity. With three sets of limbs thrashing around as if in a game of twister, we gradually all disappeared under our layers.

By 9 am our three rope teams were dressed and ready for battle. As we left the sunshine of camp and walked into the freezing shade of Denali Pass, I felt overwhelmed by the task ahead. Already in pain with abdominal cramps, I didn't feel like I had a summit day inside me, let alone the biggest of my life. Concerns about our route plagued my mind. Only two days ago the steep 50° slope beneath Denali Pass had been highly unstable and avalanching. Now, as we were about to climb it, I prayed it would hold.

As the ground steepened, I felt myself suffocating from the lack of oxygen. Just a momentary lapse in my concentration had left my breathing shallow and ineffective. Every breath in and out required a concerted effort to make it count. Starved of their fuel, my muscles were stalling, unable to generate enough power. Ninety minutes of deathly cold in the shade of Denali Pass chilled me to the core and my joints seemed to creak with the cold.

Finally, I took my first step into the morning sunshine. In an instant the transforming warmth was seeping through my icy layers. My mind exploded with gratitude. I had never felt the life-giving properties of the sun in this way before and would never take it for granted again. Strengthened by the sun, my day had turned a corner.

As we stopped for a break Ryan inspected each one of us closely. 'How's everyone going? Juliet, how about you?'

'Excellent, thanks,' Juliet replied, trying to cover the strain with a smile. Her movements had looked laboured, but she was worried about being sent back, as we all were.

'How are you, Jo?' he asked me with a penetrating stare.

'Tired but good to go,' I replied, holding his stare. I wanted him to know I was committed. My body could complain as much as it liked but I wasn't going to give in.

Rob's rope team arrived, looking equally sapped of energy. Rob's shoulders hung forwards and his axe swung limply in his right hand. 'Take a break here, Rob,' I called out, but he didn't look up.

I could hear Jo calling to me but even talking back seemed too hard. I had hit a wall at the top of Denali Pass and simply had nothing left. My body seemed to have shut down. The only systems that remained operational were my lungs, heart and legs. I felt as if there was just a dim red light on in my head and I was functioning on the last of my emergency reserve battery. I didn't know how I was going to make it any higher.

'Have you got an energy gel to hand, Rob?' I asked, helping him off with his rucksack. I needed to get some sugar inside him quickly.

'Don't know,' he replied with a lifeless voice, still not looking up. Rummaging in my jacket pockets I found two sachets and passed one to Rob. I didn't like to see him struggling. I wanted him to be strong and wished he could offer some reassurance that he was OK.

'How's it going, Rob?' Ryan asked. There was no avoiding his question. I hoped Rob was with it enough to understand the potential effect of his answer.

'Ready in one minute, Ryan.'

'Good job, man, we move in three minutes,' Ryan said.

Above the pass, we climbed a steep ridge in a series of switchbacks. This had a concertina effect on the teams, enabling Rob and me to be closer. Each time we passed we exchanged a nod or a hand signal. The energy gel had quickly filtered through to my hungry muscle fibres and even though every step was still laboured, I felt renewed strength. Rob too was more upright and his head was no longer down. Spectacular views of the Alaska range had begun to open up in front of us and a fresh wave of excitement and adrenalin surged through my body. This was why we were here. These were the sights that couldn't be bought. These were the moments we'd never forget.

By early afternoon, we'd made it past a large icy feature called Archdeacon's Tower and were finally on Football Field, where we gathered for another break. In the calm sunny weather, its gently undulating, snowy expanse gleamed invitingly, like a ruffled white satin blanket. Although it looked like the perfect high-altitude picnic spot, it felt strange to know people had died here. It was such a stunning place, yet like a femme fatale, Denali's charms could be deceptive. Having lured men in, her fickle nature could turn and mercilessly punish them.

All that now stood between us and the summit was the final headwall and the summit ridge. Ryan gave us his last words of advice. 'We're in with a chance but don't underestimate the summit ridge. It's exposed, so be on your game.' As we started up the headwall, my abdominal cramps had worsened and all I could think about was curling up into a foetal position. Every step I reasoned with myself. *Can I take one more step? Yes. Well then, take it.* I moved my right foot upwards. *Can I take one more step? Yes. Well then, take it.* I moved my left foot upwards. If I could just get to the ridge, I knew the summit would be within my reach.

Taking my final steps onto the summit ridge, for the first time I truly felt the magnitude of the mountain we had climbed. Looking straight down 6,000 metres to the tundra and beyond to the Pacific Ocean was simply a breathtaking sight.

As we climbed along the summit ridge I was surprised to feel dizzy. I had always loved the airy feeling of exposed routes but with a 3,000-metre vertical drop to my right and another to my left, my oxygen, food and sleep deprived brain was clearly overloaded. Ahead of me was the largest and most perfectly sculpted cornice I'd ever seen. Like a tidal wave frozen in time, it was a mass of overhanging, windblown snow. As I drew closer I could see dramatic patterns of rime, where snow had been blasted onto its windward edge creating a fantastical collection of feathered shapes and textures. My gloved hand was already fidgeting towards my camera. Balancing along the precipitous edge, I took as many photos as I dared. The effort of simultaneously co-ordinating my camera, rope, feet and ice axe almost finished me off, but I had to do it. I knew we would never be here again.

As we reached the top of the mountain we were able to untie and Rob and I took our last steps together to the summit of Denali.

In a state of disbelief and bursting with happiness, we held each other in our arms. We had finally made it to 6,194 metres, the highest point in North America. It was 4.30 pm on 12 June 2003. Eight months after Rob's abdominal operation he had managed the heaviest load-carrying mountain of the Seven Summits. We had never felt so alive and so truly blessed. In the magic of the moment all the fears and pain of the last few years had been swallowed up. 'We did it! Can you believe it? We did it!' Rob said, squeezing me tight. At the eleventh hour Denali had rolled back the curtains and allowed us to tread on her loftiest point.

In a state of exuberant exhaustion, we took in the sights that surrounded us. Denali towered majestically over the entire Alaska Range and beyond. Six kilometres below, the tundra merged with the horizon and was laced with thousands of lakes and rivers that dazzled like silver scarves in the afternoon sun. Giant glaciers snaked for mile after mile as their vast icy rivers flowed gracefully through the mountains.

'Good job, Rob and Jo. You did it!' Clark shouted, slapping Rob's back. After many celebratory hugs and handshakes, a small queue of eager team members clutching their sponsor flags and cameras formed in front of me. Over the last three weeks my enthusiastic snapping had earned me the reputation of team photographer. When it came to flags, Rob and I didn't have one between us. Asking a sponsor to believe in us with our history would have been laughable, so we just waved our axes instead. As we all pottered about on the small summit platform snapping away, Ryan and Clark had become concerned. They had seen ominous cloud formations in the distance and were keen to go. 'Let's get the hell outta here, gang,' Ryan shouted and before Rob and I had a chance to finish our photos, we were roping up again. Minutes later our three teams were back in action and we'd started our descent.

By the time we reached Football Field the weather was deteriorating fast. A bitter wind had picked up and the watery warmth of the sun no longer stemmed the sub-zero temperatures. Everyone was battling the intense cold. The frigid air had a bite and Football Field was no longer a friendly picnic spot. Already it felt hostile and we were still a long way from high camp.

Hours later our team toiled wearily into camp after the most exhilarating and debilitating 12 hours of mountaineering in our lives. 'That's some crazy shit up there, man,' Jeff said echoing everyone's sentiments. Ryan had warned us that we'd be exhausted but still needed to hydrate. As the minutes passed I was bracing myself for 'hitting the wall', but confusingly, instead of feeling fatigued, I was buzzing inside. I felt energised and on top of the world. Suspicious that it was a final adrenalin rush before I crashed, I kept waiting to calm down, but that moment never came. Despite my empty tanks, I was still running at full speed.

Rob wasn't in such good shape. Back at high camp, he'd quickly deteriorated. He was cold, pale and shivering, all the things that Ryan predicted. Bundling him into his sleeping bag, Juliet and I plied him with hot drinks and energy snacks. 'Is this just an excuse to have a doctor and a physio look after you?' I joked, trying to keep his spirits up, but it was several hours before he was fully revived.

Feeling wide awake and still excited, I found that trying to settle for the night was useless. I sat into the small hours of the morning scribbling in my diary while Rob and Juliet slept peacefully beside me. Outside the winds had returned with a vengeance and a maelstrom of blowing snow was now battering our tent from all sides.

The following morning, the winds had not abated, but out of food, we had to go down. The winds were so strong that even Ryan, who was double my weight, was getting blown over. As we retraced our steps downwards, the West Buttress ridge turned out to be considerably more exposed than I'd appreciated during our whiteout ascent. As it narrowed to no more than a few inches wide, I crouched over my ice axe, trying to increase my stability. The wind buffeted the massive bulk of my sack, bullying me and seemingly determined to blow me off my feet.

Hours later, as our team finally cleared the bergschrund at the bottom of the headwall, I felt relieved. But suddenly I heard Rob let out a shout above us. Whipping around, I saw him catapulting down the headwall. Above him Jack and Ed were on their backsides looking petrified. Although Rob had stopped, he was now hanging upside down. Jack had forgotten to shout 'Anchor', which had unexpectedly tightened the rope pulling Ed and Rob straight off their feet.

'Are you OK, Rob?' I yelled. He didn't reply. My heart was thumping in my chest. We couldn't afford to have an accident, not here.

'Make yourself safe here, guys,' Clark shouted to our team. 'I'm going up to help.' Quickly untying from our rope, he clipped back into the fixed lines and set off.

'Rob, are you OK?' I shouted again. He still didn't answer but finally I saw him move. Being pinned upside down by the weight of his rucksack on the near-vertical slope, it had taken him a few moments to calculate what to do. Gracelessly but efficiently he righted himself and by the time Clark had reached him he was back on his feet. He looked OK.

'Ed, get on your feet,' Clark shouted.

'I can't,' he yelled back. Above him, Jack had frozen rigid with fear. For five minutes Clark hollered at Jack to stand up and give Ed some slack; finally he got to his feet and they carefully climbed down the last hundred feet of the headwall.

Instead of feeling remote and harsh, camp three now felt safe and welcoming. Thousands of feet below the windswept ridge, we basked in the afternoon sun, feasting on snacks we'd left buried. Taking a team vote, we decided to descend to base camp in one long push even though this meant walking through the night. We were committed to getting back to base camp, whatever it took. None of us wanted to get trapped in another storm without any food. 'Look at your bird bones,' Rob laughed sympathetically as he loaded my rucksack onto my back. Packed with all the extra gear we'd left at camp three, it was now more than twice my size and looked ridiculous, its sheer weight grinding my feet deep into the snow. Swaying above my head it threatened to keel me over and I teetered out of camp like a drunken John Wayne.

With Windy Corner behind us, we tramped silently towards camp two. The low afternoon sun bathed us in its warmth and with every hour the air tangibly thickened. Stopping at camp two just before midnight, we were treated to a spectacular display of Alpen glow as Denali's western slopes were set ablaze in brilliant orange, burning pink and finally a golden glow before the sun dipped below the horizon.

With sleds loaded, we left camp two as the moon rose from the glowing embers of the sunset sky. We took our final break at camp one in the dusky light of the small hours and even in the freezing temperatures, it now seemed warm and calm. As we made our final push to base camp the full moon swung across the sky and behind it the sun rose once more. It was 4.30 am and our extraordinary night was drawing to a close.

Crawling back up Heartbreak Hill, we now understood its name. It was 8 am when we finally toiled back into base camp and I felt euphoric. We had been on the move for 24 hours and though desperately tiring, we had been treated to the most bewitching of nights. As most of the team slept out in the open, Rob and I cuddled up on the pile of rucksacks and reflected on our last three weeks. Expeditions had been demystified, we had made some wonderful friends and the spell of illness and failure had been broken. The tapestry of our last few years finally had some light woven into it.

Six hours later there were great cheers from our team as our plane finally appeared. We needed just three flights to get us all off the mountain but as the plane came in everyone stared in disbelief. The pilot was about to land without snow skis. We watched helplessly as he touched down on the sun-softened glacier and the plane's wheels drove deep into the soggy snow. Then in one dramatic move the aeroplane was catapulted through the air, landing on its nose and only propeller. With each bounce along the glacier our shocked crowd of onlookers let out cries of horror. After its fourth bounce the plane finally stopped, wedged vertically into the glacier.

A huge sigh of relief echoed around camp as the pilot climbed out miraculously unharmed, which was more than could be said for the plane. With its propeller well and truly buried and its tail high in the air, our ride home was no longer looking too promising.

Thankfully, the pilot was able to straighten the propeller and make his return flight, minus passengers, for some essential repairs. Hours later we were happy to be airborne in a freshly dispatched plane. As we flew back to Talkeetna, the endless forests of brown willow, aspen and birch had exploded into a medley of green. While we'd been climbing Denali, Alaska had been transformed from winter to springtime. At this latitude, the summers were short but the flora had adapted, managing to fit its entire growing season into half the time of its more southerly cousins.

Back in Talkeetna, every guesthouse was full, leaving us the choice of more camping or the luxurious Talkeetna Alaskan Lodge. Jack elected to camp but the rest of us needed no persuasion. The Lodge checked us in at lightning speed, efficiently whisking us and our smells away from reception. We were finally able to sample our long-fantasised pleasures – a real toilet, a shower and a soft warm double bed.

*

Over the coming weeks we experienced the delights of Alaska, coming within metres of brown bears, watching glaciers calve into the ocean, seeing whales breach and dolphins play. We kayaked among seals and icebergs, caught halibut and cooked it on our camp fire. But even as we travelled, sleeping in the luxury of a Transit van and enjoying the oxygen-rich air, our thoughts drifted back to the mountains. With Denali under our belts, we dared to wonder if our dream of travelling to the seven continents and climbing the Seven Summits could become a reality.

We were faced with a choice. If we were serious about the Seven Summits, we would have to be serious about Everest. Riding on the wave of excitement from our success on Denali, for the first time we started to discuss in earnest how to make it possible. If we were going to consider Everest, we first wanted to return to the Himalaya and attempt one of the world's 8,000-metre peaks. This would tell us if we could even survive above 8,000 metres, in the death zone. Some believe the death zone to be anything above 6,000 metres – the altitude at which hypoxia can cause severe mental and physical deterioration. But it is often considered to be above 8,000 metres – the altitude at which this process happens dangerously fast.

Two weeks later, from an internet café in Alaska we organised a trip to climb the second of our Seven Summits, Kilimanjaro, in July and arranged to join an expedition to climb Cho Oyu in Tibet that August. At 8,201 metres, Cho Oyu is the sixth highest mountain in the world and stands just 35 kilometres due west of Everest. It would be just the test we were looking for.

*

Within two weeks of leaving Alaska we'd switched cold weather gear for safari outfits and had repacked for Africa. Our first port of call was Mount Meru, a dormant volcano 80 kilometres east of Kilmanjaro. As the second highest mountain in Tanzania, it was nevertheless little known, being overshadowed by its more coveted neighbour. But less popular mountains always have their advantages, one of these being that you often have them to yourselves.

As we neared Meru's summit, ragged cliffs plummeted to our left and steep slopes of black volcanic sands eventually disappeared over more cliffs to our right. After many hours of scrambling along Meru's knife-edge crater rim in the dark, we were blessed with a spectacular sunrise and heart-stopping views. Not only was Mount Meru the perfect mountain to acclimatise on but it also gave us glorious views of Kilimanjaro – the highest free-standing mountain in the world. She looked truly regal as she rose dramatically from the hot dry plains of the Masai steppe, crowned with her signature ice cap.

Having acclimatised on Mount Meru, we were able to summit Kilimanjaro in five days, giving us time to respect the altitude and enjoy the mountain. By approaching via the quieter Umbwe route and the steeper western breach of the crater rim, we would avoid the main tourist routes and be treated to more varied terrain. Climbing Kilimanjaro was a wonderful lesson in nature, as we passed through no less than five major climate and vegetation zones. Having left the road amid scrub-land, we ascended through rich tropical forest, then moorland, highland desert and finally an arctic zone.

The climate, weather, altitude and terrain were significantly less hostile than Denali, but compared to life on the pristine snow, it was filthy with dust and mud filling every crevice. Towards the end of the trip, our entire team looked in need of a high-pressure hose down. Hiking and perspiring in the blazing sun brought back strange memories for Rob as chemical smells leaked from his pores once again. He had been warned the chemotherapy drugs could take several years to work out of his system, and two years later, he could still smell them.

With the warmer temperatures, Rob and I indulged, zipping our new, thinner sleeping bags together. Snuggling up at night in our own tent was a novelty, though my nocturnal thrashings soon left Rob complaining of grievous bodily harm. With the easier life of climbing Kilimanjaro, trivial issues bubbled to the surface. It even annoyed me that Rob got gravel in the tooth paste tube and he hated discovering my hairs in his porridge. Without the intense pressure of trying to survive, we had unwittingly become intolerant, arguing over small issues.

After an exciting scramble up the western breach under a starlit sky, we finally reached the rooftop of Africa, 5,985 metres above sea level, at 8.15 am on 30 July 2003. It was a chilly but stunningly clear day as our team celebrated with hugs and handshakes. We looked out across Tanzania, where Mount Meru and faraway Mount Kenya were the only mountains to venture above the sea of cloud. It was a privilege to have climbed Kilimanjaro while she still wore her icy crown, something that in 20 years' time may only exist in our photos. Reaching the summit had been a great day of celebration for everyone. For the rest of the team, Kilimanjaro was the highest they'd ever climbed, and for us it was our second successful summit after our Nepal disaster, confirming that our success on Denali had been no fluke.

*

Weeks later we were once again sitting opposite Dr Phillips in his consulting room at the Lister Hospital.

'My word, you do look well, Robert. This expedition life must be suiting you,' Dr Phillips said with a broad smile. 'I'm pleased to say your blood results look very good again. I really am thrilled to see you looking so healthy. What's your next adventure?' Dr Phillips had always been full of enthusiasm for our plans and it was a relief to finally return home with good news for him.

'We're heading out to Tibet to climb Cho Oyu – it's one of the 8,000ers,' Rob replied.

'Goodness, rather you than me. But I'll look forward to hearing all about it next time. Book in to see me when you're back from Tibet.'

Even though Rob was fit and well, it was always a relief to hear that Dr Phillips was happy with his blood results. With Rob's clean bill of health, nothing stood between us and the Himalaya once again.

Despite our excitement, returning to Nepal made us nervous, our enthusiasm countered by concern that some unforeseen disaster lay in wait for us. Days later, after checking the entire contents of our medical kit for the third and final time, we finished our packing, hugged my parents goodbye and were ready to go. All that remained for us now was to stay healthy, climb safely and survive the death zone.

CHAPTER 8

Shadows of Nepal

'Grasp today with all your might, it is the tomorrow you feared yesterday.'

Anon

It was late August 2003 as we touched down at Kathmandu's Tribhuvan International Airport. A year had passed since we landed there in eager anticipation of our first Himalayan peak. That endeavour had ended abruptly with Rob's life in the balance, an emergency rescue and major abdominal surgery. Now, with Rob's clean bill of health, we were back and this time to climb Cho Oyu – the 'Turquoise Goddess'. It felt like an enormous leap of faith but we were more determined than ever.

As our rickety minibus swung out of the airport drive a cacophony of horns greeted us. Swerving immediately, our driver flew straight back off the road, nearly dismantling a fruit stall but missing the cow that lay casually in the middle of four teeming traffic lanes. Within seconds we were reminded that Kathmandu's road markings were purely decorative and heavy oncoming traffic an incentive for overtaking. 'We're back!' said Rob, throwing me a wide-eyed glance.

Street sellers sat cross-legged on straw mats, their vegetables and headless plucked chickens piled just inches from gutters of raw sewage. Emaciated dogs snatched passing licks of the chickens before a few well-aimed stones sent them skulking away. As the bus turned down the narrow potholed street towards Hotel Tibet, local shop owners welcomed us, calling out *'Namaste'* (hello) in Nepali. Kathmandu was just as colourful, dirty and chaotic as we'd remembered.

Hotel Tibet was an oasis of tranquillity, with serene photographs of the Dalai Lama and devout Buddhist monks lining the hallways. On our first evening we met up with Mark Whettu. As a close friend of Russell Brice, the leader of our expedition, he would be travelling across Tibet with us before taking a smaller team to climb Shishapangma, another 8,000-metre giant. Mark was a warm, relaxed New Zealander and a veteran of high-altitude climbing. He had even survived an enforced bivouac just beneath the summit of Everest, although he'd lost all of his toes to frostbite. Tragically, the climber he was accompanying was on his seventh attempt of Everest, which became his last, when he refused to turn around. Mark's experiences were a sobering but timely reminder before our first foray into the death zone.

The night before we flew to Tibet, the entire team assembled in the Red Onion Bar opposite the hotel for our pre-expedition briefing from Russell. We had met him in Chamonix before, and had chosen to join his team because of his reputation for excellence in expedition safety and logistics. He was also a legend for his work with the Tibetans to build schools, provide work and help communities, something we were keen to support. In contrast to Mark's toned and muscular physique, Russell appeared less than fit for high-altitude mountaineering, with a small beer belly overhanging his jeans. But appearances were deceptive and he had many successful ascents of Cho Oyu and Everest under his belt, among a host of other extreme climbs.

Gathering around the bar we chatted with our new team mates we'd met the previous day – Morgens, a wonderfully exuberant triathlete from Denmark, decorated head to toe in sponsor logos; David, a quick-witted research analyst from London; Zac, a tall, athletic Lebanese who was a whirlwind of sponsor flags and video cameras; Jamie, an enthusiastic dentist who had soon briefed us on his extensive glacier travel experience in New Zealand and Richard, a warm-hearted British guide who lived in Chamonix.

Calling for our attention, Russell stood up from his bar stool and explained that he would travel overland to base camp with the equipment, while we flew to Lhasa, the capital of Tibet. We would then acclimatise as we drove across the Tibetan plateau. He gave us some parting words of advice: 'Eight thousand metre peaks are a whole new game. Staying healthy won't be easy. You need to look after yourself, so arrive well at base camp and watch your hygiene. Every little thing counts.'

With the briefing over we met the last few members of our team.

No-one had ever climbed anything as high as Cho Oyu before and everyone was excited but nervous about the six weeks ahead.

Also travelling with us to Cho Oyu were Juhanis and Merja, a Scandinavian couple. Their daughter, Laura, had gone missing after summiting Cho Oyu three years earlier and her body had never been found. Had she still been alive she would have been my age. For the first time since her death, her parents were now travelling to Tibet on a pilgrimage to her resting place.

By 10 am the following morning we were flying over the Himalaya. Rob and I sat glued to the windows, mesmerised by our first ever view of Everest. Rising from a carpet of clouds thousands of metres below, her massive black pyramid rose defiantly, head and shoulders above all else. Inside the safety and comfort of the plane, life was easy at 9,000 metres. Out there, a plume of ice crystals was being ripped from her summit, blasted by jetstream winds into the dangerously thin atmosphere. Trailing silently eastwards like an elegant prayer scarf, her icy plume looked deceptively benign.

Advancing our watches four hours to Beijing time, we landed in Lhasa, and were welcomed by the Tibetan Mountaineering Association in five mud-splattered Toyota landcruisers. The TMA would be responsible for escorting us through Tibet to our base camp. Landing at 3,800 metres on the Tibetan plateau, our bodies immediately felt the altitude and even carrying our kit bags left us dizzy and breathless. Such a big altitude jump is normally inadvisable but we'd planned to spend several days in Lhasa so our bodies could catch up.

We drove along the clean paved streets between gleaming high-rise buildings as teams of Chinese office workers robotically performed their corporate stretches outside. Later that day as we walked around the Jokhang Temple, Tibet's spiritual centre, locals of all ages swung their copper prayer wheels or lay prostrate, while just five metres away uniformed Chinese guards played cards and babbled into their mobile phones.

After a nervous 24 hours when Rob had an upset stomach, everything settled down and the following day we visited the famous Potala Palace. Having reopened in 1980, it was once home to the fourteenth Dalai Lama until he fled to India in 1959 to escape the Chinese. Built nearly 1,500 years ago and perched on a natural rocky outcrop, its 1,000 rooms and 13 floors preside regally over the Tibetan quarter of Lhasa. Just the effort of climbing the steps to the entrance had the entire team panting and nursing throbbing heads – the first signs of acute mountain sickness.

Plunging from bright daylight into the dark candlelit rooms, we were greeted with the familiar and pungent smell of joss sticks and yak butter candles. Faces distorted in demonic grimaces peered out of the gloom from great tapestries that hung from the ceilings. Alongside them were ornately embroidered swastikas, the eastern symbol of love and good luck. As our eyes grew further accustomed to the dinginess, we could make out hundreds of gold-encrusted Buddhas lining the temples, stuffed with paper prayers and holy writings. Shafts of hazy sunlight streamed through high windows, spotlighting the rich kaleidoscope of colourful paintings that adorned the temple walls.

In a seemingly hypnotic trance, monks sat cross-legged, chanting to the beat of their drum, reading prayers by the light of flickering butter lamps. A constant stream of pilgrims wound their way through the maze of rooms, stairways, corridors and temples. Passing the hundreds of altars they paid homage with innumerable rituals: spinning prayer wheels, ringing bells, lighting candles, reciting mantras and offering prayer scarves. Some moved with purpose but many were more intrigued by us than the altars that they drifted past.

Three days and many monasteries later, we set out for Shigatse, with a little more acclimatisation but a little less sleep. The entire canine population of Lhasa appeared to be nocturnal and after three sleepless nights from endless barking, plus the Chinese Army who chanted songs outside our hotel window from 5 am every morning, we were happy to be on our way. Outside Lhasa, the transition was abrupt. Beyond a few outlying settlements lay the vast empty plains, without so much as a single shrub to be seen. But after the bustle of the temples and monasteries, it felt wonderfully peaceful.

Our journey took us along the Friendship Highway westwards, though, as a potholed gravel track, it barely qualified for its name. Incredibly, Tibet is nearly the size of Western Europe and has an average altitude of 4,000 metres, yet aside from the polar regions it is still one of the most isolated and unexplored lands in the world. As we crossed the endless barren plains it was difficult to imagine that they had once been at the bottom of a massive ocean – the Tethys Sea.

But evidence of the plateau's previous marine existence was never hard to find as entrepreneurial children waved sea fossils at us in every village.

With the plateau in the rain shadow of the Himalaya, even after the monsoon season, the ground remained a desert of mud, rock and sand. The only green to be found was at the occasional village that perched on the banks of the rushing Yarlung Tsangpo – Tibet's largest river. These were supposed to be the fertile central lands of Tibet, yet even now, at harvest time, the plateau was still uncompromisingly barren and harsh.

September was harvest time and the fields were a hive of activity as everyone gathered food for the long winter. Mothers with babies strapped to their backs, small children, even the elderly did their part. Teams of horses galloped around in circles trampling barley to separate the grain. Sometimes it was even laid over the road to be threshed by the occasional passing vehicle. We felt guilty about driving over their crops but were always greeted with friendly waves and grateful cheers. Barley and millet were the only crops hardy enough to survive the high altitude and inhospitable conditions. Tragically, this knowledge was ignored in the early sixties when the Chinese insisted the locals grew wheat and rice. This alone led to over 70,000 Tibetans dying of starvation.

Once out of Lhasa, evidence of the 1950 Chinese invasion was sadly easy to find. Monasteries that had stood for centuries were no more than rubble. With over 6,000 monasteries destroyed, the Dalai Lama referred to the supposed 'liberation' of Tibet as an act of cultural genocide. Over half a million monks and nuns had been displaced by this systematic rape of Tibet's religion and double that number were simply killed in cold blood, while many more were forced into labour camps. Shamefully, by the mid 1970s fewer than ten monasteries still stood in Tibet.

After eight bone-rattling hours, we were relieved to sample the brand-new tarmac of Shigatse. As the second largest city in Tibet, it overflowed with Western-style shops and neon signs, its streets bustling with hundreds of Han Chinese. China's incentivised migration scheme was clearly a roaring success and local Tibetans in very real danger of being outnumbered. Despite bemoaning the demise of Tibetan culture at the expense of Chinese capitalism, the entire team had soon sniffed out the only Western-style supermarket in town. We hunted down biscuits, crisps and anything else that looked vaguely safe to eat. Though we loved the wildness of Tibet, our bowels were less tolerant.

The following day, just before the Lhakpa La, one of Tibet's high passes, we reached the highest settlement of our journey so far. At 4,900 metres, it was a desolate, soulless place with brown mud houses and not a single blade of grass to be seen. Even now, in late summer, a chill wind whipped across the rubbly earth and the locals were barely visible under their layers of sheepskin and yak hair. The pass itself stood at 5,200 metres and was equally barren and windswept. Prayer flags were the only sign of life, interrupting the monotone vista with a blaze of colour and a hypnotic clatter as they flapped in the breeze. The ochre plains and endless skies stretching to the distant horizon gave us the feeling that we were inhabiting a strangely empty planet.

Dropping back to the plains, we arrived at Tingri. A Tibetan version of the Wild West, it was no more than a string of houses flanking a dirt road. Dust whipped into the air and rubbish gambolled down the main street as locals trotted past in their horse-drawn carts, waving cheerfully with their broad toothless grins. Rows of whitewashed mud houses and multicoloured window facades lined the street, their south-facing walls plastered with brown discs of hand-pressed yak manure, drying in preparation for their fires. A pool table stood randomly on the side of the road, its players temporarily halting their game to eye our convoy as it entered town. As we turned into a courtyard where we would stay that night, a tiny woman with a creased, leathery face walked past clutching the severed heads of two goats by their horns. 'Hope that's not dinner,' Rob joked, but as she disappeared into the kitchen area, it didn't look too encouraging.

A week after we'd last seen Russell, he suddenly appeared in the courtyard. With his hands casually stowed in his jean pockets and his shoulders hunched against the wind, he seemed at home in this little Tibetan outpost. He had already arranged everything for our arrival. 'I've put you two in the only twin room,' he called over to Rob and me. We thanked him, feeling rather embarrassed at our special treatment, although I was secretly glad not to be in the dormitory with nine snoring, wind passing males.

'Good trip, Russ?' I asked.

'No, it was shit. We had 11 road collapses to deal with.' The spectacularly steep Bhote Kosi gorge that slices through the Himalaya linking Nepal with Tibet was notorious for dramatic landslides. Its road clings precariously to the cliffs and is frequently destroyed in avalanches of rock debris and mud. At each impasse, every barrel of expedition equipment had been carried by hand. It had been a backbreaking task for Russell and his Sherpa team.

Having escaped Chinese influence, Tingri was truly Tibetan, as was our hotel accommodation. It was exciting to be experiencing more of the local culture first hand, with the exception of the unsavoury bathroom facilities. With two nights to acclimatise in Tingri, our teams headed off en masse the next morning to stretch lungs and legs on a nearby peak. In no time at all what appeared to be a harmless hill had slowed everyone to a silent, breathless plod. Everyone, that was, except for Morgens, who had steamed ahead. The demanding life of a professional triathlete clearly had its fringe benefits. Unwittingly though, Morgens had just become like the hare at the greyhound races, while the other fit lads did their level best to keep up.

As I took my last breathless steps to the summit stone cairn, Zac excitedly thrust his camera into my hands.

'Jo, will you take my picture for me?'

'Sure, if you don't mind camera shake because I'm breathing so fast,' I said, marvelling at his unending supply of energy and enthusiasm. Having noticed I was a keen photographer, Zac seldom went an hour without asking me to photograph him. Each time he would strike some awkward-looking action pose, much to the amusement of fellow team members.

At 4,600 metres, this insignificant-looking hill was almost the height of Mont Blanc. Yet, looking south towards the Himalayan chain, we were standing on little more than a wrinkle. It was hard to fathom that we were at the edge of the youngest and fastest growing mountain range on the planet, a mere 50 million years old and still buckling upwards half a centimetre every year. Even 80 kilometres away, Cho Oyu was standing proud amidst an array of Himalayan giants. Over eight kilometres high, she was simply immense and we both began to wonder if we weren't just a little crazy.

By mid-afternoon the following day we had arrived at base camp. It was situated on the banks of a sprawling river bed and flanked by giant mountains of scree. 'Welcome to base camp,' Russell announced proudly as we settled onto the plastic chairs in the mess tent and sipped hot lemon tea. 'You'll have to make this home for the next week.'

'Could think of worse,' David chirped, having seen the luxurious toilet tent which even had a plastic lid strapped to the loo barrel.

'Don't worry, it'll get worse,' Russell said gruffly. Over the next 20 minutes he briefed us about the task ahead. 'Base camp is at 4,900 metres, higher than all of Western Europe. But you need to make this your comfort zone,' he said sternly. 'Over the next week you need to do some acclimatisation walks. But take it easy. It's not a race.'

Suddenly, our attentions were diverted as Lachu, the chief expedition cook, burst through the mess tent door. Although only five foot two, he was larger than life with an infectious laugh and the grin of a Cheshire cat. 'So, Big Boss,' he addressed Russell affectionately 'Dinner at six o'clock today?'

Lachu was on his 42nd expedition and had cooked at the base camps of all 14 8,000-metre peaks. He was a true veteran of Himalayan expeditions and as it turned out, an exceptionally talented one too. For our first evening the team was treated to the culinary delight of sizzling yak. 'Better make the most of this, you'll probably be feeling too sick for the next one,' Russell said with a knowing smile.

The next morning, there had been a dramatic reversal of the previous night's perky mood. In an ideal world it is advisable to increase your sleeping altitude no more than 300 metres in any one day but with base camp being 700 metres higher than Tingri, we were all struggling. Comparisons of headaches and solutions dominated breakfast conversation and despite the abundance of porridge, omelettes and chapattis, everyone's appetite had evaporated overnight. Pale faced and wrapped in our puffy down jackets, it was now hard to imagine what Russell had meant about making base camp our 'comfort zone'.

The locals believed that the mountain gods gave headaches to those who dared tread too high as a final warning before the punishment of death. Thankfully, the physiological explanation was a little less frightening. They are caused by the same mechanism as a hangover. In a bar our vessels dilate because of too much alcohol, at high altitude they do so because of too little oxygen. Either way, as the blood flow increases, fluid shifts into the brain, painfully elevating the pressure inside the skull. The compensation for this hangover-like headache was that it came with a spectacular view.

Although Rob and I had attempted to make our acclimatisation marginally easier by doing some climbing in the Alps after Kilimanjaro, the little we'd earned had already been lost in the two weeks since we'd been at altitude. Pushing our bodies again to adjust to the ever decreasing oxygen levels was the only way to reacclimatise. Over subsequent days the team pushed progressively higher into the mountains overshadowing base camp on a series of walks. As we inched slowly up the scree, our conversations were at best staccato and usually non-existent.

Hundreds of metres above base camp, I felt spoilt by the ever widening vistas and frequently lost myself in the task of seeking my next photographic vantage point. My obsession with taking pictures had become a fortunate distraction from the effort of climbing. For this reason alone, Rob regretted not having the same affinity for photography and he was always grateful for a breather when I recruited him to be my model.

No-one is ever exempt from the effects of altitude, irrespective of age or fitness. Each time the group stopped, everyone found that it took noticeably longer to steady their breathing and calm their hearts. The process of acclimatisation is a marvellous thing, although from the non-scientific point of view it tends to feel more wretched than marvellous. Despite there still being 21% oxygen in the air at higher altitudes, the air pressure isn't sufficient to force enough of it into our bodies. As the oxygen just meanders into our lungs and diffuses slowly across the membranes, our bodies counteract this by pushing our heart and lungs harder. After a few hours our kidneys are recruited to help with a number of cunning counter measures, including self-doping whereby our bone marrow is stimulated to produce more red blood cells. No doubt if we were airlifted to the Olympic testing committee, we'd be disqualified within minutes. Amazingly, even these incredible adaptations are just the start and the body then goes on to produce special enzymes, grow more tissue capillaries, modify cell components and even increase oxygen storage in muscles. Acclimatisation is a fascinating process and although we can never permanently adapt to anything above 5,500 metres, our bodies are without doubt wonderfully versatile. We are perhaps the finest piece of engineering on this planet.

Back at camp and tired from our walk, Rob went for a lie down while I went to collect some drinks. Once inside the mess tent, Jamie began his familiar quizzing.

'So what time did you leave camp?' he asked.

'Can't remember exactly.' I replied nonchalantly.

'What height did you get to?'

'High enough for one day,' I said, trying to remain politely evasive.

'So how was your pulse rate when you got back?' he pushed a little more.

'I've no idea and does it really matter? We've all had a good walk.' Jamie had a good heart and was great at keeping the team on its toes, but his obsession over performance was wearing. We had a different battle to fight with the invisible fears of Rob's past and the threat of ill health or injury. Our only challenge was to scale the high ramparts of Cho Oyu and return safe. Finishing my lemon tea as quickly as I could, I poured one for Rob and escaped to our tent for a lie down.

The following morning, we were woken by loud clanging as the ground shook under our tent. Scrambling outside, we found ourselves surrounded by a sea of hairy, snorting yaks. A motley crew of yak herders with their wives and children had encircled our camp and were whistling, shouting and throwing rocks to keep their beasts under control. The yaks had infiltrated camp and were now sniffing out the few blades of grass that hid among the rocks. Each had its own bell and was decorated with multicoloured pompoms. They looked distinctly huggable, with their shaggy hair and soulful eyes, but given their bull-like size and imposing horns, hugs were strictly off the agenda.

The herders' faces were weathered to the colour of brown boot polish by decades of exposure to the extreme solar radiation and the winds of the plateau. Even the babies' cheeks were ruddy and cracked. Their many layers of woollen and sheepskin clothes were supplemented with the occasional Adidas jacket, all thick with years of grime and yak grease. The men's long black hair was entwined with striking scarlet tassels and wrapped around their heads. The women, who stood some way off, giggling and smiling, wore long woollen dresses with ornate silver belts and necklaces of turquoise and amber. It was impossible to imagine just decades ago that Red Guards were severing men's plaits and confiscating women's jewellery. Tibetan nomads had seen difficult times but amazingly, they had survived, defiantly holding onto their traditions and pride.

The next day, mayhem erupted at base camp, as over 100 yaks were loaded with our barrels of equipment and food. Timid and beautiful, the yaks were also unpredictable and easily frightened. The herders constantly shouted 'Whoaaah! Shsa, shsa,' as they dodged the jostling horns. Young male yaks protested at their loads and after repeated fits of bucking even the herders stood well back until the last piece of equipment had been hurled from the animals' backs.

Several hours later the yak train was finally loaded and set off for the 22-kilometre walk to advanced base camp, or ABC as it was commonly known. At the same time our team headed up the valley to a rock wall. Russell wanted us to practise climbing vertically with our mechanical rope ascenders (or jumars), to refresh our skills before we attempted the ice and rock cliffs higher on the mountain. Russell reminded us, 'Your rope work needs to be both automatic and perfect. You cannot afford to make a mistake on the mountain, it might be your last.'

As our team walked some distance behind the yak train, we watched the herders battling to control their yaks across the river. Wading across the tumbling icy grey river was hazardous; a toppled yak held under by its load could drown in seconds and strip the herders of their precious livelihood. Suddenly we could hear shouting. It was Zac, running frantically along the river-bank. 'Stop! Wait. I would like a photo. Please wait!' But they were unable to hear him above the rushing waters, their only concern being to reach the far side intact.

After our jumar practice, we returned to camp to find a yak herder clasping blood-filled goggles to his face. His eye socket had been badly gored and his eyeball punctured by a yak horn. It turned out that he had been working for another expedition who, facing the cost and effort of medical care, had deserted him in his moment of need. He was in danger of losing his eye, or worse still developing septicaemia.

Seeing this, Russell immediately started him on strong antibiotics, dressed his eye and paid for a vehicle to transport him the two-day journey to the nearest hospital in Shigatse. Russell's tough exterior masked a passionate heart for the Tibetan and Sherpa people and he often referred to them as his 'family'.

Having spent a week at 4,900 metres, we were ready to move up to ABC. Russell had warned us not to race as it would be a long tiring day. On the morning of our departure, Rob and I were finishing our packing as some of the lads left camp in hot pursuit of Morgens. Minutes later, as Kevin, Rob and I were leaving, Russell marched past. 'See you later, I'm going to catch the lads to tell them to slow down,' he puffed, pulling away. Russell had had years of experience and didn't want any of our team to peak too early or burn out.

It was a fabulous morning and countless stops for photos had left us some way behind but the freezing rain of the afternoon spurred us to increase our pace. Suzuki, from Japan and Kevin, a jovial and chatty New Yorker had maintained a similar pace to ours but Suzuki had become worryingly fatigued. Although I'd repeatedly suggested she wear her waterproofs, she wasn't to be persuaded. Now I implored her for the fourth time.

'Too tired,' she mumbled, without even looking up.

'You'll get too cold,' I said, but this time she didn't even respond. I was just not getting through.

Rob had stopped just ahead. 'She needs to put her waterproofs on, Jo,' he called.

'I know,' I said irritably, now feeling tired and frustrated myself. 'That's what I've been saying for the last ten minutes.' Suddenly, hearing my own words, I realised that in my own fatigue I'd been totally ineffective.

'Right, Suzuki, let's get your sack off,' I said, trying to be more positive. 'Have a rest and we'll help find your waterproofs.' Even before I'd finished she'd collapsed in a heap onto the rocks. She had lost the will to look after herself and was beginning to shiver uncontrollably. We should have taken action sooner, but we barely knew her and with the language barrier, we didn't want to seem pushy.

The three of us dressed her in waterproofs and pulled her back to her feet. The temperature had dropped with our altitude gain and the freezing rain had now turned to heavy snow. With darkening skies and poor visibility the scree ridges all looked disorientingly similar. ABC was nowhere in sight and Suzuki was flagging. Time was running out before nightfall.

CHAPTER 9

Not Good Enough

'When you reach the end of your rope, tie a knot in it and hang on.'

Thomas Jefferson

WE WERE RELIEVED to arrive at ABC just before dark. From the slow movements and pained expressions of the entire team, it was clear that none of us felt brilliant. Altitude is always the great leveller. Crouching at Cho Oyu's feet, ABC was as high as Kilimanjaro, yet we'd have to make it our new comfort zone. We were now so high that even helicopters couldn't reach us. If a person were to be suddenly deposited at our altitude without acclimatisation, they would be dead in a matter of hours.

The following morning, despite the usual altitude-induced headaches, our previous day's efforts were rewarded with glorious sunshine and spectacular views. At 5,800 metres, ABC was stunningly located on the Gyabrag Glacier as it flowed from the north-western flanks of Cho Oyu. Our tents were clustered on the glacial moraines, a jumbled mass of rock debris being carried along by a great icy conveyor belt. It felt somewhat akin to setting up camp on a building site, albeit a very beautiful one, and one that was grinding slowly downhill. The giant, ice-laden 6,000- and 7,000-metre peaks that surrounded us were dwarfed by Cho Oyu. No longer simply dominating the skyline, she now filled it completely.

Our first full day at ABC was romantically 7 September 2003 – our seventh wedding anniversary. Unromantically, we spent it out of breath lugging rocks in order to make camp safe by building steps and walkways. Having pitched camp on the jumbled glacier debris, even as we stepped out of our tents we set off rock slides and risked spraining our ankles, so it was backbreaking but necessary labour.

On our arrival in the mess tent for dinner, Russell grabbed both our arms and with a broad smile ushered us to the far end of the tent. Laid out for us was our own private table for two, complete with plastic flowers and candles. Unbeknown to us Lachu's cook team had been preparing a surprise anniversary dinner. We were even serenaded by music on a small portable stereo and received full Sherpa service. We dined on garlic soup and popcorn, yak stew, cheesecake and even after-dinner mints. Afterwards Morgens gave a touching speech and made a toast with Russell's Famous Grouse. However, altitude and alcohol make a lethal combination and even though we were all supposedly hardened mountaineers, the bottle was conspicuously still half full by the end of the evening. With our cheeks aching from so many photos, we retired to our tent, having celebrated our seven years together in Tibet, in the highest restaurant in the world.

The following day we held our Puja, a ceremony in which the mountain gods are asked for safe passage. It was conducted by one of our cooks, Loppasang, who had previously been a lama. Intrigued at Loppasang's career change, I asked him why he was cooking instead of living in a monastery.

'I fall in love so get married. No more lama!' he laughed, screwing up his dark chubby face with a look of great satisfaction. Having secured the blessing of the mountain gods, we were allowed to venture onto Cho Oyu's slopes and start climbing in earnest. But, later that day, the reality of what lay ahead struck home. After a mere 60-minute stroll, our legs were shaking and our lungs felt like deflated balloons. The summit still towered nearly three vertical kilometres above our heads and we hadn't even started carrying loads.

That night, tucked inside my sleeping bag with my head torch and Bible, I felt encouraged as I read a verse from Isaiah 40: *'Even youths grow tired and weary, and young men stumble and fall; but those who hope in the Lord will renew their strength. They will soar on wings like eagles; they will run and not grow weary, they will walk and not be faint.'*

Over the next few weeks we would be following the altitude maxim 'climb high, sleep low'. This would allow our bodies to sample higher altitude by day and recover and acclimatise by night. At least that was the theory. In reality, with the altitudes we were pushing up to we would never fully acclimatise or recover. The night before our first departure, Russell announced, 'If you can't climb to camp one in five hours, you're unlikely to make the summit.' Although he had repeatedly told us to go slowly, we were about to be tested. Failure to perform might cost us our opportunity to summit. There were nervous glances around the mess tent.

We set out for camp one at nine the following morning, the Sherpa team having left hours earlier to set up the tents. The Sherpas' strength and stamina at altitude was truly astounding – even the fittest and most acclimatised Westerner didn't come close. None of us would be climbing this mountain without their help.

For what seemed like hours we climbed carefully through the moraines. They looked deceptively easy but were in reality an endless maze of unconsolidated rocky ridges and troughs, and any sudden movement converted the rocks into a layer of ball bearings that slid unpredictably across the blue ice beneath. Suddenly the sound of a small rock avalanche was followed by heavy breathing behind me. Before I had a chance to turn around, Zac came scrambling past, his legs spinning on the ice like some manic cartoon character. Thump! His rucksack swung left and clobbered me with the force of a small elephant and knocked me off my feet. Unable to get a grip, I skidded back into the trough out of which I had just painstakingly climbed.

'Thanks a bunch Zac!' I shouted, gasping for more air but he didn't hear. He had left ABC late after videoing himself shaving and was now moving like a missile to catch up with the other lads.

The last hour and a half of the climb to camp one was spent scaling what Russell had described with some understatement as a gentle scree slope. The team had more aptly named it 'the scree slope from hell', as vast swathes of the 45° crumbling mountainside would slide downhill without so much as one of us sneezing. Moving upwards was a constant battle to reverse the trend of one step up, slide two down. Rob and I were relieved to arrive at camp one after just four and a half hours, reaching a new personal best altitude of 6,400 metres. But instead of enjoying celebratory hugs we lay comatose in our tent, bearing more resemblance to two planks of wood than a pair of jubilant mountaineers.

Camp one was delicately poised on a crevasse-ridden ice cap that crowned the top of the scree slope. Above it was the north-west ridge that we would climb to access the ice cliffs en route to camp two. Descending the scree slope back to ABC, just one hour later, proved

MAP OF CHO OYU

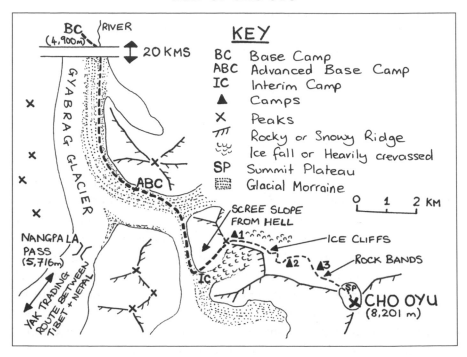

MAP OF EVEREST REGION

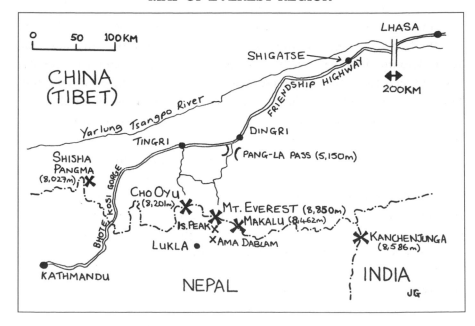

even more treacherous than our ascent and became a serious contender for a new extreme sport. After surfing a series of rock avalanches for nearly 2,000 feet, we were spat out at the bottom, miraculously unhurt but with a few more grey hairs and boots full of gravel.

The next few days were spent resting and preparing at ABC before spending our first night at camp one. Russell demonstrated how to use our oxygen equipment and the emergency hyperbaric Gamow bag. This brilliant invention looks like a large yellow body bag: a person is sealed inside and air is pumped in, artificially increasing the pressure and hopefully reversing the fatal effects of pulmonary or cerebral oedema. Russell had saved 13 lives with this bag, despite none of them being members of his team.

As we all sat feeling sobered by Russell's stories, Zac who had been busy videoing suddenly piped up. 'So Russ, how does Cho Oyu compare to Everest?' His unstoppable enthusiasm was inspirational, but now didn't seem the right time to be discussing Everest. Russell paused and looked around the group,

'Cho Oyu is a game compared to Everest'. The team was deathly silent. Even Zac didn't have any more questions.

*

With time on our hands, simple card games became the favoured form of entertainment for our slow minds, although with our international team, friendly disputes repeatedly broke out over which nation's rules took precedence. Tempers were also becoming frayed between other teams at ABC, but it was not so amicable. Russell wanted a co-ordinated approach between teams on the mountain, but he was dogged by a lack of co-operation.

'It's the same thing every bloody year,' he said with growing frustration. The low cost, budget expeditions were unwilling to pay for Sherpas to put up the fixed ropes, but they were always first in line to use them. It was also frustrating for the better organised expeditions to witness these teams leaving piles of garbage around like ugly sores; and our Sherpas were regularly dispatched up the mountain to remove their mess. Yet despite all this, if a costly rescue was required, Russell was often their first port of call.

After several days of rest, we were toiling through the moraines again towards camp one, when suddenly Jamie popped out of a gully ahead.

'What were you doing down there?' I called out, rather surprised given he'd left camp 30 minutes ahead of us.

'Got lost,' Jamie replied and scuttled off along the ridge. Confusingly just ten minutes later, he appeared again, but behind us. Stepping aside, we said our second 'hellos' as he marched past. But when it happened for the third time, it was hard not to see the funny side of it. Nevertheless we attempted to soften the awkward moment for him and just gave a casual nod. Fortunately for Jamie he was exceptionally fit, so pulled ahead with ease once more.

My second trip to camp one was proving far harder than my first. Before I'd even reached the scree slope, I could barely lift my feet and with every step up my morale sank lower. Even my breathing was more shallow and frenzied than before. As I approached interim camp at the bottom of the slope, Rob walked back to meet me without his rucksack.

'I feel terrible,' I said feebly. 'Don't know what's wrong with me today.'

'I know. You've been struggling all morning. Give me your sack.'

'I'm sorry, Honey'

'Don't worry. You've only got 100 metres to interim camp. There's a tent you can rest in.'

I collapsed onto the rocky floor of the tent and instantly fell into an exhausted sleep, barely even registering the icy cold rock under my head. Just half an hour later I'd hauled myself to my feet again and started the gruelling climb up to camp one. Deep inside I wanted to keep taking steps. I didn't like the pain but something kept drawing me higher. When I arrived at camp one after seven hours, I didn't want to see Russell. I couldn't face being told we weren't fast enough.

Staying awake for hours in a freezing, dark tent, waiting for snow to melt, was like a torturous version of watching paint dry. Despite having no appetite and feeling sick, rehydrating our bodies was not a luxury we could afford to neglect. At this altitude dehydration alone could cause a sudden and fatal deterioration. Both the barometric pressure and our breathing rate would drop overnight, making it our most vulnerable time. Fogged with tiredness, my mind went over the same thoughts like a merry go round. *Am I getting ill? What's wrong with me?* I normally acclimatised faster than Rob, yet now I seemed to be deteriorating.

'Do you think I'm hitting my personal altitude ceiling, Honey?' I asked Rob but there was no response. 'Rob,' I said flicking my head torch on. He'd fallen asleep. Though I was loathe to wake him, he had to drink.

At 6,400 metres, it was becoming startlingly obvious why the world's highest populations in the Andes and Himalaya only live up to around 5,500 metres and why, even there, they do not settle permanently. Above this altitude, the human body can't function properly, our systems start to shut down and our cells are starved of their life-supporting oxygen. The higher you go, the faster this process occurs.

With a warm drink inside me, I finally lay down on the protruding mound of snow that bulged under our ground sheet. Within seconds my already congested nose had become blocked and I was gasping for air. Thrashing back into an upright position, I slumped against my rucksack nursing my head as it pounded like a jackhammer. Shivering under my layers of down, I started to count the hours, willing the sunrise on.

By 5.30 am the miserable wait was over and it was light enough for me to start up the stove. My attempts at being quiet were thwarted by an inability to coordinate my hands and brain. After clanging the saucepan lid for a third time Rob groaned and rolled over.

'What's the time?' he said screwing his face up and clearly unimpressed.

'Early but I've had a crap night and I'm desperate for a drink,' I said hoping for some sympathy, but instead he rolled back over and wriggled deeper into his bag.

Gradually camp started to buzz as the rest of the team prepared to climb the ice cliff. After yesterday's abysmal performance I wouldn't be moving any higher today. Kevin had decided to return to ABC, which left Rob and me alone at camp one to contemplate our poor performance. I wondered if I should go down too but Russell had left the door open. He'd suggested we try the cliff tomorrow and we were happy to grab whatever crumbs of opportunity were thrown our way.

The morning passed as we melted snow ready for the team on their return and answered nature's calls. Although the short walk to the snow-hole toilet left me limp and out of breath, somehow the sun's warmth, a peacefully empty camp and views that stretched for miles across Tibet made the discomforts worthwhile.

My second night at camp one was marginally better, but after two and a half hours melting snow and gearing up the following morning I felt ready for bed rather than breaking personal altitude records. As we left camp one the ground steepened immediately. I felt as though my heart might explode right out of my chest and I couldn't shake my dizziness. Unusually, Russell was climbing right beside me. After yesterday's dismal performance, I guessed he wanted to observe me more closely.

'How long do you think to the ice cliff?' I asked him, feeling like a child whining 'Are we nearly there yet?' Looking at him for his answer, I was perplexed by what I saw. His lips were moving but I couldn't hear a word. As I stared, I felt as if I was falling into a trance. The silence was gradually replaced by an increasingly loud high-pitched buzz. I stopped in my tracks and looked for Rob. Something was very wrong. My vision was blurred, everything was moving in slow motion. My hypoxic brain finally twigged. I was about to faint, and that was a very big problem. I was flanked either side by cliffs that plunged away for thousands of feet and I was not attached to a rope. Summoning every ounce of concentration, I tried to get some words out before it was too late. 'Russ, Russ, stop. I can't hear anything you're saying,' I murmured.

Before I'd even finished, he had grabbed my waist harness. 'We're going down,' he said, turning me around on the spot. I willed myself to stay upright as I teetered down the slope and Russell delivered me to our tent door. Collapsing inside, I felt a confirmed and wretched failure. I had just proved everything Russell might have suspected. I didn't have it in me.

Rob had only made it about 50 metres farther before he too gave up exhausted. For both of us it had been a feeble and heart-wrenching morning. Even with an extra day of rest, we were still not making the grade. As we melted snow, Russell came over for the chat we'd been dreading.

'Thanks for getting me back safe, Russ. I'm sorry I nearly lost it up there,' I said, feeling very pathetic.

'Don't worry, Jo ... when is your period due?' he asked me. His question took me by surprise.

'Umm, don't know, not sure.' I felt even more stupid, but I'd lost all sense of time. I didn't even know what day of the week it was.

'We need to think about how things are going for you both.' I knew precisely what was coming next and there was no avoiding it. 'The fact is neither of you are performing well enough at the moment.'

'Yeah, we know,' Rob said. I nodded in reluctant agreement, trying to hide my intense disappointment and desire to burst into tears.

'Based on your current performance, it's unlikely you'll summit,' he continued. After that I didn't absorb anything else he said. The words dug into my heart like a knife. Even Rob, who was normally so level headed, struggled with the reality of Russell's comments.

The altitude seemed to be affecting my emotions as strongly as my physical abilities. Every emotion was exaggerated, yet it was impossible to change how I felt. Hearing Russell's verdict had sent my mood plummeting and I could see Jo was doing no better. The ramifications of our failure went far beyond just Cho Oyu. If we couldn't summit Cho Oyu then Everest was definitely out of the question. If Everest was out of the question, then so were the Seven Summits and our dream would have to remain a dream.

Whatever the reasons for our poor performance, we both had to descend to a lower altitude. Neither of us could think straight and simply staying alive for two days at 6,400 metres seemed to be stretching us too far.

Safely back at ABC later that day, it was a haven of comfort. It no longer seemed hostile, cold and barren, and felt like coming home. With the thicker air, everything about life was easier and our troubles quickly faded. I realised that defeatist thoughts had been swamping my mind. Rather than seeing camp one as a failure, I resolved to look at it differently. Our bodies were simply acclimatizing slowly and we'd have to be patient. I hoped Russell would share this view.

At 9 am prompt, Russell called a meeting to brief us on his summit plan. The first team would move from ABC through camps one, two and three, summiting on the fourth day. Assuming there was then a second weather window before the winter winds arrived, the second team would do an additional acclimatisation climb to camp two and then make their summit push. The second team, was to include Kevin,

Suzuki, Rob and me. We squeezed each other's hands tightly as the significance of what Russell had said hit us. He was willing to give us a second chance.

Seeing the excitement on everyone's faces, Russell was swift to keep our feet on the ground. 'No matter how bad you've felt so far, it's gonna get a lot worse. And remember, you're only successful if you come back from the summit.' With that he finished his briefing and returned to watching a team of Korean climbers through the telescope. They were taking the huge risk of attempting Cho Oyu's north-west face while it was still laden with the late monsoon snows.

That afternoon, I made a simple discovery, but one that revolutionised my life. I'd just started my period. Unlike on Denali, I couldn't take the pill on Cho Oyu because it was too high, so I had to let nature run its course. Even at sea level I became tired and breathless just before my period started, and I now realised why I'd nearly fainted above camp one. Having excitedly told Rob, I raced off to inform Russell. He wasn't surprised. 'Just as well you'll have a few more days in the second team. I've seen women fail because of their period, that's why I asked.'

Normally, to have a period while camping is a severe nuisance, but this time I couldn't have been happier. Maybe I had, as it were, fallen but I hadn't yet failed. I was going to get back up again and give it everything I had.

My initial exuberance was short lived though as I soon remembered that the very thing my body had been slavishly producing in response to the altitude was more red blood cells to carry the oxygen. Now, just before our summit attempt, I was about to lose precisely what I needed most.

*

Several days later, Rob and I left ABC early to give ourselves the psychological boost of not being last to camp one. After several hours, with just 50 metres to go, I was on a high and I felt like a new woman. Reaching the final traverse, I became aware of furious panting and coughing behind me. It was Jamie, seemingly desperate to catch me up. But feeling so pleased at my morning's performance, a mischievous moment overcame me and I cranked up my pace just enough to reach camp first.

'Well done, Bird Bones', Rob puffed as he arrived moments later, 'I could see you had the bit between your teeth.'

'Yes I did . . .' I chuckled, '. . . but isn't it great to arrive only feeling out of breath, instead of needing full cardiac resuss!'

The next morning, every step above camp one was a new altitude record. While it was desperately hard work, I was making steady progress. As we neared the ice cliff I could see Rob was flagging. I was already carrying all my equipment plus our medical kit and camera gear but I insisted on taking some of his weight.

'You don't have to do this, Bella, really,' he said.

'This is no time for heroics. You helped me the other day, so why can't I help you?'

'You can't carry any more.'

'When you see me on all fours, then you can take some weight back. How's that?' I said.

'OK, it's a deal. And you're not allowed to argue, understood?' Rob knew my stubborn streak all too well.

'Understood,' I replied, relieving Rob of his oxygen mask, metal regulator and some food. Every gram at this altitude made a difference. I was now 100% focused on reaching camp two. If we failed this time Russell would almost certainly say no to our summit attempt.

Moving up the steep snow slope beneath the ice cliff, I drew parallel with Suzuki. She'd made no appreciable height gain in the last ten minutes and was still well below the ice face. Wailing and groaning, her arms and legs flailing, she was using vast amounts of energy but to no avail. Like everyone else who climbed past, I tried my best to encourage her, but it was a lost cause. Minutes later Russell caught up with her and sent her down.

A 70-metre ice cliff was the biggest obstacle en route to camp two and we were both eager to get past that section of the climb. Like a giant dam, millions of tonnes of snow and ice forming Cho Oyu's north-western face lay behind that cliff. Periodically and without warning it would collapse, releasing vast quantities of lethal ice blocks onto the slopes below. And when that happened, the trick was to be nowhere around. But it was a lottery.

With Rob ahead we moved quickly along the traverse to the shortest section of the cliff. As he kicked his crampons into the vertical blue ice, debris flew in all directions. Standing diagonally beneath him I thought I'd be safe, but I was wrong. With one big kick he launched a mass of ice missiles into the air. Instead of falling down the gully they ricocheted out, smashing into me in three places. Rob heard my yelps and shouted from above but I couldn't say a word. Every last morsel of air had been sucked from my lungs as my right shoulder and thigh screamed with pain.

'Are you all right, Jo?' he shouted again. I was delicately balanced on a ledge no more than four inches wide, above a drop that would whisk me thousands of feet back to ABC, with no stops. Instinctively tightening my safety lines, I pressed my nose into the ice cliff on my right as I tried to regain my composure.

'Jo. What's happened?' I could hear the worry in Rob's voice and knew I had to answer.

'I'm OK,' I whimpered back as loud as I could muster and promptly burst into tears. My arm had gone numb with the pain and I was scared that it was broken. I winced and tried to test it to see if there was any bone movement. It was OK, I was still in one piece. But there was nothing I could do and nowhere to go. I couldn't even curl up to nurse my leg. I forced myself to continue. My encounter with three cricket ball sized fragments of concrete-hard ice made climbing the cliff itself doubly hard. After a rest at the top, I clambered back to my feet and resumed my gruelling plod, albeit with an additional limp.

Moving up at a gentler angle, I could see someone ahead lying in a crumpled heap on their rucksack. As I drew near, to my great surprise it was Zac.

'Jo, I need your help,' he said with a forlorn expression.

'What's up, Zac?' I asked, worried that something was desperately wrong.

'You need to radio the Sherpas for me.'

'Why what's happened?' I asked.

'I can't go any further, I need them to bring a tent here. I've never felt like this before. I don't know what's wrong with me, I'm usually first.' I was taken aback by Zac's words but crouched down on the snow beside him.

'Look at me, Zac, I'm half your size. If I can do this, so can you.'

'I can't, Jo, I'm telling you, I feel terrible.'

'I'm sure you do, but that's normal. Plus I don't think the Sherpas will bring a tent here anyway. You can do it Zac. Come on, let's go'. But he didn't want to move, saying he needed more rest. Rob was right behind me and took over the encouraging and we were both relieved when eventually he got back to his feet.

Eight hours after leaving we pulled into camp two. It was situated on a broad bench above more ice cliffs and just left of the avalanche-prone north-west face. As I dropped my heavy sack onto the snow, my brain banged constantly as if it was inside an empty tin can, but I didn't care. We had finally made it to 7,100 metres. Inside I felt like dancing but lighting the stove and melting snow had to suffice for the evening's entertainment.

After a few hours, though our water was finally ready, we both felt uncomfortably bloated. Flatulence is a common affliction at altitude. At our current elevation, any trapped intestinal gases would triple in volume making HAFE – high altitude flatulence emission, something of a blessing.

Sleeping on oxygen for the first time was an unsavoury experience. No matter how I lay or positioned the mask I felt as if I was suffocating. Every time I moved a pool of semi-frozen saliva slurped out of the mask down my neck, or worse still into my mouth. After a wakeful night, the effects of the dry air and oxygen had dried my throat to a crisp and I was desperate to make a drink. Rob hadn't slept well either, but I was too wrung out to offer sympathy. My emotions had gone into a Neanderthal survival mode.

Kevin had suffered a bad night too, so bad that he'd decided to quit. 'I'm outta here, guys, and I'm taking all my gear down to ABC.' By taking his kit back to ABC, the decision would be sealed. Kevin's trip was over.

Hours later as the 'A' team prepared to leave camp two we wished them good luck for their summit push and I gave Morgens an especially big hug. He was going to attempt to summit without oxygen, and even being a professional triathlete, it would test him to his very limits. Shortly after, Rob and I set out for ABC and Rob quickly started to fall behind. I continued down, hoping the sight of me ahead would encourage him on, but in the end I was uncomfortably far ahead. Slumping onto the snow, I waited for him above a steep section.

'Are you OK, Rob?' I called as he drew nearer.

'No, I'm knackered. Got nothing left,' he replied weakly.

'Big push to camp one. Then we'll take a break.'

'I'm finished with this,' he said emphatically.

'Finished with what?' I asked.

'This bloody mountain!' Pausing to catch his breath, he continued, 'There's no way I'm coming back up here again. I'm done with 8,000-metre peaks.' I was stunned by his outburst but didn't dare say a word. As I watched him sway on the spot, his head hanging, I suddenly realised that if I didn't encourage him to descend quickly, he might deteriorate too far for me to help him. At these altitudes, even the Sherpas couldn't carry people. I had to get him down fast.

CHAPTER 10

Beyond Limits

'There is nothing to fear except fear itself.'

Franklin Roosevelt

Rob DISAPPEARED OVER the edge of the ice cliff and I nervously watched the ropes twitching as I waited for my turn. Abseiling down on any rope requires the utmost care; one mistake with your harness or rope will be your last. The ice cliff was the final obstacle before reaching camp one. Once there I could let Rob rest a little, but then we'd have to push on.

Despite my own state of exhaustion, I somehow found the necessary reserves to keep Rob going. Once we had negotiated the ice cliff safely, I felt ten feet tall inside and my resolve was stronger than ever. I was going to get Rob to the safety of ABC, come what may.

The next day at ABC was wonderfully lazy, a fitting reward for our efforts. Most of it was spent horizontal or grazing on Lachu's endless supply of snacks. Despite the pleasures of ABC, I was in an emotional no-man's land after Rob's declaration of the previous day. Was he serious about not going back up? I knew we risked failing if we tried again but we risked disappointment and regret if we didn't. I was desperate to encourage Rob and bolster his mood but now wasn't the time. He had gone into his cave for a private board meeting and trying to talk him out of it before he was ready wasn't going to help. Hard as it was, I would just have to hold my nerve, say nothing and hope he'd come around.

As the day wore on radio transmissions indicated that Richard was unwell and descending from camp two. When he finally arrived he was haggard and pasty, looking 20 years older than when he left three days ago. He had developed a chest infection and though harmless enough at sea level, it could easily develop into HAPE – high altitude pulmonary oedema, a lethal condition in which the victim drowns in their own body fluids. If not treated immediately, it will kill within hours.

We didn't sleep well that night worrying about Richard and wondering how the first team were doing. They were due to set out for the summit around 3.30 am and I kept unzipping the tent door to check if the stars were still visible. We prayed they'd have good weather to summit. At 8,000 metres the weather alone could make the difference, not only between success and failure but between failure and catastrophe. Around 6 am, as we lay buried in our sleeping bags, Rob made a surprise announcement.

'I'm going to take up more of those noodles next time. That's all I can eat when we're up there.'

'You're OK to give it a go then?' I was startled.

'Yeah, just had to clear my head,' he said. Rob had seemingly had a cathartic change of mind and was now fine, but after the emotional rollercoaster of the last few days, I felt ecstatic and wrung out all at the same time.

Getting to camp two, sleeping there and coming down again had been too much. I'd had enough. I could see it was difficult for Jo when I said I was finished but I needed to reboot my system and start again. With the thicker air of ABC, the world seemed a different place and I wasn't going to be beaten. I was ready for the summit push.

It was a pensive morning at ABC as we waited for a radio call from the first summit team. The sky was heavy with dark storm clouds and snow squalls buffeted the mess tent. We huddled together around the radio set hoping for news. At 8 am the radio finally crackled into life. To our surprise Russell announced they were bathed in glorious sunshine high above the sea of cloud that enveloped ABC. Sadly, he also told us that he'd sent David down. He'd fallen over several times while putting his crampons on, and to have continued up could have been a death sentence.

Throughout the morning there was a kaleidoscope of emotions in the mess tent. Richard still felt awful and was fed up knowing he'd not be well enough to join the second summit team. Kevin was struggling to remain enthusiastic with his own attempt over and Rob and I were feeling down, having heard the latest weather forecast.

Jetstream winds were predicted to return in the next few days, not only preventing our summit attempt but also potentially destroying the high camps. There was nothing we could do but watch the minutes tick by while we waited for further news.

Finally, though, the empty static was interrupted, as one by one, great whoops of joy came over the radio as each team member reached the summit. Even Morgens, who had been the slowest because he wasn't using oxygen, had made it. But many hours later the happy mood reversed. Ian, a property developer from the UK, and a member of the summit team, had gone snowblind just above camp one. Despite wearing goggles, his corneas had been severely burnt by the high UV levels and although it would be a temporary condition, it was an excruciatingly painful one.

The team descended from camp one the next morning with Ian blindfolded and braced between two Sherpas. They were jubilant on their arrival back at ABC but they'd all aged dramatically. Ravaged by the rarefied air above 8,000 metres they all bore the hallmarks of the death zone. Several hours later, David was still nowhere in sight and a search party was about to depart when he drifted back into camp. As I chatted with him he seemed slightly drunk, clearly an overdose of altitude, though I was relieved to see his sense of humour remarkably intact. The decision for him to descend had clearly been the right one.

Despite the jetstream forecast, Russell was optimistic; he believed we'd have an opportunity to summit before they hit. Our small team had now dwindled to just Rob and me as that morning, Russell had told Suzuki that she wasn't competent to attempt the summit and she'd be a danger to herself and others. She didn't agree. After much crying she marched off and made tearful pleas to the Sherpas for private payment to get her to the summit. But Suzuki was lucky – they refused to help. If she'd had her way, the climb could have cost her dearly.

Kevin was now regretting his decision to quit, but with all his gear off the mountain, he felt there was no way back. Sensing Kevin's regret and that he was about to miss the opportunity of a lifetime, I had a chat with Russell on his behalf and a plan was agreed. Kevin would receive extra Sherpa help to carry his gear back up the mountain. When Kevin heard this good news, his mood was instantly transformed. He was thrilled to have a second chance.

That night at dinner the first summit team were bubbling over with enthusiasm. We were keen to hear their stories, but knowing how hard it had been didn't comfort our already anxious minds. As I left the mess tent to get an early night, someone grabbed my arm.

'Didi.' Straining to see who it was in the dim moonlight, I realised it was Serin, one of our Tibetan cook assistants. He had started copying our Nepali Sherpas and cooks, who had given me the name, which means 'elder sister' in Nepali. In the dark his beady eyes and toothless grin were just visible and although neither of us could communicate verbally, we had got to know each other well with smiles and sign language. Gently lifting my arm, he placed his prized *dzi* stone into my hand and excitedly pointed to me and then up towards the blue moonlit slopes of Cho Oyu. The *dzi* is a traditional Tibetan piece of jewellery made from a round agate stone. It carries a black and white design that is supposed to protect its wearer from catastrophe. Serin wanted me to carry it to the summit of Cho Oyu. Thanking him as best I could, I promised to take it with me. I felt deeply honoured.

The following morning Kevin, Rob and I were itching to make our fourth and final journey to camp one. After a never-ending team photo session, we said our goodbyes and left ABC. As we departed, Tom, a car mechanic from the States who had just summited, gave us a verse from Psalm 37: '*Be still before the Lord and wait patiently for him.*' As we plodded up the moraines, I couldn't help but wonder at its significance.

Our night at camp one was spent hoping our tent wouldn't get ripped off the mountain. By dawn, loose guy lines and prayer flags were lashing around camp like wild animals. We were afraid to leave the tent for fear it would blow away and we communicated with Kevin by radio, even though he was only ten metres away. Russell was monitoring the radios at ABC and we agreed with him that we'd wait one more day to see if the winds dropped. We spent the day being bounced up and down on the windward side of the tent while listening to the deafening rattle of the fly sheet and watching the radio swing hypnotically from the roof of the tent. With little to do and our minds dulled by the altitude, I found myself spending hours just counting the seconds between the blasts of wind. It seemed as if the high winds had struck as predicted and we sensed it might be the end of our summit bid. Remembering Tom's Bible verse, all we could do was be patient.

The winds continued to batter camp all night but amazingly, as the next day dawned they'd diminished to no more than a light breeze. It was time to go. Being better acclimatised, we were now able to move at a slow but steady pace. Knowing we could make it to camp two gave us a confidence we'd not felt in over five weeks. We arrived in six hours – an encouraging improvement on our previous time.

Moving up towards camp three the following day we were now using oxygen for the first time while climbing. Wearing the large MIG fighter pilot masks felt suffocating, yet every time I instinctively ripped it off, I had to relearn that there was even less air outside. On reaching high camp there was much celebration and we hugged each other as tightly as our oxygen masks and equipment would allow. Seven and a half kilometres above sea level, we were now in position. Nothing but the weather and our own abilities lay between us and the summit.

Camp three was precariously positioned on a steep snow slope directly above a cliff, with tents pitched on tiny dug-out platforms no bigger than a kitchen table. One moment of inattention would send us straight back to camp two in serious need of medical attention. Having elected not to use oxygen while resting inside the tent, we had freedom to move about but everything happened in slow motion. Even removing our boots left us breathless and in need of a lie down.

Sitting side by side in our tent vestibule we soaked up the views. The clouds stretched to the western horizon, glistening with the low afternoon sun. Shishapangma, another mighty 8,000-metre peak, was the only other mountain that ventured above them into our lofty realm. With adrenalin flooding my system for the big push ahead and seeing sights that I'd only ever dreamed of, I felt as if I was flying.

As the sun dipped below the horizon, the temperature quickly plummeted to −18°C and we started to prepare for our departure. At this altitude, eating was a functional task to be endured rather than enjoyed, our objective being to consume the maximum number of calories without making ourselves sick. We force fed ourselves half a packet of plain noodles, but couldn't stomach any more. Tonight would be our first encounter with the death zone. No matter how well acclimatised anyone is, climbing above 8,000 metres is dangerous and must be limited to as few hours as possible. From the moment you venture into it you deteriorate rapidly, both physically and mentally. We had the hardest hours of our lives ahead of us and no matter what our preparation, it would be uncharted territory. All our fears and anxieties of the last five weeks were now totally focused on the next 24 hours. We knew we had to perform like we'd never performed before.

Somehow between nightfall and our 3 am departure we had lost time. We hadn't managed so much as ten minutes' sleep to restore us and getting dressed turned out to be far harder than we imagined. A combination of three sleepless nights plus the lack of oxygen had slowed our brains to a crawl. Even deciding how to thread a buckle was confusing, while calculating our hours of available oxygen at different flow rates felt like advanced mathematics. It took 30 minutes to put our harnesses on and 40 to sort our crampons and oxygen equipment. It was already 3.20 am and we were late for the biggest mountain of our lives. In our high-altitude stupor, time had just slipped through our fingers.

Crawling out of our tent I gazed upwards hoping for a clear sky, but what I saw took my breath away. There were thousands upon thousands of stars, each one so clear and bright. I had never seen anything like it and struggled to absorb the immensity of what I was witnessing. I felt small and insignificant and yet so alive.

'OK, Didi, we go now,' Loppasang called, bringing me back to the reality of the task ahead. I turned towards Rob and tugged on his rucksack straps.

'Are you set?' I asked from behind my oxygen mask.

'Yeah. Is your oxygen flowing OK?' he asked, pointing to my tube.

I glanced at the flow gauge window halfway along my tube. 'It's flowing OK. Love you.'

'Love you too. Be careful.'

It was 3.30 am when Kevin, Rob and I, along with the two Sherpas Loppasang and Karsang, started up towards the notorious rock bands. As a thick layer of yellow limestone that slices through the upper mountain, the rock bands are awkward and broken cliffs and the most intimidating obstacle on summit day. Sealed inside the cocoon of my goggles, mask and hood, my movement and vision were restricted as if in deep-sea diving gear. My world was now reduced to the lonely beam of my head torch.

Thirty minutes out of high camp I had reached the rock bands but felt panicky. My breathing was still frenzied, I'd found no rhythm since leaving high camp and now I had to climb. I slid my ascender up and scrabbled for purchase on the snow-covered rock. Even my first few moves left me limp. Groaning inside my mask I fought for every move, then hung in my harness, unable to lift hand or foot. Devoid of strength, my legs were shaking and hauling my weight up with my arms was agonising. I forced myself upwards once more and sank back in my harness again. I fumbled to adjust my goggles and mask but with clumsy mittened hands, I just made things worse. Thoughts screamed inside my head. *This isn't possible. It's too hard. I've reached my limit.*

Russell's words that Cho Oyu was just a game compared to Everest reverberated inside my dulled mind, taunting me. *If Everest is harder than this – it's inconceivable, impossible. It will kill me for sure. There's no way I'm doing Everest.* My mind raced in a blur of unanswered questions and declarations. I was about to expire with the effort. I'd never given up in my life, yet even in my state of high altitude oblivion I felt strangely relieved to have made the decision. Saying no to Everest, I felt as if I'd come to my senses. I'd discovered my limits and I could finally be at peace.

As my mind had been working, my body had continued robotically clawing its way up the rock. With each desperate move I was still gaining height and the long-feared rock band was passing beneath me. Bracing myself against the steep snow, I was breathing so fast my throat felt narrowed to a crack and my rib muscles burned with the effort.

'Sorry Loppasang,' I gasped, 'rest here, please.'

'OK,' he replied. Loppasang was breathing hard too behind his oxygen mask, but his presence was calming. Looking around I decided this was a safe place to turn back. *I could give up now and stop all this pain. Yes, this is a good place to halt this nonsense before it's too late.* But as if reading my mind, Loppasang breathlessly announced, 'Climb now better, Didi.' Before my brain could even engage, his comment rekindled a fire inside me. My heart surged with excitement and within seconds my mind had leapt over an abyss. I'd never felt so utterly incapable of taking another step, yet I was doing just that. In my abject weakness, a primitive desire had kept me going through the torturous rock bands and now I was ready to push for the summit. Nothing was going to turn me around.

Heaving myself back upright, in the black freezer of the night, I started up the steep ground of snow and rock slabs. Though every step was laboured, my panic had subsided and I felt strangely calm. A breeze had picked up and was burrowing into the flesh of my right cheek. A minute sliver of skin, exposed between my goggles, mask and balaclava, felt stiff and immobile, and the rubber of the oxygen mask had frozen to it. As I continued to take weary steps, I tried to decide what I should do. With my chunky mittens I knew I wouldn't manage such a delicate task but I daren't risk taking them off. I yanked my down hood forwards and to the right, trying to shield my face from the bitter west wind. It was the best I could do.

Chasing the dark, brooding night away, the first signs of dawn finally broke across the icy world. The five of us gathered on a small platform of ground jutting out above the rock slabs. It was the first safe place to sit, but even here we couldn't let our guard down. Only the sharp points of our crampons held us onto the slope. Turning to Rob I noticed a six-inch icicle hanging from his mask. I snapped it off and he reciprocated. He rubbed my knee with his mittened hand. I knew he was doing well.

As I looked out from Cho Oyu's north-west face for the first time that morning I forgot my heaving chest, shaking legs and numb feet, stunned by what I saw. Stretching beyond the horizon and piercing the dawn sky was the peak's colossal triangular shadow. For the first time we were confronted with the massive proportions of the giant upon which we now perched. I waved my arm towards the vista below, and Rob nodded at me. No words were necessary. The ochre-brown plains of Tibet lay like a bed of crumpled velvet beneath us, glowing a burnished bronze as the golden rays of dawn danced across them. To our left the rocky spires and giant cornices of the vast Himalayan chain stretched west. I felt utterly puny, yet immensely grateful that we were allowed a glimpse of such inaccessible places and astonishing handiwork.

As we stood again, a long steep slope stretched out of sight above us. From the top we would gain the summit plateau. Despite our agonisingly slow pace, five breaths for every step, we soon caught up with three other climbers who were not using oxygen. I was shocked by their frail and deathly faces, their uncovered cheeks and noses waxy and white with frostbite, their beards thick with frozen saliva and mucus. With the wind chill it was −35°C and as I passed, I tried to warn one of them. 'Your nose is white,' I shouted weakly through my mask, pointing with my mittens to my masked nose. His eyes drifted slowly towards me like a man too drunk to focus. With as much volume as I could muster, I shouted again, 'Your nose. Frostbite!' It was no use. He didn't even seem to register my presence.

Higher up, two men sat hunched over their axes. They too had no oxygen and were drugged under the influence of the rarefied air. One man's jacket flapped open in the viciously cold wind. He didn't move an inch, unaware of the icy blast. Another moved jerkily, looking for something in his pocket. Plastic food wrappers spilled onto the snow and were whipped away by the gusts, but he was too tired to care. Seeing these men so reduced was horrifying. Their lives seemed to hang by a thread of consciousness. They were all firmly in the clutch of the death zone. One small mistake up here would be their last.

Nearing the summit plateau, our team had split up. Rob had pulled ahead with a renewed determination in his step. I was 50 metres behind and the others were out of sight below. The summit was just half a kilometre away, though it would take an hour to reach. My steps remained painfully slow but my mind had changed gear. After all the doubts and questioning, after always being in the second team, it finally seemed as if we were going to get there.

Then, at 9 am, after nearly six weeks of struggling, I'd finally arrived at the prayer flags marking the summit of Cho Oyu. Falling onto my knees I rested motionless for what seemed like an eternity. I breathed my oxygen in slowly and deeply, my mind and body feeling completely empty. The altitude had ground me down and I had nothing left. Rob, who had summited 20 minutes earlier, walked slowly towards me. Helping me to my feet, he wrapped me in his arms. Rob had performed like a Trojan. He'd been faster than anyone on either team.

'Congratulations, Bella!' he said.

'You too, Honey!' I said as my eyes filled with tears, 'I can't believe we're actually here.'

It was 27 September 2003 as Rob and I stood in each other's arms, more than eight kilometres above sea level. Cho Oyu had saved the best for last and today the weather was perfect. With a gentle breeze and not a trace of cloud to be seen, the sky was an endless cobalt sea.

It was the most glorious day we could have hoped for. To the north, the vast emptiness of the dark Tibetan plains stretched away. To the south, the jagged peaks of the Himalayan chain dazzled us with unheralded glory, and to the east, beyond Cho Oyu's prayer flags, stood the gleaming hulk of Everest. To see her this time, we were no longer in the comfort of an aircraft but had fought every step to be here. It was surreal to be finally face to face with the Goddess of the Sky.

Shortly afterwards, Kevin joined us at the summit, elated and weary. There were emotional hugs all round. The Sherpas had been a pillar of strength for all of us, whether assisting us on summit day or setting the ropes and camps ahead of us in the preceding weeks. With the excitement of the summit behind us, and our energy levels at their lowest, we had to be on top of our game for the descent.

'Please be careful,' Rob said, as he helped me untangle my camera strap and oxygen hose.

'You too, remember to keep your feet wide,' I said. We both knew the majority of climbing accidents happen on descent. Walking with an artificially wide gait would prevent our tired feet from catching crampons in our trousers and causing a potentially fatal fall.

Russell had encouraged us to descend as far as possible after summiting. He had suggested we head for camp two but Rob and I had already agreed we'd aim even further and get to camp one if we could. Once off the summit plateau we descended the steep north-west snow face. We were at our most vulnerable at the top where we had no ropes to clip into and the slope ended in a cliff. With my head down I lowered myself into the steps that had been kicked into the snow. Every step required careful placement. It was mentally and physically exhausting and my thighs shook with every step.

Before long I was alone with everyone else ahead. Suddenly the snow steps disappeared and the task of descending had become tortuously awkward. Looking up, I realised why. Kevin, in his exhaustion, was sliding down on his bottom, smoothing the steps. My heart sank. I had no energy to cope with this extra demand. Endangering himself, he was also making it virtually impossible for the ailing climbers still ascending. I called out but my feeble voice was muffled by the mask. Ripping it off, I called again, this time my words just vanished with the wind. I felt delirious with exhaustion, but steps or no steps, no-one else but me could get me safely down. All I could do was focus my fear and make every move count.

It was gone midday when we finally toiled back into high camp. After a brief stop to collect gear, we continued to camp two. Arriving there by mid-afternoon, we silently collapsed, face down, into our tent. With rucksacks still on and encased in our oxygen masks, we lay with our crampons and legs lying outside in the snow.

Rob broke the silence. 'I don't know if I've got camp one left in me.'

'Me neither,' I whispered. We fell silent again. Another half hour passed and still we hadn't moved an inch. My body felt like lead.

'We should go,' I mumbled into my mask. Rob grunted in agreement. Heaving ourselves onto all fours, we reversed out of our tent. Kevin had also collapsed in the tent next door.

'Kevin, we're heading to camp one. You coming?' Rob called.

'Yeah,' he groaned. The ice cliff was still beneath us, and we had to get past it before nightfall.

Hours later we staggered into camp one. The horizon glowed a crimson red and the evening stars twinkled above us in the inky black sky. After 15 gruelling hours we'd reached our camp for the night, but our day was far from over. We were still high and also dangerously dehydrated. Our water bottles had remained frozen all day and our throats were raw, stripped of moisture. In a comatose stupor we lit the stove and coaxed each other to stay awake, knowing that gas poisoning from stoves is an insidious killer of exhausted climbers.

Heading back to ABC the following morning, just hours after feeling at death's door, the most peculiar and uninvited thoughts popped up on the screen of my mind. *Well ... you've managed Cho Oyu, so why not Everest?* I couldn't believe my own thoughts, let alone comprehend them. Could something inside me really be contemplating Everest? How could the slate of my memory be wiped clean, and so soon?

As we plodded wearily back into ABC, the rest of the team welcomed us with congratulatory hugs and back slaps. It was wonderful to be safely home with our friends. The indefatigable Lachu had even cooked a celebratory cake for us on his gas stove. It was good to be back. The thicker air, our restored appetite and the ability to sleep were precious gifts. That night, after we'd turned our head torches out and wriggled into our sleeping bags, we prayed together and thanked God for the privilege of what we'd seen and for keeping us safe to the end. Climbing Cho Oyu together pushed us further than we'd ever imagined possible, but with the difficulty, came the greatest reward. To share this experience was an immeasurable blessing.

Over the following days we returned to base camp and finally started our journey home to Kathmandu. Instead of flying from Lhasa, we drove all the way completing the world's longest descent from the Tibetan plateau in just two days. As each day passed, the difficulties of the climb grew dim, leaving nothing more than wonderful memories and a bronzed glow on our weather-beaten faces. Climbing above 8,000 metres had forced us through a new pain barrier. We'd learnt to push with our minds as much as our bodies. Only by going to our physical limits could we discover the possibilities that lay beyond them. Summiting Cho Oyu had opened a door and while Everest still seemed out of our league, we finally believed we'd earned the right to try.

As we waited at the border post between Tibet and Nepal, the subject of Everest came up with Russell. In his familiarly blunt style he gave us his verdict. 'Your rope work and technical skills are solid, you're good in the team and you've managed to climb above 8,000 metres, but . . .' he paused to look up at us, 'If you're going to stand a chance with Everest, you've got to really want it.'

Looking at each other, we already knew the answer. Rob drew in his breath, 'Yes . . . we really do want to climb it.'

Russell looked at me as I nodded in full agreement and that was it. We had finally declared that we wanted to climb Everest. For the first time our dream had become a tangible possibility.

'Great, it'll be fantastic having you guys along. I'll put you in the 2004 team,' Russell said with a broad smile. 'Of course, I don't know if you've got what it takes to summit Everest, but if you are successful, I promise it will change your lives.'

CHAPTER 11

Frozen Planet

'The heavens proclaim the glory of God; the skies proclaim the work of his hands. There is no speech or language where their voice is not heard.'

Psalm 19 vv 1 & 3

Cʟɪᴍʙɪɴɢ ᴀʙᴏᴠᴇ 8,000 metres on Cho Oyu had ravaged our bodies of muscle and fat. Between us we'd lost 12 kilos and now we had just six weeks to nurture and train ourselves back into shape ready for climbing Vinson, the highest mountain on the world's most hostile continent, Antarctica. Travelling to Antarctica was a once-in-a-lifetime opportunity, so we planned to savour it for as long as possible. After Vinson, we were hoping to climb Mount Shinn and some of the Patriot Hills, as well as skiing to the South Pole.

By late November 2003, after rigorous training, frenetic eating and endless preparations, it was time to head south. With three expeditions to pack for – Vinson, the South Pole and Aconcagua in Argentina – we had swamped my parents' house with 100 kilos of equipment. My medical and photographic kit was conspicuously in excess of requirements, as was our spare glove collection. History had left us feeling like incurable hypochondriacs and now we were travelling to the coldest continent on the planet and climbing its highest mountain, where the temperatures would be at their worst.

On 25 November 2003, our last full day in the UK, Dr Phillips gave us the good news that both Rob's blood tests and scan results were clear. We were free to go. Mum held me tightly at the front door. 'We'll be praying for you,' she said with a concerned smile. 'Cheerio then,' Dad said with a cheeky grin, as if we were just popping out to the shops. As had become our ritual, we pulled off our wedding rings and gave them to Mum. Not only would the metal conduct cold, but if we developed swollen frost-damaged fingers they would restrict vital blood flow and jeopardise our fingers – an outcome that no jewellery was worth.

Once at Heathrow, we met our guide Stuart, who had been recommended by our expedition agent. Realising we would soon wave goodbye to civilisation, we treated Stuart and ourselves to a celebratory champagne lunch at the seafood bar. It seemed a fitting start to our weeks of roughing it and dehydrated rations.

The subject of a guide for our Antarctic expedition had been a moving feast over the past 18 months. For our previous expedition, cancelled after Rob's illness in Nepal, we were going with our guiding friend Nick Banks, but his new duties as President of the British Guides Association, prevented long overseas expeditions the following year. Our second plan was to go alone, knowing Vinson was technically well within our climbing abilities. However, increasingly strict insurance policies for remote locations soon put an end to that idea. Our third plan was to go with Ryan Campbell, with whom we'd become good friends since our Denali expedition. He was experienced in high latitude and arctic style guiding and seemed the perfect fit. But our British agent wasn't so sure. 'He's probably not suitable. You need to go with someone who has polar experience. We'll find someone for you,' they advised us. We felt grateful for any advice, especially after our previous cancellation and heavy financial losses. Everything about this expedition had to be absolutely right.

Two days later we arrived in Punta Arenas, a small Chilean city that sits on the southernmost tip of South America. The bleak landscape and stunted, listing trees bore testament to the unrelenting wind that blew from the Drake Passage, the roughest stretch of water in the world. The hardy locals had made valiant attempts to counteract the harsh climate with brightly painted corrugated iron roofs and colourful buildings. Though, no doubt it was the pisco sours, their local beverage, that cheered them up as much as the bright paintwork.

Our first two days were spent preparing food, finalising equipment and receiving our briefing from Antarctic Logistics and Expeditions. ALE is the sole operator for flying non-government, private and commercial expeditions to the interior of Antarctica and as such enjoy a happy monopoly over activities and prices. Meeting the four other expedition teams I nervously scanned the conference room to see if there were any other females amongst the bearded athletic throng.

'Everyone looks so fit,' I whispered to Rob.

'Don't worry, Bird Bones, we'll tie you to the end of the rope so you don't blow away,' said Rob cheekily quivering his eyebrow at me.

Later that day, we had buried the local supermarket cashier behind a mountain of cakes, biscuits, chocolate, butter and porridge. It was a dietician's hell, but the perfect menu for surviving and working in the frigid temperatures that awaited us. Rob was glad of the cashier's inattention, though, as he passed several kilos of baby food, which Stuart had persuaded us would make a good alternative to porridge. After hours of ration sorting, I was stranded on our hotel bedroom floor amidst a sea of dried fruit and nut bags. Meanwhile Rob had developed a prematurely snowy appearance from bagging up dried milk and Stuart was meticulously weighing our gear to avoid the $65 per kilo excess baggage charges for our flight to the ice.

Our flight to Antarctica, scheduled for 30 November, was disappointingly cancelled on our third and supposedly final day in Punta. There were reports of 70 kph winds driving across the blue ice runway at Patriot Hills camp, making it unsafe to land. Three days later, after a false alarm of better weather had sent us all racing to the airport, we started to appreciate the nature of the game we'd engaged in. Landing in Antarctica was both difficult and unpredictable and accurately summed up by Roald Amunsden's observation that 'at best, the climate in Antarctica is about the worst in the world'. It seemed the odds were stacked against us even getting there.

Having downgraded to the cheapest hostel available, we were unable to stray far in search of entertainment and had to be on standby for regular phone calls updating us on the weather and flight status. After completing a thorough survey of all the eating houses in Punta, the best place was a burger joint called Lomit's, though sadly even that was soon renamed Vomit's. So I resorted to a spot of home cooking in the hostel kitchen, which met with mixed approval.

'Suppose we're going to be eating this sort of food for weeks,' Stuart said glumly, poking my pasta around his bowl. Rob was a little more measured, thanking me and doing the washing up. Like the good husband that he is, he wisely understood the repercussions of complaining about the food I'd cooked.

With time on our hands we exchanged expedition stories with

Stuart. We already knew he had managed sizeable teams on expeditions with all the corresponding staff of porters and cooks and we were keen to hear more.

'So when did you get your polar experience?' Rob asked.

'Oh, I've never been to the polar regions before,' he replied. Rob and I both shot each other a glance. 'So this will be a learning experience for all of us,' he continued casually, seemingly unaware of our discussion with the agent. As the conversation continued he told us about his recent efforts towards a guiding qualification, though impressed on us that his line of work didn't pay well and wasn't always much fun. Doing our best to sympathise, we consoled him saying that not many people had the mountains as their office.

At 7 am on our ninth day of waiting, we all sat expectantly in the airport departure lounge once again. But as Mark, the ALE representative, approached us, the grimace on his face said it all.

'Sorry guys, its been called off again.' The winds had died down but there was now poor visibility and snowfall, with a massive system sitting over the Ronne ice shelf, Antarctic Peninsula and Ellsworth area. Mark explained that ironically with the snowfall, we needed high winds to clear the runway, putting us back to where we started over a week ago.

On the bus journey back to Punta, undercurrents of disappointment soon errupted into agitated discussions between other teams and the ALE operations manager. The subject of refunds had become a thorny issue. Many worried about what to say to sponsors if they lost their money. For us it was a more straightforward, but still painful problem.

'You know our trip insurance only covers us for about 10% of the costs if we cancel,' I said gloomily.

'I know. If we fail this time, that's it. We can't try again.' We both felt equally despondent at the thought of our hard won savings being swallowed up by a second failed trip.

'Of course, even if we do get to Antarctica now, our Aconcagua expedition will have to be cancelled. We're already going to be two weeks late,' Rob noted. Demoralised, we sat in silence for the rest of the bus journey home.

By the afternoon we were wandering through the main plaza, as were other teams, trying to kill time. Many were queuing to kiss the shiny bronze toe of an Indian statue, which local legend says will guarantee your safe return to Punta. Neither Rob nor I felt our future could be particularly assured by kissing a statue's toe, besides which, given our dwindling chances of leaving Punta, focusing on coming back seemed a little premature.

*

We'd been waiting in Punta for exactly two weeks when a call came through at 9 pm.

'Well . . . the sky's clear and wind's down to 16 kilometres an hour,' the expedition representative reported optimistically.

'Great! So are we going then?' I asked excitedly.

'Not yet. Don't get too excited. There's still too much snow on the runway,' he replied. Tantalising us with the news of clear skies if we couldn't use them seemed terribly cruel, but he offered consolation. 'The team at Patriot Hills are going to try and clear the runway overnight.' It sounded a little ambitious, given that it was a job normally reserved for the strong katabatic winds generated by the Patriot Hills, and neither Stuart, Rob nor I were convinced. But at 7.10 am the following morning we received our third call to go to the airport. 'We'll pick you up in 20 minutes. Don't be late.'

Despite our scepticism, excitement finally began to mount as we climbed the ladder of the Ilyushin 76, a Russian heavy cargo plane. Even though I knew the flight could be aborted part way, we were nearer to Antarctica now than we'd ever been. The cargo hold was like a dingy warehouse with fuel drums, sleds and crates piled under webbing and strapped to the floor. A tangled jumble of wires, pipes and cranes hung from the roof. Clouds of cigarette smoke wafted out of the cockpit and next to it hung a poster saying 'Thank you Colonel Gaddafi'. With only two porthole windows giving light, I carefully picked my way through to the seats, which consisted of little more than a metal shelf bolted to the fuselage. It was going to be an uncomfortable five hours, but none of us cared. As the plane taxied down the runway, our cheering and clapping was drowned by the roar of the engines and at 9 am we left the green land beneath us far behind.

Clambering over two sleeping pilots squashed into coffin-sized berths, I squeezed into the cockpit. The flight crew were from

Kazakhstan and made the toughest-looking expeditioner among us look a softie. They took a relaxed attitude to our wandering into the cockpit, probably aware there was little likelihood of polar adventurers having terrorist tendencies. We had all found healthier ways of purging our souls. I spent half the flight sitting in the observation bubble, supported thousands of feet above the deep blue Southern Ocean by a single sheet of bulletproof glass. As we approached the edge of the Antarctic ice sheet, its shattered ice floes littered the ocean like broken china. Beyond, there was nothing but a brilliant and blinding world of white.

Five hours later we were just seconds off touchdown. My stomach was clenched in anticipation. Rob squeezed my thigh tightly and shouted into my ear, 'Hope they paid attention in flight school!'

Boom! We hit the ice. The rumbling and banging was deafening. The plane shook and the engines screamed in full reverse thrust as we careered down the corrugated blue ice runway. To use the brakes would spell disaster. I just hoped we'd stop before the three kilometres of ice ran out.

Eventually we came to a halt and the back of the aircraft opened and lowered onto the ice. Squinting through watery eyes, I was mesmerised by the dazzling Antarctic light as it streamed into the darkened cargo hold. Even as my eyes adjusted, all I could see was a gleaming white desert that stretched to every horizon. In front of us the wind-scoured runway was a glassy, turquoise blue and looked like ripples on wet sand. We were awestruck.

We stepped carefully off the ramp, remembering Mark's words at the briefing. 'Take extreme care when you step onto the blue ice. We've had broken arms in the first minute before. If that happens – it's home you go.' The Ilyushin's engines were still running because of the extreme cold and away from the warmth of the cargo hold the icy air suddenly hit us. 'Bit nippy here!' I shouted to Stuart and Rob over the drone of the engines.

Even with the glaring sun and not a breath of wind, it was −15°C outside and the sudden change made me shudder. I wondered again how we'd cope with the cold. Rob's nerve endings were still sensitive from his chemotherapy and my circulation was poor enough that even my doctor had warned me against polar expeditions. But as quickly as my concerns had arisen, they were swallowed up by the thrill of being there. Even just standing on the ice runway, Antarctica was truly breathtaking.

The Patriot Hills camp was a good 20 minutes from the runway and while Stuart excitedly dashed off to take his photos, Rob and I loaded the skidoos with all our kit. Patriot Hills is a temporary camp constructed as a base for expeditions, and in just two months it would be dismantled again at the end of the short Antarctic summer. For the rest of the year, temperatures and winds are too hostile for survival, and permanent darkness envelops the continent between March and October.

Five hours after our arrival, the good weather was continuing to hold as we loaded the rugged Twin Otter plane parked beside camp, for our flight to Vinson base camp. A small but sturdy propeller plane with skis, it is the perfect workhorse for polar regions. With a throaty roar, its engines blasted clouds of snow behind us and we bounced off down the snow runway. As we headed north, the rocky peaks of the Ellsworth range pierced the ocean of ice. Gaps between the peaks acted like giant sluice gates, where the frozen sea of ice burst through and tumbled east towards the plateau below. After an hour of flying and just minutes away from base camp, the visibility had deteriorated significantly and clouds enveloped the Vinson Massif. Our Canadian pilot leant round and swirled his finger in the air. We had to abort. It was no longer safe. Rob and I shook our heads at each other. Antarctic weather systems had a habit of persisting for days, if not weeks.

'Hope this isn't a repeat of Punta!' Rob shouted in my ear.

Back at Patriot Hills it was still a gorgeously sunny day at well past midnight. With 24 hours of daylight and still feeling excited to be there, it was hard to convince my brain of the need to go to bed. I stayed up enjoying the sunshine and taking photos before finally being chased to my sleeping bag at 2.30 am by the sub-zero temperatures.

The next morning was again frigid but clear, and we were relieved that our second attempt to fly to Vinson base camp was sucessful. Landing on the lower Branscomb Glacier we taxied steeply uphill and having disembarked we quickly set to work building camp to stay warm. Even at just over 2,000 metres the temperature had already dropped to −22°C. The snow was so dry that it squeaked as if cutting styrofoam, and could be sawn into satisfyingly perfect blocks. In a matter of hours our walls were built, the tents were up and we had a brew on the go. Cup of tea in hand, I wandered away from our tents, relishing the peace and isolation. Across the Antarctic ice sheet, not one thing in the vast wilderness made a single sound. The silence was so complete, only my breathing and the blood pumping in my head were audible. Looking out across the most pristine continent in the world, I feasted my eyes. I mused over how to record what I saw. Even the best photographs and superlatives would never do justice to this magical kingdom of ice. Suddenly I realised I was shivering and, despite my countless layers, standing still for just a few minutes had left my feet and hands painfully cold. I scurried back to our tent, swinging my arms furiously and stamping my feet.

As we packed our sleeping bags the next morning we could still hear Stuart snoring in the tent next door but we were both cold and keen to get going. I hadn't slept well again. Ever since we'd started expeditions I'd felt in a permanent state of sleep deprivation. I'd considered it good training for if and when we had children but it was nonetheless physically and mentally debilitating. After many weeks of sleep deprivation on Cho Oyu, Rob's rather scientific appraisal of the situation was that I had gone slightly 'ga ga'. I hoped this trip would be better.

Fighting to get our feet into our huge double layered boots left our hands like blocks of ice, even though we had gloves on. By 10 am, with steaming porridge inside us, we loaded our rucksacks, clipped into the sleds and set off for camp two. We had an ambitious plan for the day; we were not only skipping the normal location for camp one but were moving everything in one load instead of two, our logic being to maximise the good weather and push as high as we could.

The cold made us want to keep moving but after several hours of slogging up the Branscomb Glacier, we needed a break. Planting myself onto my sled, I found a packet of nuts, the only food that hadn't frozen in my breast pockets. Dropping some on the snow, I fumbled as I tried to pick each nut up with my heavy gloves. With no animal or bird to scavenge for thousands of kilometres, to leave anything felt like a crime. It would become a permanent addition to the continent.

As we followed the Branscomb, it began to bear left and climbed more steeply. The snow slope gradually became a lethal mass of ice,

MAP OF ANTARCTICA

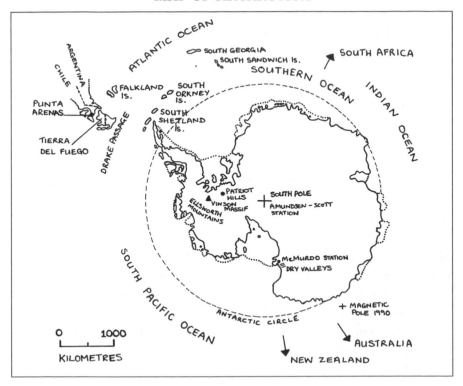

MAP OF VINSON

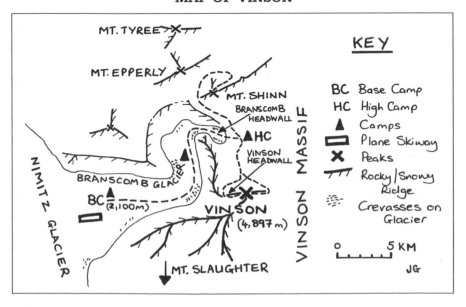

scoured and polished by the wind. The decision not to use crampons or a rope was now problematic and as I started across, I immediately regretted not heeding Rob's advice to purchase new walking poles for Antarctica. The sharp metal tips of the ones I was using had been worn to a rounded stump on Cho Oyu; they were fine for rock, but useless on ice. The £60 I'd saved would have made my life so much safer and easier.

The polished ice only covered an area the size of a tennis court, but it was like trying to walk across a sloping ice rink in wellington boots. With my blunt poles skidding on the ice, the only thing affording purchase was the occasional patch of snow. But I wasn't even half way when my sled whistled past me. Flipping over, it whipped me off my feet and I slammed down onto my coccyx with an excruciating thud. My smooth Gore-tex clothes unhelpfully provided zero friction and along with my sled and my rucksack, I shot downhill in very much the wrong direction. Knowing there was a high probability of crevasses, I scrabbled to stop, like a cat clawing on glass. Eventually I hit a snow patch and dug my feet in. Heart racing, I caught my breath and looked up. Some way ahead, Rob and Stuart were lost in their own worlds, quite unaware of my bottom skating antics. Gathering my poles, I inched my way back up muttering to myself 'No, really, I'm fine. Don't worry about me, I'm doing great down here,' and gave my sled a few good kicks.

By the time I'd caught Stuart and Rob up, I'd thrashed out my bad feelings towards my sled and could see the funny side of my little trip south.

'You were a long way behind, were you taking pics?' Rob asked obliviously.

'No, I was just admiring the texture of the ice at close quarters' I said, too out of breath to explain. We sat for another break and though we were all tired, Stuart complained again about his heavy rucksack. 'At least you're over six foot, mate. I reckon Jo's probably got the heaviest load.' Rob winked at me and whispered 'Mighty mouse.'

After seven hours of sled hauling and pack carrying, we finally reached the location for camp. With the tent up I was happy to stay outside, cutting snow blocks for the stove and taking photos. I'd never seen snow sparkle with so many different colours. I wanted to run and jump for joy but I checked myself. I was still on a glacier and if I suddenly disappeared down a crevasse, once the novelty value of my vanishing had worn off, I knew it would actually be quite frustrating having to search for me.

Before long, I was crawling back into the tent almost in tears, with painfully cold hands and burning red cheeks.

'Put them in here, Bella,' Rob said, gesturing towards his groin and armpits. *No greater love has a man than to put blocks of freezing flesh down his pants,* I thought.

'You deserve a medal for this, Honey,' I said struggling to smile with my frozen cheeks.

Within minutes I was experiencing the hot aches as the small blood vessels in my fingers and toes began to dilate again. It felt as if I was undergoing a 20-digit amputation and the pain was considerably worse than the numbness I'd felt outside. But I only had myself to blame. My body shape isn't exactly suited to the cold. Unlike the Eskimos with their high volume to skin ratio, I have long, thin fingers and toes with a high surface area. I am precisely the wrong design for retaining heat and even with two months of frenzied eating after Cho Oyu, I was still frustratingly underweight according to my trusted body mass index chart.

When we woke the following morning it was −21°C in our tent. 'Do you realise it's colder in here than in the freezer at home?' Stuart said as he thawed the stove's frozen fuel pipe with his cigarette lighter.

'Yeah . . . the so-called Antarctic summer comes a poor second to the Aussie one,' Rob replied. I unzipped the inner tent to check my thermometer and discovered it was an even chillier −30°C in the vestibule. Being in the shade, our tent wouldn't warm up until the sun reappeared from behind the Vinson massif. Of course, it would have been particularly useful if we had been endowed with natural antifreeze in our blood, like so many Antarctic sea creatures, but as it was, we just decided to stay put and wait for the sun.

'Bugger,' Rob said pulling his socks off the line in the tent. Having forgotten to dry them in his sleeping bag over night, the sweat had frozen them into a rigid board more akin to a cricket bat than a pair of socks.

'Isn't that your only spare pair of socks?' I probed with a suspicious eye.

'Yes, yes, I know. I won't do it again,' he retorted.

As we packed our load to carry to high camp I smeared generous quantities of half-frozen factor 40 suncream over my face. The icy air had masked the sun's strength the previous day, which had left me looking like Rudolf the reindeer, albeit a little off track. We'd been warned about the lethal combination of the ozone hole, high altitude and the thin atmosphere near the Pole, each one of which significantly increases the UV radiation.

After a few hours on a pleasantly gentle incline up the Branscomb Glacier we reached an ice debris field at the foot of the headwall. Overhanging ice cliffs above had periodically broken away, shattering into millions of fragments subsequently polished by the wind into a wonderland of ice sculptures. Whether the size of trucks or like tiny polished marbles, they all glowed an extraordinary luminescent turquoise. But being in the debris field was as unnerving as it was entrancing. We were standing in the equivalent of a firing range, except instead of bullets, we might be obliterated by house-sized blocks of ice. Our sole comfort was that the extreme temperatures prevailing all year round maintained the structural integrity of the ice.

Roped up, crampons on, we started towards the headwall. The glacier reared up for 1,000 steep feet above us. To the right were deeply fractured ice cliffs and to the left a chaotic waterfall of tumbling ice. The only potential route appeared to be a steep central ramp. We knew there could be massive fissures at the top where the ice had torn apart but there was no way of knowing exactly what we'd find. No-one else had trodden there for a year. Seeing how steep it was going to be I called to Stuart.

'Why don't we get our axes out here?'

'We'll be fine. It's not very steep,' he called back, but in less than ten minutes it had steepened dramatically.

'OK, let's stop and get our axes out,' Stuart shouted down to us. Taking our cumbersome rucksacks off now, with the ground falling away beneath us, was awkward. I wished I'd followed my gut instinct and done it earlier. I could see Rob wasn't happy either but we were too far away on the rope to help each other. Eventually, ice axes in hand, we started to make our way up.

After nearly six hours we had reached the upper headwall and saw what I had suspected. Bottomless crevasses opened in front of us where the ice had ripped apart as it rolled over the edge of the high col. Thankfully their openings were narrow enough for us to jump them even with our rucksacks on.

High camp was nothing but a deserted windswept snowy col that sat between two mountains, Vinson and Shinn. The only sign of any life was a block of yellow ice standing proud where the wind had eroded the snow away, converting a pee hole from the previous year's camp into an ugly, protruding monument. It offered stark justification for the 1959 Antarctic Treaty. Any contamination of the pristine Antarctic environment is permanent, sealed in time by the constantly freezing temperatures. With the exception of urine, all trace of human presence had to be removed from the continent, including solid human waste. Defecating into a plastic bag and carrying it has never been a mountaineer's favourite pastime, but here it was the only honourable – and legal – thing to do.

Digging our gear cache into the ground, we marked it with a bamboo wand for our return the following day. As we descended the steep headwall Stuart remained in front. Our configuration on the rope seemed unusual and we exchanged questioning looks. For steep descents we'd both been accustomed to guides taking the higher rear position, from where they could stop a fall or at least prevent it gathering momentum. Rob and I had never fallen but we felt far from invulnerable, especially when we were so tired.

As I was now at the back, I tied a quick prussic knot around the rope, that could act as an easy grab handle to maintain rope tension and then called down to Rob, 'I'll keep the rope tight.' Rob was steady on his feet but he'd never liked long, steep runouts. Just knowing someone above him had a firm grasp of the rope increased his confidence. I loved being able to help him but I felt nervous that I was almost too tired even to control my own legs. The thought of being able to hold two men, if one or both slipped, was laughable, especially when their combined weight was more than three times mine.

The following day we made good time back up to high camp and spent a further three hours digging and sawing blocks of snow to build a fortress around our tent. On such a clear, calm day it was hard to imagine raging winds, but in Antarctica's fickle and inhospitable environment, I sensed our efforts wouldn't be wasted. With our walls finished we took a few moments to enjoy the view. As the sun dipped behind the ridge we were plunged into Vinson's freezing shadow and in ten minutes the temperature had plummeted to −30°C. Cuddling together in all our down layers we looked out beyond the eight-kilometre-wide Nimitz Glacier. What had initially appeared to be a sea of dappled cloud beneath us turned out to be the ice sheet itself. It seemed to lap at the feet of the Ellsworth mountain range we stood on, extending into its valleys like frozen fjords.

As I pondered the captivating views, I concluded that if an estate agent were to advertise our location, they would no doubt have an instant property auction on their hands. Our property was by any standards impressive ... Stunningly located with breathtaking views over the Ellsworth mountain range and Antarctic ice sheet. Spacious grounds with over 14 million square kilometres of potential roaming, conveniently located just two camps from the runway, 24-hour solar power and unlimited free supply of the finest water on the planet (stove required). Viewings by request with six months' notice. Warm clothes and extended training required plus disclaimer signatures in case of unexpected moments of hardship. Quite tempting I thought, although the small print might read a little different. Stunning views but ... permanently freezing with constant risk of frostbite and loss of digits, no toilets – please bring your own plastic bag, constant house rebuilding required and possibility of annihilation during storms, no washing allowed, potential transport delays for weeks or months, permanent darkness for half the year, risk of cabin fever and psychosis amongst even close family members. Rob rubbed my arms, jolting me out of my daydreams. 'Come on, Jo, you're shivering. We need to get inside and warm up.'

It was always a monumental effort in the mornings to crawl out of our warm sleeping bags into the freezer of a tent and I tried to remind myself of the immense privilege, though my body was less convinced. However, today was summit day and feeling excited we both started to pack. As we coaxed Stuart out of bed for the fifth day running, we were both frustrated that he had overslept again but we had been blessed with perfect summit weather and wanted to get underway.

By 10 am, we had climbed onto the high plateau with Vinson straight ahead, but it appeared curiously insignificant compared to the mountains nearby. With the extreme clarity of the air it was difficult to appreciate that our objective was still many kilometres away. Everything glistened and the snow sparkled, even in our shadows, like multi-coloured sequins. The holes where my crampon spikes had pierced the snow glowed bright blue, as if fluorescent lights were buried beneath.

The final hours of our ascent took us up Vinson's headwall and along a breathtaking ridge before we negotiated the final summit cornice. The headwall had been stripped to bare ice and it was so hard our crampons barely penetrated the surface. I found concentrating on speeding up, and slowing down, to maintain the right rope tension, was a useful distraction from my crashing headache. High on Vinson's west ridge we were exposed to an icy southerly wind, blasting from the disconcertingly named Mount Slaughter. Even with my hats, hoods and mask the cold still drilled its way through. My teeth jangled and my ears throbbed. So far, by regularly checking each other, we'd escaped facial frostbite, but today was turning out to be the coldest summit day we'd experienced. Rough globules of frozen breath that had formed inside my mask were pressing against my nose and cheeks. I tried to chew the ice off the inside of my mask but it froze to my lips. Levering it off with my tongue, I gave up and pushed it away, hoping my skin would survive.

With the wind chill, it was now well below −50°C. When I swallowed, I felt as if I'd been eating sand. The air was too cold to retain any of the vital water vapour that normally lubricates our respiratory tract. Even after eight hours of exercising, the muscles in my legs felt stiff with cold. I couldn't remember exactly when I'd last felt my toes. Unable to communicate with Rob, I hoped he was doing OK. My numb hands and feet worried me too, but there was nothing I could do now except keep moving. We were just minutes from the summit.

At 4.05 pm on 15 December 2003 we took our final steps to the summit of Vinson. At 4,897 metres, Vinson is the highest mountain in Antarctica. Although she was one of the lower Seven Summits, she had not given herself up easily. The altitude had still proved hard work and my headache was a testament to that. Added to which Vinson's apparent altitude, from a barometric perspective, was higher than her physical altitude due to the proximity to the Pole. This is because the earth's spin causes the atmosphere to bulge at the equator, leaving a thinner layer near the Poles.

Rob and I embraced each other and kissed through our ice-encrusted masks. We'd deliberately avoided outward affection for weeks, not wanting Stuart to feel like a spare part, but this was a moment of celebration to be enjoyed. We shook Stuart's hand and shouted congratulations to each other across the wind.

My brain still felt as if it was in a vice but my elation at reaching the summit was undiminished. The mountains had once again repelled and attracted us. As the physical discomforts had intensified, so had the rewards of gaining new heights. Today was the first day that Vinson had been climbed in a year and it was only 37 years since the first ascent.

Tucking my back snug against Rob, I hid in his wind shadow while we shared our few precious summit moments. Fairytale pinnacles pierced the ice with their indigo shadows and coppery shale, the only colour for thousands of kilometres. Boundless expanses of ice merged with the sky in every direction, surrounding us with seemingly infinite space. We gazed out for nearly 300 kilometres in every direction; it was like trying to comprehend eternity. Looking out to the flawless ice plains was as if we were sneaking a glimpse inside the engineering rooms of geology. As the ice sheet neared the Ellsworths it began to buckle and crumple. Unobstructed by vegetation, rivers or man-made structures, every movement of the naked ice mantle was clear to see.

Unzipping my jacket I fumbled for my camera.

'Time for photos,' I called to Rob over the wind.

'Quick as you can. I'm already freezing,' he replied, swinging his arms. My fingers were numb but I took the plunge and ripped my large mitts off. The wind sliced through my two thin pairs of inner gloves. They were no match for the conditions. Fighting against time, I struggled to exchange frozen camera batteries for warmer ones. My fingers became stiffer with every second and even with 'warmer' batteries, both my digital and compact cameras quickly died. I reached inside my jacket for my third and final camera, my trusted manual Nikon. Even with its battery dead I could guess at the exposures and it still worked. Taking three shots, I slowly wound the film on only to feel it rip inside. The extreme temperatures had made it too brittle. At the same moment the shutter froze. That was it. No more photos. Every piece of camera equipment had seized up and I was beginning to seize up too. It was time to go.

CHAPTER 12

Trapped in an Icy Hell

'We take risks not to escape life but to prevent life escaping us.'
Anon

LEAVING VINSON'S BEAUTIFUL but desolate summit, we were desperate to escape the biting wind and made a rapid descent down the steeper eastern ridge. Sharp rocky blades thrust from the ridge crest, making it look like the back of a stegosaurus. Twisters of snow spun off its edge, vanishing as quickly as they had formed. For the sake of our fingers and toes we had to be fast. My eyes watered from the bitter wind as it funnelled through my goggle vents, but if I closed them, my goggles would instantly steam up and freeze. Crusty frozen tears irritated my eyes. I was desperate to rub them but I had to leave my goggles on or risk becoming snowblind.

Clear of the exposed summit ridge we crossed under the shadowy north face. The wind had eased but still blew the glistening spindrift in ghostly patterns. Snaking just inches above the ice it danced like shifting sands. All around the snow had been exquisitely sculpted into wood-grain patterns and sastrugi – wind-eroded snowy wave formations that lie parallel to the prevailing wind. As we walked west into the afternoon sun, its warmth was feeble against the onslaught of the cold.

After 13 hours in Vinson's deep freeze we arrived back at our tent. Feeling hypoglycaemic from my low blood sugar levels and with wobbling legs I collapsed inside. Shuffling wearily into our sleeping bags, we all lay in silence listening to the friendly hiss of the stove. Feeling unhinged from my headache I craved painkillers, but the water I'd left in my sleeping bag was frozen. I'd have to wait.

Having spent a deliciously lazy rest day buried in our sleeping bags, the following morning we set off for Mount Shinn, a beautiful snowy pyramid accessible from Vinson's high camp. The weather looked less stable and with a strengthening breeze it was a challenging morning. As we left the security of our camp, we hoped the weather would hold long enough for us to get back, dismantle tents the next day and descend to the relative safety of camp two.

Directly below Mount Shinn we crossed a smooth ice platform, littered with serac debris, that tilted towards plunging ice cliffs. Above us soared colossal pillars of fractured ice. Feeling vulnerable, we moved as quickly as possible. We now felt strong and better acclimatised. Under our feet, chunks of aquamarine ice from the cliffs were embedded deep in the snow. The unrelenting winds had scoured them to perfection, like an exquisite palace floor with sapphire mosaics set into white marble. It was a crime to tramp across it in our rusty crampons.

Four hours later we had reached a dead end and were standing below Shinn's north-east face. The summit pyramid rose up for several hundred metres and needed to be climbed using a belay system. This entailed placing loops of rope around spikes of rock as we climbed upward. These loops, or slings, formed anchors enabling us to attach ourselves to the mountain. The climbing rope, which was tied to the next climber, was then pulled through a friction device to keep the rope tight as they climbed up. In the event of the climber falling, this friction device would lock the rope. It was the first time we had climbed using a belay system on the expedition and I felt a buzz to be climbing again.

As I finished my last move of the second rope pitch, I shuffled my feet on a small rock to find a more stable position.

'Can you clove hitch me into the anchor, Stuart? I can't reach it from here,' I said.

'Don't know clove hitches, so I'll just do an overhand knot,' he replied.

'You don't know how to tie a clove hitch?' Rob asked in surprise.

'Nope. You could show me a clove hitch, Italian hitch, anything like that and I'd forget it immediately. I just use a figure of eight or overhands,' he said. Clove and Italian hitches are basic climbing knots. Rob and I fell silent, trying to assimilate what he'd just said. Seconds later, I was unnerved by what I saw. A cobweb of tangled ropes lay piled at Stuart's feet as he tried to unravel them. We had never seen anything quite like it. 'I need you both to untie so I can sort the rope out,' he announced.

'Untie?' Rob exclaimed. 'Is there no way we can sort it without untying?'

'Not that I can see,' Stuart replied.

It was extremely unusual to be untying, especially for this reason but we had no time for discussions.

'Give me your sling, Jo,' Rob reached down to me, 'I'll clip you in while you untie. We'll do it one at a time.' His tone had changed. He was not comfortable at how events were unfolding and neither was I.

After some delay we were moving again. Keeping a watchful eye on Rob, I could see from his stilted movements that he was becoming increasingly nervous. Then suddenly I saw a chunk of rock the size of a cricket ball whistling towards me. As if an enemy attacker had just appeared on my radar screen, I automatically took evasive action. Throwing myself forwards, I buried my face in the snow as I braced for the impact. Thud! I was yanked backwards and my feet jolted down beneath me. Thankfully, the rock only clipped my rucksack. I looked around to see it bouncing 20 feet high as it ricocheted off the slabs below.

Several hours later we reached Shinn's summit at exactly the same time we'd summited Vinson just two days before, but our position was far more tenuous. A stunning but deadly cornice crowned the ridge, overhanging precipitously for its entire length. Needing to rest, we perched ourselves delicately on a sliver of sloping ground between the fragile cornice lip and the tumbling slopes below. At 4,660 metres, just 250 metres lower than Vinson and eight kilometres farther north, we were privy to incredible views over Mounts Epperly and Tyree, both razor-sharp black pinnacles.

By the time we had completed our descent of the summit pyramid, strong winds had risen and twisters of snow were spinning across Shinn's slopes. As we passed to its west, Vinson came back into view. We stopped in our tracks at what we saw. Massive lenticular clouds were ominously capping her summit and were now starting to form over Mount Shinn too. A big weather change was afoot and it wasn't for the better.

Hours into our descent, we were caught in a raging ground storm. The visibility was now severely restricted and most of our earlier tracks had been obliterated. As I was now at the front of the rope, it was my job to find the way home. Using my compass, I also stopped regularly to stare into the whirling snow, looking for any evidence of our tracks. Each time I spotted crampon holes I'd start off again hoping to find some more. After several hours my eyes grew bleary and tired of the featureless ground but the atmosphere was captivating. All around us, the air glowed with a maelstrom of airborne snow crystals, glinting in the watery sun as if we were trapped in a world of glittering candy-floss.

Having walked for some time without seeing any tell-tale crampon holes, I was increasingly nervous. Had I deviated off course? I turned to Rob and Stuart but they both had their heads down, wearily following in my tracks. I prayed I would find our tent soon. It was getting late and even the benefit of the watery sun would soon disappear as it moved behind Vinson's ridge.

After another hour of battling the elements, the swirling snow parted in front of me. There, in the distance, was our little red tent. Overjoyed, I shouted back to Rob, but he couldn't hear. Ten minutes later we finally arrived, relieved to be back at our tent. With the weather deteriorating fast, high camp was no longer a safe place to be. But with the cold already biting at our fatigued bodies, we had to rest, now wasn't the time to be dismantling tents. We hoped it would blow through soon.

Overnight the barometer plummeted and the wind continued to howl around our puny shelter. We were trapped in the full fury of an Antarctic storm. To attempt an escape from high camp now would be foolhardy in the extreme. Fingers and toes would be lost and our tent shredded before we'd even left. Our chances of surviving outside would be zero. This is why no life prevails in Antarctica's interior. High on Vinson and with no natural protection, we hoped we'd be able to out smart our opponent. Though the thin nylon shell of our tent could be ripped apart in seconds, we were now glad of our efforts to build sizeable walls – they were our only protection. Savage weather imprisoned us and rescue was not an option. Our only task was now survival.

The following day, wind continued to shake the tent ferociously. We were constantly showered by hoar frost, formed by our moist breath freezing onto the tent fabric. Our conversation soon drifted into desultory 'I spy' games but when one of these ended in a domestic dispute, I decided to venture outside to dig away the drifting snow.

After half an hour of puffing and panting, I was dressed in every item of down gear I possessed and looking like the Michelin man. A wall of snow three feet thick pressed against the front door and I slowly dug and burrowed my way through until I could climb out via a tiny hole. As I squeezed out, I felt like a hibernating arctic ground squirrel that had accidentally woken in the middle of winter.

With digging soon completed, in a moment of extreme optimism I seized the opportunity to answer nature's call with the privacy of being outside. As I attempted to walk to the pee hole, I was buffeted into a jog by the wind. Whipping my layers down, I yelped from the fierce wind and stinging ice on my bare skin. My salopette straps lashed violently and within seconds my pants were full of snow and my bottom felt mysteriously detached. Moments later, while battling to control the effects of the cross wind, a gust sent me skidding across the yellow pee ice. It was time to quit and return to using my pee bottle. Going to the toilet had become bracing, even by Antarctic standards and was promptly added to my growing list of new extreme sports.

That night I was still awake at 3 am listening to the roaring wind and snapping tent fabric. Even with a balaclava, a hat and ear plugs the noise was deafening. The winds slammed into the tent again and again, buckling its tiny poles. By the next morning the weather had further deteriorated. We wouldn't be moving anywhere. Rob agreed to take the morning shift of digging and I would do the afternoon. As we sat planning the day's menu, the most exciting part of our day, Stuart handed me two blocks of frozen cheese and salami.

'Get those down your thermals, Jo,' he said.

'Do I have to?' I whined, knowing the answer full well. Shoving them in between my fleecy thermal layers to rest on my thighs felt no better than having wine cooler blocks in my pants – not something most people would want to do, even for a party trick. But it had to be done, otherwise we'd all end up with broken teeth. However, I was flattered it was my thermals that were considered best for the job.

With our morning brew on the stove, clouds of steam spewed into our tent swallowing Stuart and Rob up in our regular breakfast whiteout. To satisfy our bodies' craving we chomped with relish through our morning slab of frozen butter, high in fat and with more calories per gram than carbohydrates or protein. I would happily have eaten half a pound if we'd had it, but rations didn't allow. In fact rations were a moot point, as we were about to run out of both food and fuel.

Heading out on my afternoon digging shift, I pulled my third hat on and gathered our full pee bottles for emptying. Rob checked to see that my mask and goggles were perfectly sealed. With the winds having strengthened yet further, I would now suffer frostbite in seconds if any skin was exposed. I zipped myself into the vestibule, which now acted as a kind of decompression chamber. Such was the force of the snow eddies outside the front door that if both the inner and outer zips were open just a fraction, vast quantities of snow would instantly funnel inside. With our down bags already dangerously damp, I couldn't allow that to happen.

Fifteen minutes later, with the digging complete and zipped safely back in the tent vestibule, I took a moment to use our plastic toilet bag before going inside. With certain danger of frostbitten bottoms outside, we now had no choice but it rated at the extreme end of my 'horrid tasks' scale. With the barometer still falling, we'd stared at the ceiling for yet another day and cabin fever had set in. We finally burst forth lustily with a Monty Python song, 'Always look on the bright side of life . . .' accompanied by the best whistling we could muster through our giggles and numb lips. We weren't alone in our madness, though, as even Captain Scott in his last few days wrote 'We are in a desperate state, feet frozen, etc. no fuel and a long way from food but it would do your heart good to be in our tent to hear our songs and cheery conversation.'

Suddenly there was yelling outside. Luis, an American guide, and his team had been climbing Vinson as we climbed Shinn and like us, they were trapped at high camp. Digging to find our door, he crashed inside, looking like a wild snowman.

'Brought you a love package,' he said, brandishing a bag of food. Bowled over by his generosity, we found something to reciprocate with. Both our teams were fast running out of food and fuel. Luis knew of an emergency cache buried near high camp and suggested he and Stuart should try to find it if we were still stuck the next day. 'Well, I can honestly say this is the worst storm I've been caught in,' Stuart said, brushing the snow off his sleeping bag. His words weren't comforting and we all hoped the emergency cache existed, or we would be in serious trouble.

Just an hour later with our walls collapsing again, I headed out to dig, this time taking the anemometer, our hand-held instrument for measuring wind speed. Wind gusts in excess of 70 kph meant there was a wind-chill temperature of at least −67°C. Even under my countless layers, the cold was vicious and gnawing. If this was just the Antarctic summer, I couldn't begin to imagine what Shackleton's men had endured through the winter. With the sun about to disappear behind the ridge, I shuddered to think how cold it would soon be. Even with the furious work of digging, the altitude left me breathless before I could generate sufficient heat. Banging my hands together, they refused to warm up. The snow found its way inside my goggles and swirled distractingly in front of my eyes, while spindrift blasted through my mask holes, pricking my lips like hundreds of needles.

The third day of the storm arrived and it hadn't relented at all. The wind roared like jet engines and the ground shook beneath our mats. For the entire night it had been like trying to sleep on a runway. I couldn't help worrying that we'd unknowingly built our camp over some monstrous crevasse. Every so often our hopes were raised by the occasional lull but it was always followed by an almighty crash as even stronger gusts pounded the tent. Lying beside me, Rob peeled my sleeping bag down and stared into my eyes. We were both praying the guy lines would hold.

Suddenly there was muffled screaming outside and frenzied digging. Our zip was ripped open and a hysterical Luis burst inside, 'We're gonna die! We're gonna die!' Under his goggles his eyes were wide with panic. Wrenching his face mask down, we all stopped dead. Beneath the layers, his face was plastered with the grin of a lunatic. We all erupted into laughter, and congratulated Luis on making us victims of his irrepressible sense of humour. Our ability to laugh kept us all going in the face of our predicament – we were down to our last day of food.

'Stuart, how about helping me look for the food and fuel cache?' Luis suggested. But Stuart was in his sleeping bag and reluctant to go outside in the storm. Sensing this Luis reversed out of the tent, 'I'll go and see if I can find it' he offered. Rob and I felt awkward but didn't want to cut across the situation by offering to go.

At midday a very cold and iced-up Luis burst into our tent dragging behind him a frozen cache bag. Our tent immediately converted to Aladdin's cave as we excitedly pulled out soups, dehydrated meals and fuel. Wanting to repay Luis for his kind efforts, I suggested he and Anthony, his tent mate, should come over for cocktails and nibbles the following day. Resulting from our shortage of drink containers and an inability to wash up, our cocktails tended to consist of a curious mixture of porridge, soup and tea. I hoped it would be the thought that counted. With the emergency supplies our situation was looking brighter. Even if the storm continued we could now survive for almost a week. Feeling very fortunate, our plight was far removed from that of the early polar explorers like Shackleton whose team was reduced to eating their own dogs.

As Luis left us, Stuart let out a sigh of relief. 'I'm glad he's gone, I've been dying for a pee all morning. I couldn't move with all those bags in here'. After weeks of continual complaints we felt exasperated and finally vocalised our thoughts. Living on top of each other created its own tensions, and our frank discussion didn't make it any easier, but for the first time since the storm had started, he volunteered to go outside and dig. By the time he'd returned, the air had cleared and I was busy creating a Vinson board game. Remembering it was just five days till Christmas, I introduced a little Christmas cheer into our stormbound home, with some polar Christmas carols. With little else to do, the three of us practised 'the Antarctic Twelve days of Christmas' and then performed a rendition, with much guffawing, for our video camera memoirs.

On the morning of the fourth day the winds had abated. Dressing up for the morning dig, I was eager to inspect the eastern skies, out of which the storm had come. Outside, the air was still filled with blowing snow but I could see through it, as if it was a veil of lace. Gleefully jumping up and down, I punched the air with my fist. For the first time in days I could see blue sky. In high spirits, I rushed over to Luis's tent to share the good news. Our moment of escape had finally arrived. We dismantled the tent while remnants of the strong winds still tried to prise it from our wooden hands. Although it was considerably warmer than previous days, by the time we'd finished, we were still chilled to the core.

We descended past the ice cliffs, their silhouetted forms standing like giant tombstones. Shafts of cold white sunlight pierced the haze above, lighting up vortices of spindrift that twisted through the icy graveyard. Away from the bleak plateau at high camp, the Branscomb Glacier below was a different world. As we entered the enchanting garden of blue ice sculptures once again, our time trapped up high already seemed distant. At midnight, after two cache stops and 2,000 metres of descent, we arrived safely back at base camp. It was 21 December, and as the last clouds evaporated, we revelled in the return of the sun as it circled at its highest elevation for another year.

By 2 am, with the good weather holding, the Twin Otter had been despatched to collect us. Hours later we were back at Patriot Hills camp. At just −15°C, the temperature was mild compared to Vinson. I wandered outside, relishing the freedom of wearing only one hat and one pair of gloves. Our experiences of the last few weeks in the Ellsworth range had been more than we'd bargained for, but to have survived the storm and escaped intact had taught us much. With the South Pole still ahead of us, we were glad of a few days to recover from our foray into the mountains before departing to ski the last degree of latitude south.

When my confused biorhythms woke me early the next day, I paid a visit to the weather and communications tent where Jason and Yaco, the radio and meteorology experts at Patriot Hills, were already up. Joining us, the ALE operations director had some bad news concerning our ski to the South Pole. 'Geoff Somers told me the sastrugi in the last degree were the worst he'd ever seen.' On Geoff's recently completed expedition their fibreglass sleds, otherwise known as pulks, had been so badly damaged, they needed a pulk re-supply after just one week. Geoff Somers is one of Britain's, indeed the world's, most experienced polar travellers. He has an impressive array of accomplishments behind him, perhaps notably the 1990 International Trans Antarctica Expedition that made the longest ever traverse of Antarctica, covering 6,000 kilometres in just 220 days with a team of huskies. With an MBE and Polar Medal Geoff's experience was vast, and hearing his verdict was disturbing. Not only would it make our skiing more arduous, but more importantly the ground might be so rutted and broken up that it would be impossible for the Twin Otter to land. If that was the case, our ski to the South Pole would be over before it had even begun.

CHAPTER 13

Vanishing Horizons

'If you don't know where you are going you will probably end up somewhere else'.

Lawrence J. Peter

'CAN'T GUARANTEE WE'LL be able to land,' the pilot said as we loaded the last pulk into the plane.

'How much time can you spend searching for a good landing area?' I asked hopefully.

'Not long, Jo. We'll be tight on fuel,' he replied. I tried to ignore the implications of his answer.

'*Que sera, sera,*' Rob said pragmatically. I always envied Rob's ability to accept reality rather than worry about circumstances beyond our control.

As we flew south, I was once again mesmerised by the dazzling ice below. It stretched from horizon to horizon like a vast windswept ocean. The unrelenting polar winds had scarred the ice, combing it into waves and deep striations; the Thiel mountains the only disturbance in the infinite white desert.

Six hours later, we were approaching our drop-off location of 89° south, still uncertain if we could land. Even from hundreds of feet above, the wind-sculpted sastrugi were clearly visible. The pilot circled three times, and brushed the surface with the plane's skis before committing. He had to be sure. 'Bumpy landing,' he finally shouted over the drone of the engine, and signalled us to tighten our seat belts. Gliding the final few feet towards the snow, we hit with an enormous jolt. The engines roared and my heart pounded as the plane slammed into the ice ridges and banged across the snow before bouncing to a halt. A sigh of relief rippled around the cabin, shortly followed by cheers. We had made it. Our journey could begin.

We watched the plane vanish over the northern horizon, the faint hum of its engines disappearing last. We were adrift in an ocean of ice. I turned through 360°, straining to see or hear anything, but there was nothing. Endless ice melted seamlessly into an endless sky. The five of us now stood alone in a vast and empty space.

'Guess we'd better get going then!' said Stuart, bringing me back to the task at hand. Bruno and Jason, a father and son who were Italian by heritage but lived in Montreal, had joined us from Luis' team. They too had been trapped in the storm at high camp, but we'd only met them for the first time as we descended Vinson. Bruno was in his mid forties, a similar age to Rob, and he looked like a tousled version of Richard Gere. He owned various businesses but constantly reminded us with a twinkle in his eye that he'd grown up as 'a poor boy in a poor village in Sicily.' Jason was in his early twenties and ran a film company and despite being Bruno's son, was frequently reining in his father, who was like a mischievous child.

It was a perfect day to start skiing south. Crystal clear, a manageable −23°C and not a breath of wind. With our skis on and pulks in tow, we took our first steps across the shining desert. I had always enjoyed nomadic holidays, travelling with everything I needed, and I had romantically imagined that dragging all my possessions without a cumbersome rucksack would be easy. Within minutes I realised how wrong I was. After just two kilometres I was regretting the six kilos of photographic gear that I'd packed. Contrary to expectations, my pulk's runners wouldn't glide smoothly and I felt more like I was dragging it through porridge than over silky snow. Moreover, the terrain was anything but smooth. It looked like a sea of lumpy ice cream. The small amount of sled pulling that we did on Vinson proved woefully inadequate training.

To navigate accurately we used the sun, combined with a compass and GPS. Our compass bearing to the Geographic South Pole was 122° rather than 180°, as one might imagine. Had we followed the latter bearing we would have missed the Geographic South Pole. But perhaps more significantly, we would have run out of food and got very wet, en route to the magnetic South Pole – 2,800 kilometres away in the Antarctic Ocean.

On clear days the GPS and compass would be largely redundant as we could navigate by the sun. Every 24 hours the sun made a complete circle around our heads, moving 15° every hour. By using

our shadows like the hands of a 24-hour clock, in combination with
the exact local time according to our longitude, we could easily and
accurately navigate south. With the sun circling above, it made the
earth's rotation feel almost tangible, although at other times we felt as
though we were just walking in circles.

Our accommodation consisted of two tents. Bruno, Jason and
Stuart shared one while Rob and I had the other. It was bliss to have
our own tent and we hadn't felt quite so excited since we'd moved
into our new home after getting married. But at mealtimes, with just
one stove between us, all five of us squashed into the chaps' bigger
tent.

'So, Mr Rob, how can I make more money in the markets?' Bruno
said in his strong Italian accent, with a cheeky smile. But before Rob
had even finished chuckling at his random question, Jason had called
us all to order. 'We need to cover a lot more ground tomorrow,' he
said. Jason was eager to make faster progress and affirmative
murmurs echoed around the tent. We had only done six kilometres in
our first half day, and still had over 100 kilometres to go, and we
didn't want to run out of food again. By the end of our discussion
we'd agreed a minimum daily target of eight 50-minute marches with
a ten-minute break between each one. Why we called them 'marches'
when we were clearly skiing was beyond me, but like so many
traditions, we had adopted this one without asking any questions.

The next day was Christmas Eve and although we were
surrounded by the largest amount of snow in the world, without so
much as a tree or a piece of tinsel in sight, it didn't feel very
Christmassy at all. I had imagined I'd spend the day romantically
skiing next to Rob and chatting about festive things, but reality
proved a little different. My lower back was becoming increasingly
painful and the gap widened between me and the team. I normally
loved being at the back – it gave me the freedom to linger and take
photos – but now it felt like a jail sentence. I couldn't catch up even if
I wanted to. I longed for Rob to turn around, rush back and be
sympathetic but I didn't want Bruno and Jason to see me languishing
on our second day.

*I was worried about Jo. She had been skiing bent awkwardly and
I hadn't seen her find a good rhythm all day. Even after the last break*

her movement still looked laboured and painful. Every time I offered
help she insisted she was fine but she was going to hurt herself if she
carried on the same way. I just hoped she would see sense and give me
something to carry.

By the end of the day I was in agony and demoralised. The muscles on the left side of my lower back were burning and locked in a painful spasm. I'd always had a scoliosis – a curvature of the spine – and it had caused me occasional problems. But I'd never anticipated the severity of what I now felt.

As we huddled together in the lads' tent, Stuart announced we had managed a slightly more respectable 14.7 kilometres, but we all agreed it still wasn't enough. We'd have to ski faster still tomorrow, Christmas Day. Our new target of 16 kilometres worried me. In the warmth of the tent I was eager to please, but I was already struggling to keep up and in reality I was scared I'd agreed to an impossible goal.

Having 'washed' my underpants in snow that night, by the following morning they were solid and I childishly delighted in waking Rob by snapping them loudly next to his ear. 'Happy Christmas!' I said, pressing my cold nose against his. As it was 25 December, we attempted a cheery rendition of 'We wish you a merry Christmas', but the dry air had left us feeling as if we'd been chewing on silica gel all night and after a series of unintelligible croaks we gave up.

As we tucked into our rations of porridge, cake and butter, Bruno started mischeviously grilling Rob once again about matters of business.

'I see you're starting early today, Bruno,' Rob laughed. Bruno's questions were as unrelenting as the polar wind but never failed to entertain.

By the end of our first march, Rob's thick fleece jacket was covered in beautiful ice flowers which had formed as his perspiration escaped and froze in situ. The giant sastrugi were equally impressive, but as the scenery grew ever more beautiful, so dragging our pulks became increasingly arduous. We were now skiing through a tumultuous ocean of ice, its frozen sastrugi waves tortured and chaotic like wind against tide. The twisted ice capsized our pulks time after time. Gradually I fell further and further behind and struggled alone with my pulk. Initially I was embarrassed at the thought of slowing the others down; minutes later I resented being left so far behind. Soon after, I found myself revelling at being alone in such a starkly beautiful place. Confused by my own schizophrenic emotions, I eventually gave up trying to figure myself out and diagnosed myself with a new disorder – 'poleitus'.

By our third march, however, my back muscles were rigid and every step caused a stabbing pain. I felt sick and the only relief was to flex right and stretch. With five marches to go I felt like sitting down and giving up. Hot tears rolled down my face and froze as soon as they contacted my goggles. With bleary vision and fogged goggles, I started to twist my ankles on lumps of snow. Feeling like a pressure cooker inside, I turned to Rob, who was faithfully keeping me company at the back. Signalling for him to turn away, I ripped my bindings open, unclipped my skis, yanked my harness off and hurled it as far as I could. Running towards it I leapt from a great height and proceeded to jump up and down on it.

'I hate you. Nasty, nasty, evil harness!' I shouted. By the time I'd finished my harness was satisfactorily buried and out of sight. Feeling limp and exhausted, I walked back to my pulk totally breathless. Despite being well acclimatised for the 3,000 metres of the Polar Plateau, there was still insufficient oxygen to support my harness abusing activities.

Rob stood in silence, not daring to intervene. Once I'd finished he quietly dug my harness out of the snow and laid it by my feet.

'Thanks, Honey. I'm sorry. It's my back. I just don't know what to do with myself,' I said, leaning over my pole to try and stretch. Begrudgingly I put my harness back on and Rob clipped my traces back in place. I started pulling again but had to ski flexed to the right to prevent my back seizing up. With my uneven stride and awkward stoop I felt I should be starring in a 'Quasimodo goes to the pole' movie rather than trying to ski there for real. Thankfully Bruno, Jason and Stuart were some way ahead and seemingly unaware of my harness tantrum. I felt extremely inadequate at pulk pulling and began to wonder if I would have fared better with my equipment in a Tesco's shopping trolley mounted on skis. Shortly afterwards Rob drew alongside me.

'This is silly, Jo. Let me take your pulk, I can drag both for a while.'

'You're joking. You can't pull both!'

'Yes I can, I'll be fine. Come on, I insist.' After minutes of haggling, I finally relented and handed my pulk over for the next 30 minutes. I felt a terrible failure and the day had just become my worst Christmas Day on record, and by a significant margin. Apsley Cherry Garrard once noted that 'polar exploration is at once the cleanest and most isolated way of having a bad time which has ever been devised', and at that precise moment, I completely agreed.

I'd never seen Jo get this mad, she was obviously in a great deal of pain. She's too stubborn for her own good though and it was a crazy fight to persuade her to relinquish the pulk. Having done so, dragging two pulks turned out to be a nightmare. Not only did they fight against me, but they fought against each other and by the end of the march I was sweating like a dog. I offered to do more but Jo was already feeling guilty and insisted on taking it back, which was actually a great relief.

Thankfully by the afternoon I had my skis on, my pulk back in tow and felt much calmer. Venting my emotions had been cleansing and I even felt amused by the morning's events. I marvelled once again at the pristine beauty and the privilege of being in Antarctica. Although I was in pain and sometimes at my wits' end, I wouldn't have given it up for anything. I loved Antarctica and every second was a gift.

For our penultimate march I sang nursery rhymes as a distraction from my back. My favourite being an extended version of 'ten green bottles' – 'fifty green bottles'. It was long-winded and mindless, the perfect antidote. Having filled the entire march with one nursery rhyme, I proudly announced this to the team and instead of questioning my own sanity, I even felt rather clever. I had attempted to use my time more constructively, contemplating world poverty, education and such like, but by the last march all I managed was to count my 3,800 steps.

That evening the five of us celebrated Christmas Day and our new distance record with some swigs of Stuart's whisky stash.

'So Rob and Jo, I have a proposal for you,' said Jason with a glint in his eye that made us suspicious.

'I'd like to make a film and use you two as the main characters', he said thoughtfully stroking his beard. 'The story will be based on Rob

having a cancerous brain tumour and he is on a journey to the South
Pole to try and find himself and come to terms with dying'. Shooting
each other curious glances, we wondered if Jason knew about Rob's
medical history and was having some kind of a joke. After hesitant
um's and ah's, we realised he was being serious.

'Have a think and let me know tomorrow' Jason said. Play acting
as if Rob had cancer again felt a little too real; we were still happy to
forget about it. However, we didn't want to disappoint Jason or his
filming ideas, so agreed to think about it.

After dinner Rob and I crawled back into our tent for our own
Christmas celebrations. I'd been saving some Christmas cards from
our family plus an extra helping of nuts and beef jerky especially for
that moment. I presented Rob with a folded scrap of diary paper from
which I'd made a Christmas card.

'Here you are. From Antarctica with love.'

'That's awesome. Sorry I haven't got one for you,' Rob said, giving
me a cuddle.

'Forget it. I'm the one who should be sorry after my harness
moment today. Thanks for helping me,' I said, giving him a kiss.

With the sun streaming through the sides of our tent it was an
unusually balmy +5°C inside. Taking advantage of the heat wave, we
treated ourselves to a Christmas Day wet wipe wash. Peeling our
layers off became a journey of discovery as to which parts of our
bodies were falling apart. Rob's groin was cracked and red raw from
chaffing and I found purple frost spots on my thighs from the cold.
With my hairy legs and our skin that was flakier than soap powder,
we were not only the perfect candidates for a day at our local spa, but
also the farthest from it. Removing my balaclava for the first time in
days, I discovered my head was a giant ball of matted fluff and quickly
replaced it again, deciding to let sleeping dogs lie.

Boxing Day started well. We'd already made a special Christmas
satellite phone call to Rob's family before leaving Patriot Hills and
now it was time to call mine. Everyone was gathered at my parents' –
brothers, wives and kids. Knowing Mum always liked to hear we were
eating well, I dutifully informed her we were chewing on frozen pear
for breakfast.

'Well we're about to tuck into roast turkey but I don't suppose you
wanted to know that!' Dad chimed in. Hearing them so clearly on the

sat phone was strange but wonderful. We imagined how cosy they all were sitting around the open fire and for just a few moments, we envied their comfort before saying our goodbyes.

With a combination of painkillers, some DIY boot insoles made from my foam sleeping mat, a hand warmer taped to my back and a lighter pulk – courtesy of Rob who now had my sleeping bag and shovel – I even made it to the second march before my pain reared its head. The constant polar breeze had strengthened overnight and the cold stung like acid on any exposed skin. Even Jason with his thick beard was hidden beneath his mask. With numb cheeks it was impossible to feel whether our skin was exposed or just cold, so at repeated intervals we called out 'Flesh' to each other to warn of any exposed skin we could see. In spite of our constant vigilance, a small area of Rob's left cheek became frostbitten, quickly blackening and scabbing over.

Even the air was different on Boxing Day. It sparkled with millions of suspended ice crystals, each one refracting the sunlight and creating heavenly atmospheric effects. The sun was surrounded by a gleaming halo and arcs of light, otherwise known as parhelia and sun dogs. Beneath it was a pillar of dazzling light, creating an extraordinary mirage on the horizon. It was a spectacular light show.

We were able to navigate as much by the wind as the sun on Boxing Day. The sastrugi were also a good guide with their consistent angle. Spindrift whisked along channels between the sastrugi and danced around my ski tips. At times I was in a trance-like state, hypnotised by the rhythm of my skiing and the veil of blowing snow that caressed the landscape. The smallest of drifts grew into elegant ridges and waves before my eyes and we seemed to be crossing living fields of ice that marched relentlessly with the wind.

By the fifth march of the day, my body's trade union threatened to strike due to inadequate time off, poor conditions and lousy sustenance. In response, I promised better times ahead, reminded it there was no such thing as a free lunch in this life and provided entertainment by composing polar songs. But my body wasn't to be persuaded.

Our breaks were like a crazy game show. In a few frantic minutes I'd have to eat, drink, answer nature's call, take photos, fiddle with gloves, goggles, masks and clothing layers, adjust my harness for the umpteenth time, clip my traces and strap my skis back on. With the day's icy wind, breaks had become even more challenging and despite our religious wearing of gloves plus thick mitts, everyone suffered hot aches for the first 30 minutes of each march. Rob and I could never decide whether our fingers felt on fire, trapped in a vice or simply severed. However, excruciating as it was, it was strangely comforting, as to have felt nothing would have meant our fingers were literally freezing to death.

With enforced shorter breaks due to the bitter wind, we finally exceeded our daily target that day, skiing 16.7 kilometres and in the face of the abnormally arduous sastrugi, we all felt pleased with the day's work. In a moment of misguided celebration, I offered to sing one of my polar songs. In spite of my obvious lack of singing talent, the team graciously applauded me, but were swift to break into conversation to avoid further scary renditions. Broaching the subject of Jason's filming request, Rob explained his medical history.

'Gee Rob, I had no idea. I totally understand why you're saying no,' Jason said apologetically.

'No worries, mate, you weren't to know,' Rob said, '. . . but happy to help so long as it doesn't involve me dying!'

The next morning we packed up camp in a disorienting whiteout. Our lives had gradually become a polar version of 'Groundhog Day'. We had the same routine, the same scenery, the same company, the same food and even the same looking poo. The only thing that changed was the weather, but now the whiteout had further increased our sensory deprivation. In addition to hearing nothing except the swish of my skis, smelling nothing except myself and feeling nothing except pain and cold, I now couldn't see anything except the person in front of me.

With no sun and no visible landscape features, navigation had to be done in pairs with the rear person shouting 'Right' or 'Left' if the person in front deviated from a straight line. The absence of any contrast from the monochromatic sky and snow made it impossible to discern the projecting sastrugi and we all slipped and tripped our way south. I was grateful for the terrible visibility though. It slowed our progress and enabled me to keep up.

Now that the horizon had vanished we'd lost any visual goal. Skiing to the pole was in all respects an utterly different sport to

Sunshine belies the bone numbing -55°C wind chill on 15 December 2003 as we reach Vinson's summit – the highest point of the most hostile continent on earth.

Rob on the Branscomb Glacier headwall, with the Antarctic ice sheet behind.

A spectacular sun halo and vast nothingness fill our day as we ski across the polar plateau to the South Pole.

Rob and I represent our respective northern and southern hemispheres at the Geographical South Pole ceremonial marker.

The South Pole dome – an underground village, currently being crushed by the moving ice sheet and soon to be decommissioned in place of a new station built on stilts.

Rob asleep in the foreground amidst a pile of bodies and gear, en route from Antarctica to Chile in the Russian cargo plane.

With the breathing difficulties of high altitude exacerbated by my tonsilitus, we snatch quick summit photos on Aconcagua, 26 January 2004, before descending.

Feeling like a mule, I move a second load to our fifth camp (camp one) on Aconcagua.

March 7 2004, on Mount Kosciuszko, wearing in our heavy, double-layered boots in preparation for Everest.

A team member climbing 'the gap' on Carstensz Pyramid's summit ridge (the other seventh summit).

The three kilometre high north face of Everest and her summit plume seen from 15 kilometres away at the blue moraine lakes near base camp.

Giant ice penitentes tower above me on the East Rongbuk Glacier, en route from the interim to advanced base camp.

Camp one on Everest's North Col at 7,100 metres. The magnifying effect of the thin air belies the fact that camp two is still seven hours' slog away. (Camp four, high camp, is still out of sight on the north face.)

At camp three on Everest's north ridge, Rob forces his half of our shared plastic bag dinner down for some much-needed calories.

At nearly eight kilometres high, just the act of taping my fingers to prevent my nails peeling off in the dry air has left me in need of a rest.

At 8,800 metres, already higher than any other mountain on earth, Rob, Kili Pemba, Nawang and I traverse towards the final rock gully on Everest's north-east ridge.

Along with one of our Sherpas, Nawang, we squeeze onto Everest's small summit on 24 May 2003 – exactly three years after Rob was declared in remission from cancer.

In a state of happy disbelief, we summit Elbrus in Russia on 20 July 2004, and in so doing complete the Seven Summits.

Rob leaves our precariously perched camp two, on Ama Dablam – a 6,856 metre mountain known as the Matterhorn of the Himalaya.

Rob on the south-west ridge of Ama Dablam, en route to camp three via the 'gendarmes' (pinnacles) that plummet for thousands of feet to the valley below.

I tuck into my favourite snack of condensed milk. As our bodies consume themselves at high altitudes, it is a constant battle to stop losing weight.

Taking a breather as I climb the Yellow Tower at 6,000 metres on Ama Dablam.

One of the many leads (broken ice revealing Arctic Ocean) we encountered as we skied to the North Pole.

On top of the world ... but quickly drifting away from it on the floating pack ice.

Subzero temperatures and frigid Arctic winds cause swollen eyes but are no dampener for our North Pole celebrations.

climbing. It was a solitary pursuit – unroped, marching south in each other's tracks for hour after hour, day after day. Mountains normally offered visible goals. There was always the summit, while a plethora of ridges, valleys, cols, glaciers, rock faces and pinnacles provided varied scenery and objectives. The novelty of a flat horizon for 360° and of skiing south day after day was wearing thin. It was more a journey of endurance, routine and mind over matter. Climbing and arriving at a higher camp or summit was a far more tangible reward than a new GPS reading. Mountains give a great sense of achievement and unique rewards – sights no-one else could see, places no-one else could reach without hard work. The journey to the South Pole was different. Not only would the view be the same as every other day but also tourists could fly right to it. They could step out of a warm plane for a few brief hours and then fly home again; see Antarctica, yet not fully experience it. It would be the equivalent of arriving at Cho Oyu's summit by cable car, although that in itself would be impossible as you'd pass out long before you ever got there.

Nevertheless, in spite of the unchanging scenery we were still drawn to each new horizon and intrigued by what lay beyond it. Fridjof Nansen believed it was the power of the unknown over the human spirit that drove men to polar regions and perhaps he was right. Insatiable curiosity is a powerful motivator.

By the end of the eighth march a fresh breeze had developed and putting the tents up was punishing. With all of us spinning our arms to fling blood back into our fingertips, we looked like a gaggle of distressed penguins. That night the winds continued to strengthen and we were glad to have our skis as bomb proof tent pegs. There was not so much as a single shrub to stop the winds as they raced across the polar plateau for hundreds of kilometres before slamming into our tents.

The following morning our temperamental stove finally blew up and with a whoosh ignited the entire vestibule. As flames engulfed one end of the tent, I immediately unzipped the other end for a quick escape.

'My hair is burning!' Bruno shouted, furiously patting his eyebrows.

Stuart hurled the flaming stove and mat outside. 'That was lucky,' he said, inspecting the tent. 'The material isn't damaged at all.'

Fortuitously, the thick coating of hoar frost inside the tent had acted as a temporary flame retardant. We laughed nervously at our near disaster. Losing a tent would have been inconvenient and treating severe burns almost impossible. Besides which, getting burnt to a crisp in the coldest place on earth would have been the height of carelessness, and made for an embarrassing story back home.

With camp dismantled once again, we were on the move. The strong winds overnight had cleared the low cloud but they'd brought a cruel windchill of at least −40°C. A continuous blast from the east made my entire left side stiff and awkward as I skied. Snow was falling, although rather than falling from the clouds it had most likely been blasted into the air by the recent high winds. Antarctica is the world's highest and coldest desert and only receives two inches of precipitation annually in its interior. Incredibly, places like the Dry Valleys hadn't seen snowfall for over two million years, so it was unlikely we were experiencing the real thing.

In the diffuse grey light the ice fields appeared desolate and sterile but we were glad of the improved visibility. However, as the pace had increased once again, Jason had pulled a long way ahead. Unlike the laboured polar plod that the rest of us were doing, he skied upright with robotic movements and never seemed to tire. I envied his strength and the ease with which he hauled his pulk. Today the sastrugi were more stunning than ever, their elongated wave crests shaped by the wind into fragile overhanging arcs of beautiful crystals. It felt criminal to destroy them with our clumsy pulks and skis and I found myself plotting a convoluted path to try and leave them untouched.

Despite the extra effort, I found that just altering my direction regularly brought a little relief to the repetitive movement of skiing. When climbing I could change the angle of my feet and the loading of my rucksack but with skiing I felt like a train on rails. By the end of each day we had completed about 30,000 steps and with my slightly different leg lengths, my knee joints felt as if they were grinding like an ill-fitting machine part.

The next day, 29 December, we were blessed with the return of indigo skies, dazzling sunshine and clear horizons. 'I can see something over there,' I said excitedly to Rob as we packed our tent away. Rob peered out to where I was pointing but saw nothing.

'There, that black pin dot on the horizon,' I said jumping up and down. 'That's got to be it. It's the South Pole. We're nearly there!'

Eight hours later that barely perceptible dot turned out to be just that – a tower used for scientific research at the South Pole station. It was the first day we'd had anything to aim for, final confirmation that we hadn't been walking round in circles.

In preparation for arriving at the Amundsen-Scott American station at the South Pole, we had been given a briefing document the size of a small thesis. As non-government visitors we were subject to strict regulations. There were rules for everything, including how we circumnavigated the eight-kilometre ground antennae, how and where we crossed the runway, sectors where it was forbidden for humans to tread, who would meet and escort us inside the station. It even specified which toilet we would be allowed to use, though sadly the rules only permitted using it once. In addition, we could not expect any medical or logistical support, irrespective of any emergency. This rule sounded harsh at first but it was the only way of protecting the station against irresponsible, freeloading expeditions with no rescue plans.

After days with an unblemished horizon for 360° it felt strange to come across buildings sitting in the middle of nowhere. As we neared the station we could see the silver geodesic dome, radar dishes, towers and antennae. In spite of all the buildings it was eerily quiet, almost like a deserted space station. Skiing in single file beside the edge of the runway, we found ourselves floating effortlessly along. The groomed runway snow and absence of sastrugi made our skis race and the pulks glide freely. It was pure joy.

As we set off across the runway in accordance with instructions, we were suddenly aware of loud engine sounds and shouting. Snowmobiles appeared from nowhere and people were running towards us, frantically waving their arms. We stopped in our tracks, uncertain of whether to proceed. Finally they were close enough for us to see under their hats and goggles. They were laughing and smiling. 'Welcome to the South Pole!' one shouted. 'Congratulations guys, awesome job!' another called out.

We definitely hadn't anticipated being welcomed as minor celebrities. Within seconds we were surrounded by cargo handlers, scientists, logistics staff, physicians and station managers, all bursting with enthusiastic questions and wanting to take our photos. After the warm work of pulk pulling, standing still for 15 minutes left us shivering. Thanking them for their welcome, we excused ourselves and headed off to erect our tents alongside the Twin Otter runway.

Skiing side by side Rob and I chattered away excitedly and some minutes later we arrived at the ceremonial South Pole. It was an incredible feeling to see the short barber-striped pole with its chromium globe and the arc of 12 national flags. 'We did it, Bella!' Rob said, wrapping his arms around me.

I buried my face in Rob's chest and let out a huge sigh of relief as he held me.

'I'm so glad to be here. No more pain!'

Dumping our skis and pulks, we walked to the official Geographic South Pole marker. Our GPS read 89°59'·999 south, the nearest it could compute to 90° south. With back slaps, hugs and handshakes we all congratulated each other. It was so cold that without our face masks our cheeks had quickly frozen into permanent grins and my nose crunched when I twitched it. Gripping the marker pole, I spun myself around it. Within seconds I'd crossed all the lines of longitude and spun through every time zone in the world. It was a scrumptious moment.

The station manager called over to us. 'Do you guys want to come inside the dome for coffee and cakes?' He'd barely finished asking before we were eagerly striding towards him. A glistening tunnel of ice led down to the dome. Inside were stacked numerous building like portakabins, their doors the same as industrial freezers but designed instead to keep the cold out. From rumours of previous expeditions we had braced ourselves for a frosty reception, yet once inside we were welcomed like VIPs. We were lavished with refreshments and treated to a question and answer session with the station managers, along with the directors of both the new station building and scientific projects. We talked about everything from Mars research and solar weather, to 'pole fever' and greenhouse therapy.

Twenty-four hours later we had barely slept, having spent hours touring laboratories, peering down ice holes two kilometres deep and discussing cosmic neutrinos and quantum physics. Talking to the scientists was humbling and their knowledge was astounding. Having spent so many days in a mental vacuum such conversations were both riveting and baffling. Our stay at the South Pole station was a fascinating insight into another world.

*

Over a week later our time in Antarctica had finally come to an end. It was 2.30 am on 8 January 2004 and we had just lifted off the blue ice runway at Patriot Hills. Inside the warm cargo plane the rest of the team quickly fell asleep. I sat perched high on a pile of rucksacks and fuel drums with Rob's head resting in my lap, my mind still bursting with all we'd seen and done. It had been a magical journey, one that we would never forget.

Landing back on terra firma the sweet smell of the vegetation and soil was overwhelming and the wind felt warm and damp. As we sat in the bus driving back to Punta, our next challenge sharpened into focus. Antarctica already felt like a dream.

'You know we're three weeks late for our Aconcagua expedition, don't you?' I said to Rob.

'Yeah, we need to try and get to Argentina this afternoon if we can.' Before our ski south we had made contact with our friends by satellite phone to warn them we'd be many weeks late. We had been thrilled to discover that they were keen to wait, so we could all climb Aconcagua together.

Within a matter of hours we were flying to Mendoza. It felt absurdly luxurious to be reclining in soft seats and having in-flight food delivered to us. We drifted in and out of sleep. Our bodies were yearning for a little more pampering and laziness but our minds were hungry for the next adventure.

At nearly 7,000 metres, Aconcagua is the highest mountain in the southern and western hemispheres. It is also the highest mountain outside the Himalaya. We both wondered if we were being overly ambitious by climbing the second highest of the Seven Summits just two months before Everest. We didn't want to jeopardise our attempt of Everest and there was some logic in favour of resting and retraining, but inspite of this neither of us wanted to give up on Aconcagua. We'd always seen the Seven Summits as an opportunity to combine travelling and climbing. Irrespective of whether all seven were possible, we wanted to enjoy the journey. We'd read so many stories of people who had sacrificed everything, even relationships, for the sake of Everest. Yet if they'd failed, they had nothing left. We wanted Everest to stay in its rightful place – as another mountain on our journey. If it didn't happen, we'd still be doing what we loved. We were committed to climbing Aconcagua – if we backed out now we'd let friends down, lose money and potentially never return. It was an opportunity neither of us wanted to squander.

CHAPTER 14

No Half Measures

'The best things in life are not things.'

Joann Davis

SINCE LEAVING ANTARCTICA we'd travelled 5,000 kilometres to the heart of the Andes and had traded one desert for another – ice for rock and plains for mountains. With the sun scorching down on us for a second day, I was grateful for the breeze that funnelled down the valley. We had just one more day's hike to reach base camp, from where we'd start our climb of Aconcagua. I swigged the last dregs of my sun-warmed water to rinse the dust from my throat. Our next camp, Casa de Piedras, was still hours away.

I felt naked as I walked in my shorts and T-shirt and relished the novel sensation of warm air on my skin. It felt just like the first bikini moments on holiday when the novelty of being so scantily dressed, yet not getting cold, is delightful. My fingertips, however, were still numb from frost damage, as were Rob's, but overall we'd escaped Antarctica relatively unscathed. Our attention to detail, clothing systems and careful monitoring of each other had all paid off. We'd also been incredibly lucky.

The sun made me feel soporific and carefree but Aconcagua was not to be taken lightly. Ominous statistics bandied about by other climbers suggested that for every eight people attempting the mountain, just two would summit and one perish. Climbers regularly paid the price for underestimating Aconcagua's altitude and hence it had one of the highest mountain death tolls in the world. Though her summit lay just below 7,000 metres, her latitude and proximity to the ozone hole made her the equivalent of a 7,500 metre peak. Some even called her a small 8,000er. Over the years her 'Viento Blanco' or White Wind had severely punished those who ignored her warnings and had filled the Cementerio del Andinistes on the outskirts of the nearby town, Punta del Inca.

We were now a team of six. We already knew Ryan and Clark, who we'd first met as our guides on Denali. They had brought their girlfriends, Sherrie and Lisa. In just a matter of days they too had begun to feel like old friends. Sherrie, from Alaska, fitted her temporary jobs around her hobby of rock and ice climbing, Lisa, a tree planter from Vancouver, used her work to fund surfing and snowboarding trips around the globe. To be travelling in a team of three couples was both novel and wonderful.

Ryan was the only one in our team who had climbed Aconcagua before. Though Sherrie and Lisa were experienced in the mountains, they'd never been that high and for us it was our first time in the Argentinian Andes. While they were patiently waiting for us, they'd spent several weeks rock climbing and surfing and their bodies were lean, fit and tanned. Our pasty, white, scrawny bodies were a sorry sight by comparison. Our only saving grace was that we were acclimatised to 3,000 metres. It was a small benefit but at least it had helped us for the first few days.

It was mid afternoon when we arrived at our second camp, Casa de Piedras, at 3,240 metres. Tomorrow we would complete the final leg of the Vacas valley and reach our so-called base camp. By now Rob had developed a nasty case of giardia and by the next morning the same symptoms were plaguing me, but my turn for the worse had been strangely reassuring. It confirmed that Rob's intestines weren't knotted again and with a swift application of antibiotics we were soon on the mend.

As we left camp on our third day, we parted from the main trail that led to Plaza Argentina, the second most popular route on Aconcagua. We were taking a new route, only discovered a few years ago. It was longer but more scenic, and by approaching Aconcagua from the north we'd escape the busy camps and accompanying litter of the standard routes. We were excited to break away from the main trail and head up the deserted Vacas valley, knowing it was unlikely that we'd see anyone else until summit day. We all loved the solitude of the mountains and were happy to leave the other jostling teams behind.

Having started the day in perfect sunshine, we were later drenched by rain, battered by hail and finally treated to a snowstorm. Waterfalls materialised out of nowhere and the red buttresses flanking the valley were transformed into snowy towers. The next morning we woke to a sparkling wonderland with a fresh blanket of snow covering the ground, crowning the high rock walls above camp and filling every crevice.

For the first three days we'd used mules to ferry some of our kit to base camp, but after that it was too high and steep for them and it was our turn to be mules. We planned to do a traverse of the mountain, which meant even heavier loads than normal because everything had to go up and over. There would be no easy stashing of gear at lower camps. We'd move much the same way that we had on Denali – caching our gear the first day and moving camp the next. With this routine we'd also be repeatedly climbing high and sleeping low, our preferred method of acclimatisation.

Several days later, as we carried our first load towards camp two, we were the sole life form at this height. We hadn't seen any vegetation for days, not even a single weed. We were climbing in a high desert, albeit a rocky one. Even in the Himalaya there had been some vegetation up to 5,000 metres but here the low relative humidity and thin ozone layer had prevented it reaching beyond 3,500 metres. The only living or moving thing seemed to be the streams and waterfalls, but even they were frozen most of the time. Waterfalls hung like fairytale chandeliers from the cliffs high above us, while glassy swirls and globules of frozen water laced the stream beds like polished gemstones.

Even at 4,800 metres, the height of Mont Blanc, we were still in a deep valley surrounded by Cerro Fitz Gerald, Zurbriggen, Ameguino and the master giant, Aconcagua. Our original plan was to climb several of these outlying peaks before Aconcagua, but being behind schedule we'd elected to climb just one, Cerro Fitz Gerald. Her intimidating east face now hung above us; like nature's cathedral, her buttresses soared skywards and frozen waterfalls clung to her walls like giant frescos.

Rob and I wondered if we were biting off more than we could chew and should stick to our main objective. I mulled Ryan's words over and over. 'It'll be more technical than Aconcagua, but you'll love it and it will help us all to acclimatise'. Although it sounded perfect, a combination of our tiredness and anxiety quickly converted our discussion into argumentative conversation. But a few hours later, we had both made our peace and resolved we were still keen to climb Cerro Fitz Gerald. In the end, neither of us wanted to concede our attempt of such a beautiful mountain.

Two days later, the six of us were enmeshed in a giant penitente field en route to climbing Cerro Fitz Gerald. Having started as a field of snow, years of erosion by the sun and wind had weathered it into thousands of ice pinnacles known as penitentes, some several metres in height. We clambered through the jungle of ice spikes, its labyrinth of snow sculptures was hypnotically beautiful, luring me to go deeper and explore, but it was a death trap. The latticework of spikes was poised on a delicate veneer of unconsolidated snow that camouflaged deep cavities.

We emerged from the ice field on to a loose scree slope. Tiptoeing our way across, we traversed the scree and then a 60° snow slope, reaching a steep couloir that would lead us to the summit ridge. Rob was ahead in Ryan's team, moving tentatively and obviously nervous. I hadn't seen him like this for years, at least not until recently on Mount Shinn when the rope handling had unnerved him. I could hear him discussing the quality of the anchors with Ryan, who was reassuring him in his usual jovial and relaxed manner.

I felt old emotions rising inside. Rob's fear of heights had sometimes frustrated me because there was so little I could do. I'd had expectations on how he should behave and deal with his fears. It was always easy to let those expectations become unrealistic. I didn't want to allow myself to get sucked back into those thoughts. I knew I couldn't change Rob but I could change myself. Clearing my throat, I called out encouragement to Rob up ahead, but he was too deep in concentration to hear me.

Over the years, I'd slowly learned to control my fear of heights and had climbed mountains I'd never imagined possible, not even in my wildest dreams. Despite this, our climbing in Antarctica had unexpectedly resurrected my old insecurities. As we climbed Cerro Fitzgerald's south face, a deep-seated, irrational fear had gripped me and I was struggling to shake it loose. I was frustrated that my enemy had been reawakened but I knew that if I worked at it, my confidence would return. It was only by confronting my fears again and again that I eventually gained control of them.

Moving in two rope teams, we slowly made ground up the 300-metre couloir to the rocky summit ridge. It was 1.50 pm when we made our final scramble to the summit of Cerro Fitz Gerald at 5,600 metres. There was a dented, rusty metal box resting near the summit which contained a log book. It had only ever been climbed by two other teams. It wasn't quite a first ascent but it was special none the less. Cerro Fitz Gerald is impressive, but being an outlying peak in the shadow of Aconcagua she had been neglected. Right now we were all grateful to Aconcagua for her distraction. She had given us the whole of Cerro Fitz Gerald to ourselves and we'd probably be the only people to climb it for years to come.

Taking what looked like a short cut, we descended quickly via a long scree gully and a snowy couloir. Arriving at the top of a gently sloping snow field, we started to make our way across it, but our short cut soon came to an abrupt end. We had started to punch through into holes, disappearing up to our waists in unpredictable snow. The afternoon sun had caused a strange pattern of melting below the surface and the entire slope seemed little more than a hologram, disappearing the moment we trod on it. 'Hey guys, this is no good. I'm going to check it out over there,' Ryan shouted.

The rest of us continued slowly across, but within minutes we gave up fighting our way out of holes and turned back. The snow field was a deceptive veneer hiding a maze of cavities. We couldn't risk going further. 'Where's Ryan?' Sherrie shouted to us.

We turned expecting to see Ryan behind us but saw nothing. Something was wrong and Sherrie knew it instantly. She was already scrambling back up to us. Within seconds we were all hollering Ryan's name out across the snow. There was no answer. We waded back to the last place we'd seen him.

'Where the hell is he? He never just disappears like this!' Sherrie said with panic in her voice. Cupping her forehead in her hands, she scanned desperately back and forth across the snow field. No-one said a word, but we all suspected what had happened.

Within seconds we had set up a rope and were belaying Clark across the fragile snow field towards our last sighting. He moved further and further away, continuing to shout Ryan's name. Still there was no sign.

'I need more rope, make a new anchor,' Clark shouted to us. We hurriedly made another anchor point and Sherrie took over belaying lower down.

'Where the hell are you, Ryan? Come on,' Sherrie said, her voice audibly wavering. As Clark moved across the snow field, time was running out, there were only a few metres of rope left. Sherrie yelled out to Clark, 'You've got five metres left Clark . . . four metres . . . three . . . two . . .' Within seconds he wouldn't be able to continue. If Ryan was injured, every minute we lost could endanger him further. And wherever he was, we were now certain he'd fallen into a very deep hole.

Suddenly Clark whipped round. He was shouting and pointing excitedly at the ground. Ryan had fallen 25 feet through a snow bridge, but by some miracle he'd landed on a desk-sized platform of ice, while his poles had tumbled further into the abyss below. He was not only conscious but had only sustained a minor injury to his elbow. With difficulty, Ryan had managed to put his crampons on without dislodging the delicate snow shelf and then climbed out with just one ice axe. He'd been very lucky, as indeed we all had. Clark threw Ryan the rope to tie in and we were soon reunited as a team.

With Ryan safely back, Sherrie dropped the rope and flung her arms around him. Ryan was visibly shaken by the ordeal. 'Shit, man, I thought I was toast. This place is lethal. Everything's unstable. We'll have to head back to our other tracks.'

Retracing our steps along the high traverse was a small price to pay for escaping the snow-field intact. Ploughing our way back up we repeatedly punched through the soggy, unconsolidated snow. Each time I dropped into an empty space my stomach turned and when I hit the bottom of the hole I let out a nervous sigh of relief. By 5 pm, the sun had dipped behind Aconcagua's north-west ridge. We'd finally escaped the minefield of chasms and wearily negotiated the last scree slopes back to camp two.

Three days later we'd moved to camp three at 5,600 metres, the same height as Cerro Fitz Gerald's summit. The weather had turned foul higher on the mountain and from our protected location we could hear the ferocious 'Viento Blanco' blasting her upper flanks. High clouds tore past her summit and looking up it seemed as if the whole mountain was toppling towards us. Summit winds frequently reached speeds in excess of 100 kph on Aconcagua and a *National*

Geographic photographer once recorded them at 260 kph when his powerful twin-engine plane started to go backwards over the summit.

From camp three our intended route over the Polish Glacier had come into sight, but we could see it was out of condition. Its upper section was a vast swathe of wind-polished, steep, bullet-hard ice. In this state countless climbers had been killed, falling thousands of feet. Only the lucky ones had been found and gone home in body bags.

Our only option was to join the standard route for summit day. That would entail climbing the infamous Canaletta – a 300-metre couloir of steep, loose scree. Positioned above 6,500 metres, it was the crux of the route and led directly to the summit ridge. More often than not the Canaletta was the cause of failure or difficulties high on the mountain. It was also where we'd potentially get caught up with other teams. But we had no choice.

The following morning I woke with a sore throat. My body had finally rebelled against the weeks of unrelenting hard graft. Several days later, after our carry and move to camp four I was running a fever and my tonsils were white and furry. But I wasn't alone in feeling below par and the entire team felt rough at this altitude. That evening all six of us sat quietly with our legs criss-crossed over each other. Instead of our normal colourful banter and card games, we nursed our headaches while discussing the route and made plans for our summit push later that night.

'You know if you're not up to it, Jo, we can try again next year,' Ryan said. I nodded reluctantly but felt dispirited that Ryan was even suggesting we might give it a miss. Rob and I had already decided this was our only shot at Aconcagua. We had dreams of travelling elsewhere, we needed to get back to work, we even hoped to have a family. This was a precious season of our lives, but it had an expiry date. It was unlikely we'd return to this mountain.

I was already awake when my alarm went off at 3 am. After two weeks working our way up the mountain, we had finally made it to summit day. But now I felt as though I had razor blades in my throat and I was cold and shivery before even venturing outside. The gusts that buffeted the tent all night hadn't eased at all but we decided to get ready in anticipation of it improving. With bleary eyes and fuzzy heads we climbed into our many layers.

'How's your throat?' Rob asked but as I tried to answer, I could barely talk. 'Jo, if you need to turn around today, I'm coming down with you.'

I shook my head furiously and croaked, 'No, I want you to go up.'

'No, Jo. We've said this for every other mountain – if one of us has a problem, we'll both turn around. I'm not about to change things now. It's not a discussion.' Hearing Rob so resolute in his decision to stick with me, I was determined not to let him down. I wanted to give it everything I had.

By 5 am we were all outside in the frigid and blustery morning. 'Ready to roll, gang?' Ryan called, flashing his head torch around the team. After five muffled affirmatives from behind our masks, we set off into the night. The wind whistled eerily, funnelling through the rocky towers around high camp. Wrapped in my layers, the only other sound I could hear was the frozen snow crunching beneath my crampons and my heavy breathing. No matter how beautiful and benign a mountain seemed by day, in the black of the night it always felt dangerous and malevolent. I longed for the sun.

With two masks on to protect my throat, I was having to suck in air as if being strangled. If I'd felt this way on any other expedition, I would most likely have given up but I was gradually learning not to allow my body to dictate to my mind. I followed Rob's torch light as it bobbed up and down in the darkness above. Clark was hot on my heels and regularly encouraged me from behind. 'Good job, Jo.'

I appreciated his words, but I knew I was going too slowly. By 6.30 am, as I'd been expecting, he stopped me. 'Jo, you need to tell me how you're feeling. Be honest.'

Swallowing hard and trying not to wince with the pain, I forced my words out. 'I am OK to continue . . .' I swallowed again. 'My throat's just making it harder to breathe, that's all.'

'Look, you can't go on if you're going to get worse. Let's reassess in 30 minutes.' Clark's seriousness about turning me around jolted me out of my altitude-induced haze. Whipping off my gloves, I frantically felt around in my pocket for some more painkillers and forced two tablets down with a swig of my slushy iced water.

Thirty minutes later the pre-dawn gloom was eclipsed by the blazing orb that crept over the horizon. Our world was transformed as golden rays streamed across the morning sky. Everything was bathed in the sun's brilliance – the mountain tops glistened, rising like dazzling pyramids from the golden clouds. Aconcagua's mammoth triangular shadow stretched dramatically west, far across the Andean chain. The sun felt like life itself, infusing my body with a new energy. The sunrises we saw on summit days were like no others on the planet, and this one was no different.

Any moment now I knew Clark would stop me and ask for an honest answer. I struggled to focus my mind. I couldn't lie – I felt no better and I knew it would be foolhardy to continue if I got worse, yet the dawn had rekindled my will to go on. I prayed, hoping for inspiration. I didn't want to endanger the others, but I didn't want to give up too quickly. Although I didn't receive any thunderbolts or blinding visions, as the minutes passed I did feel at peace. When Clark stopped me again, I'd resolved to continue.

Approaching the crest of the north-west ridge we started across Aconcagua's colossal north-west face via the so-called Windy Traverse. The traverse is nothing more than a narrow, crumbling ledge hanging above a plummeting scree field of monumental proportions. As I poked my head above the parapet of the ridge, a wall of wind slammed into me, knocking me backwards. It blew my legs around as if they were no more than flimsy flags and it was a fight just to place them where I wanted. The Windy Traverse was living up to its reputation.

By the time we'd reached the foot of the Canaletta it felt as if the air was freeze drying my throat. Ryan had stopped up ahead. I could see he wanted to talk. 'Are you sure you can do this, Jo? Have you got enough to get down?' he asked with a penetrating and serious stare.

Rob gripped my arm. 'I'm happy to turn around any time, Bella, you've got to be sensible.' Taking a deep breath to speak through my inflamed throat, I felt like I was breathing in through a straw. I gave Ryan and Rob the thumbs up and managed a husky 'I'm sure,' hoping I wouldn't need to speak again. But even as I said so, questions plagued my mind. *Can I really guarantee this? Am I absolutely sure?* When things went wrong at altitude, they happened fast. I couldn't afford to make a mistake now, I'd endanger the whole team. I prayed again that God would help me to be sensible and keep us all safe.

Our team had spread out. Sherrie had gone ahead as it was too cold for her to wait. Clark and Lisa were some way behind but still moving steadily. Ryan, Rob and I started up the Canaletta. Rob continued two steps behind me all the way. Just knowing he was there gave me strength. I wanted to keep going for him.

Jo was always strong and capable in the mountains but now she was a different person. Summit days were always the hardest and even her playful jokes would take a back seat, but today was worse than normal. She had totally shut down. I hated seeing her like this, but she was determined to go on and I trusted her judgement.

Several hours later, I was in a state of disbelief as I scrambled up Aconcagua's last few rocks. For so long this moment had seemed elusive and impossible. I had made it. In spite of how I felt, my mind was soaring. It was 26 January and we had the whole of South America at our feet. As we gazed westwards across Chile, the Pacific Ocean was only 130 kilometres away. At 6,960 metres and being so near to the Chilean Trench in the Pacific Ocean, we were standing on top of the earth's biggest wrinkle, 14 kilometres in height. Invigorated to be finally there, the last seeds of doubt had evaporated and a new wave of energy surged through me.

After ten minutes and hasty congratulations, I wanted to get down quickly while I was still firing on all cylinders. I needed my adrenalin levels to stay high. We passed Clark and Lisa on the final traverse, encouraging them that the summit was not far. As we exited the Canaletta and rejoined Windy Traverse we were shocked to see climbers still ascending so late. Some of them wouldn't make the summit and would have to turn around. Some would get seriously ill, maybe too ill to descend. It was madness but it wasn't for us to try and stop them. Up here everyone was free to make their own choices. The mountains are the ultimate democracy where no-one can hide from taking responsibility for their own choices.

By late afternoon we were all relieved to be safely back in high camp. Crammed into one tent in a pile of exhausted bodies and tangled gear, we celebrated our summit success with Thai noodles and peanut sauce. It had been a long hard day and though I'd been forced to examine my actions every step of the way, in the end I'd trusted my intuition and was amazed to have pulled through.

The following day, with all our equipment piled high on our backs like a mobile junk shop, we dropped in one long descent through four camps to Plaza des Mulas, nearly 2,000 metres below. Experiencing the normal route was far worse than we'd imagined. The north-west side of the mountain was a barren, windswept heap of scree, lacking any of the stunning terrain of our northern approach. The sprawling, ugly, busy camps were littered with rubbish and human detritus. Wherever we looked there seemed to be climbers vomiting or staggering around. Only now could we truly appreciate our experience in one of Aconcagua's remote and unfrequented valleys.

After hours of bone-crunching descent my knees felt as though they were glowing in the dark, but by 5 pm we had finally arrived at the Plaza des Mulas base camp and celebrated being safely off the mountain. It had been a wonderful three weeks with our friends in the mountains and all that now stood between us and a shower, toilet and comfy bed was a 25 kilometre walk to the road head.

*

One week later we were back in the UK. After our back-to-back expeditions we had lost weight and felt in need of a serious rest, but with Everest looming just seven weeks away, we had no time to lose. Packing our bags for Australia, we relocated to Sydney for two weeks of food, sleep and beach therapy, followed by a month of intensive training. On 7 March we celebrated reaching the top of Kosciuszko, Australia's highest mountain at 2,228 metres and the fifth of our Seven Summits. As we enjoyed the thick sweet air of its lower elevations, it was easy to forget that even though it was the smallest of the Seven Summits, Kosciuszko was still nearly twice the height of Britain's highest mountain, Ben Nevis.

By the end of March 2004, Rob's mother had done a fabulous job of feeding us up. We'd regained all our lost kilos and had even added a few extra in muscle bulk. The extreme altitude on Everest would cause our bodies to burn muscle for fuel, so every extra gram would tip the scales in our favour. A week after leaving Sydney we had spent a weekend in the UK collecting our gear, a few days in Kathmandu meeting the team, and three days acclimatising in Lhasa. Now we were once again bouncing across the dry and dusty plains of Tibet. Ready or not, the challenge of our lives was beckoning us.

CHAPTER 15

Snakes and Ladders

'He who has a why to live can bear almost any how.'
Friedrich Nietzsche

IT WAS EXACTLY six months since we'd last crossed Tibet en route to Cho Oyu. Though we had no idea what lay in store for us on Everest's slopes, it was reassuring to have Russell Brice at the helm of the expedition again. Our entire team was crossing Tibet in a convoy of seven landcruisers. Rob and I were travelling with Cecilie and Richard in our jeep. Cecilie, the only other female in our team, was attempting to be the first Norwegian woman to climb Everest; and Richard was hoping for better luck after his chest infection on Cho Oyu.

Last August after the monsoon, the Tibetan plateau had been wildly beautiful. The rich ochre plains had rolled to the horizon and golden barley fields had clustered around villages like highlights on a dark canvas. Now, with the frigid winter winds still blowing, it was a truly stark landscape, devoid of vegetation, dust eddying uninterrupted across the plains. Since our last visit to Tibet, some parts of our route were barely recognisable. The Chinese were making unnervingly fast progress with new roads and electricity pylons now lacing the barren plains.

As we entered the foothills, millennia of precipitation had carved ragged gashes into the hills. The gravel road we clattered along clung to loose shale slopes as it wound its way along deep gorges. Wrecks of trucks below were evidence of those carried away by a sudden landslip, or as our driver reliably informed us, too much *chang* – the local brew. Lurching our way steeply down to cross another parched stream bed, sitting inside the landcruiser was like being below decks on stormy seas. Anything loose was hurled around the cabin before being caught on the rebound, while our driver's miniature Buddha whipped frantically from side to side on the dashboard as if in some maniacal dance.

With the droning engine and rattling suspension, conversation was drowned and my mind drifted back to a discussion we'd had that morning. We had joined some fellow British travellers at breakfast in Shigatse, one of whom had failed on Everest the previous year. His words kept replaying in my head: 'I caught a cold from trekkers who visited our base camp. It cost me Everest.' That cold had not only prevented him performing, it had also left him dangerously ill at high altitude. Although Russell was due to be managing a few trekking groups that would pass through our base camps, he had been at pains to point out that he would be keeping their facilities separate from ours for that very reason. We all appreciated his advice, born not least from over ten Everest expeditions. Ironically, despite all these warnings, I already had an ominously sore throat. Spending the last week on various aeroplanes, or giant flying petri dishes as Rob called them, was probably the cause. With the countdown to base camp ticking away, I was beginning to feel increasingly uneasy.

As the plateau slowly gained height towards the Himalaya, we reached the Gyatsola Pass at 5,200 metres. From here, what appeared to be mere ripples in the plains amounted to snowy giants of over 6,000 metres. From the pass we began our descent to Dingri, which we quickly renamed 'Dingy', our last port of call before base camp.

Hotel Qomolungma was rumoured to have hot water and electricity and we raced eagerly inside, keen to enjoy our last good wash and the opportunity to charge electricals. But brown, tepid water and a single light bulb that glowed dimly between 7 and 10 pm wasn't quite what we'd hoped for, but it was the gale howling under our door all night that was the most unpleasant. Having been parcelled away in our convoy by day, dinner times were a welcome relief and an opportunity to get to know one another. Russell had split us into two climbing teams of ten. Team Karsang, consisted of people who had climbed or attempted an 8,000-metre peak before and we all knew each other. Of the ten on our team, Richard, Jamie and Ian had all been on Cho Oyu with us last autumn. Team Chhiring were new to each other and to the world of 8,000-metre peaks, with the exception of Andy, another Australian, who had been to 8,027 metres on Shishapangma. Team dynamics already had a different flavour from most of our previous expeditions. With a peppering of supremely confident men, there was a distinct aroma of competition even before we'd reached Everest. But beneath the bravado, uncertainty about the weeks ahead plagued us all. There was only one thing we could be certain of – to expect the unexpected.

After our second night in Dingri, we just had one day's drive left to base camp. As our convoy reached the Pang-la Pass at 5,150 metres, we were greeted by an uninterrupted view of the Himalayan giants. Gazing south there were 8,000-metre peaks in abundance; Makalu, Cho Oyu, Shishapangma and, standing proud in their midst, the colossal gleaming pyramid of Mount Everest, the jewel in the crown. Even from 65 kilometres away her icy plume trailed far into the eastern sky, as if she were a giant belching volcano. She had no delicate features, rocky spires or fine needles; even alongside the other 8,000-metre peaks, she was bulky and monstrous. Only such a perfect pyramidal structure could support her sheer immensity. Neither the name Everest, nor her previous functional name of Peak 15, did her justice. But the natives had long recognised her supremacy, calling her Chomolungma, Mother Goddess of the Universe.

In the six months since we'd decided to attempt Everest, many friends had asked us 'why?' George Mallory's reason was beautifully simple – 'because it's there'. Others have answered 'why not?' For us, though not profound, the answer was equally simple – we loved the mountains. They are an enchanting kingdom of incomparable beauty, endless light, space and air. This combined with the physical and mental challenge they provide makes for a powerful cocktail of experiences which are deeply energising.

A few have asked us why, with Rob's chequered health history, would we want to test our lives to the very limit on Everest? It's true we could have chosen to wrap ourselves in cotton wool, hoping the cancer wouldn't return. But if we had done that, its spectre would have controlled our lives. It would have won. Cancer, like terrorism, would only win if we allowed it to put fear in our lives. Even with the threat it could return at any time, we refused to throw our freedom away. Neither of us were ready to roll over and play dead.

Back in our dust mobiles, we wound deeper into the chocolate brown foothills. With every glimpse of snow-clad mountain tops, my spirit began to rise. I felt as if I was coming home. It was good to be back. As we turned into the final valley that would lead us to Everest, our journey across Tibet was nearly complete. For us, it had taken a mere week in the comfort of landcruisers. Eighty years previously Mallory's expedition had walked for five weeks from Darjeeling just to get here. Our last stop before base camp would be the Rongbuk monastery. It was here that the Rongbuk Lama reluctantly but graciously blessed the first British expedition of 1920, on their pilgrimage to Everest. At over 5,000 metres it is the highest monastery in the world and the sacred threshold to the north side of Mount Everest.

As we left the monastery behind, we also left the last permanent dwelling place for humans. Beyond this we would be venturing where no man could live, into the throne room of the mountain gods. The Rongbuk valley was desolate, like a moonscape, but as we juddered the final kilometre across a rocky river bed to base camp, a comfortingly familiar sight came into focus. Rows of cheerful red tents were neatly lined up and the Sherpas and cook team were rushing over to greet us.

As we peeled ourselves out of the landcruisers, I recognised a voice behind me. '*Namaste*, Didi. Lemon tea inside.' I turned to see Kul Bahadur, or KB as we called him, with his beaming mouthful of shiny gold fillings. He'd been Lachu's cook assistant on Cho Oyu and would be the head cook for our team. Touchingly he'd remembered my fetish for lemon tea and pointed us towards the mess tent where hot drinks and lunch awaited. Our team filtered excitedly into our new home. Murmurs of delight and relief rippled around the team when we found a fabulous spread of tuna, chips, coleslaw and yak cheese sandwiches.

Our base camp lay at the foot of Memorial Hill, a heap of terminal moraine which is sprinkled with memorials dedicated to climbers who have perished on the north side of Everest. Some were shiny plaques, festooned with wafting prayer scarves, but many were nothing more than a small, unnamed cairn. Looking down over base camp, it looked more like an entire tented village. We had invaded the sprawling glacial moraines with a vast army of tents and equipment. Twenty-four climbers, 23 climbing Sherpas and a multitude of cooks with over 400 barrels of supplies – enough food to feed one person for nearly 15 years. Everything had been scaled up for this expedition. There was no mistaking – think Everest, think big.

Having seen so many photographs of Everest, we'd wondered if familiarity would dampen our experience. But now we were at base camp, we realised no photograph could have prepared us for seeing her in the flesh. Even from 15 kilometres away, her vast scale is deceptive. The Hornbein and Great Couloirs appear insignificant blemishes, yet in reality they are mammoth gashes that tear deep into Everest's three-kilometre-high north face. Approaching Everest from the north felt like being allowed to glimpse the most precious of jewels. From the more popular southerly approach, she hides behind the giants of Nuptse and Lhotse. Only from the north were we privileged to see every inch of her elusive flanks as she rose heavenward in unveiled glory. Here Everest's supremacy was undisputed – the valley belonged to her alone.

It would take nearly two months to adapt our bodies to the thin air and even then we would still need supplemental oxygen up high. At the summit there would only be one-third the level of oxygen available at sea level and we'd be at the very limit of our existence. Had Everest been even a fraction higher, it would never have been possible to climb her. At 8,850 metres, she is nearly halfway to the point in the atmosphere at which our blood would simply boil and vaporise. Neither of us knew how we'd cope. On Cho Oyu, we'd briefly entered the death zone and had stolen ourselves away intact. Now we faced camping higher than the summit of Cho Oyu, spending at least one night in the death zone.

The following morning we were woken at 7 am by scuffles at our door. 'Tea, Didi?' It was KB and his cook assistant, Chakra, on their rounds. Bed tea is a tradition of Himalayan expeditions and a very nice one too. Since our first expedition, I had long since been encouraging Rob in these local traditions, though to not much avail. I was clearly losing my feminine touch, or maybe we had just been married too long! As I sipped my bed tea I pondered on the meaning of the day, Easter Sunday. It was a fitting start for our new life at base camp.

After a lazy Sunday morning, we gathered in the mess tent for our welcome briefing with Russell. Although our team was familiar with his military style of operation, we were reminded of camp operating procedures for the communications tent, generator, mess tent and toilet. Russell was very particular with all issues of base camp management, right down to the disposal of waste. Locals paid to transport barrels of excrement to Beiijing, two weeks away, would quickly empty them en route, reusing the barrels to make local brew. While Russell had become wise to their tricks, some other expeditions had not. For that reason alone, it was good to know the locals' credentials before sampling any of their home brew.

As Russell introduced us to our Sherpas, it was wonderful to see so many familiar faces. Many of them had worked with him for years and it was easy to understand their unswerving loyalty. He provided a unique system of financial support for the Sherpas and their families, plus good quality expedition equipment and clothing. He'd seen too many Sherpas afflicted with frostbite because of substandard equipment. Lost fingers meant lost livelihoods, along with the ability to support their families. For these reasons, as well as his safety record, we had chosen Russell.

One major consequence of being on Russell's expedition was that we would have to climb Everest from the more difficult northern side. In contrast to the south side, our high camp was considerably higher at 8,300 metres, forcing us to spend much longer in the death zone. Summit day also presented some formidable obstacles. Instead of snow, we'd mainly be climbing on awkward rock due to the strong winds that continually scoured Everest from the north. We would also have to ascend three rock steps, each one greater in height than the snowy Hillary Step of the south-east ridge. Despite these technical difficulties, our northern approach had advantages. We would be missing the dangerous Khumbu iccfall and we'd also benefit from being on a quieter side of the mountain.

Climbing Everest would be different from many of our previous expeditions. Normally, we moved together as a team but as on Cho Oyu, our movements would be more independent. Russell would give us guidelines and dates for moving camps, allowing everyone to set daily schedules to suit their own acclimatisation. Questions started around the mess tent, many focusing on the infamous Second Step, the crux of the north east summit ridge. Percy Wyn Harris once described it as a 'dark, grey precipice, smooth and holdless' and it gave us pause for thought that Russell's descriptions sounded no better. But as he finished the briefing his final words focused us back to our immediate objective. 'Living here might seem difficult now, but you need to make base camp your comfort zone in the next week. Your body does its most effective acclimatising at night, so get plenty of rest and stick with a partner for your walks.'

With our official briefing over, conversations broke out. In Russell's earshot, I innocently mentioned having fun.

'Fun? You're not here to have fun,' he said in a gruff tone.

'Surely it'll be a bit of fun?' I joked.

'No, I'm serious. You won't enjoy it.' Several other conversations in the tent had stopped as people listened in. I didn't like the sound of Russell's prediction but he knew the mountain, I didn't. In a small way his predictions were already coming true. As soon as we had arrived in Kathmandu, Jamie, Rob and I had been asked to deal with the issue of team selection for a certain individual. Much as we wanted to be helpful, being team members ourselves made it an awkward task and it was a far cry from the early team bonding I'd romantically envisaged.

Later that afternoon, Graham, who had climbed Everest previously, led a small group of us on a delightful stroll to the shimmering dark-turquoise waters of the blue moraine lakes. Graham was here in his capacity as a director with the BBC. He was the grand-nephew of Howard Somervell, who in 1924, on the third British expedition, had attempted Everest with Major Edward Norton. Their attempt had been just days before their team mates, George Mallory and Andrew Irvine, went missing. Graham was searching for Somervell's camera, which had been handed over to Irvine before their final summit climb. Finding this might unravel the mystery of whether Mallory and Irvine were the first men to summit.

The morning silence was broken the next day by yak bells and the cries of herders echoing up the valley. I was already up after a fitful night's sleep, occupying myself around camp. Having tidied the mess tent, I was sticking up some colourful paper with humourous climbing quotes to brighten it up a little. By late morning, base camp had become a maelstrom of activity and noise as nearly 100 yaks were loaded with supplies. They would spend the next few days being herded 22 kilometres to advanced base camp – ABC. As the yaks and their bells clanged out of camp, Teams Karsang and Chhiring set off in small groups for our first big acclimatisation hike. The Rongbuk valley was flanked by steep slopes of loose rock. Climbing these was like walking the wrong way on an airport conveyor belt tilted to 45°, dodging the occasional rock that someone might dislodge above you. It was hot work, but a delightfully cool wind kept our temperatures down.

For a handful of the men on both teams, leaving camp for a hike had been like bursting out of the starting blocks. Everyone was keen to perform, but a few eagerly sought to establish their position in the herd. For us, we knew we had to treat it as a marathon, not a sprint. Burning out and peaking too early on long expeditions was a very real risk. But even if we paced ourselves, we still had no idea if we had what it would take to go the full distance.

Resting again in our small group of six, we were now at the height of Kilimanjaro and were all feeling the altitude. Each time we stopped, it took noticeably longer to steady our breathing and calm our heart rate. Having just climbed 600 metres, the sprawling villages of base camp were now discernible only as sprinklings of coloured dots on the valley floor.

'Thought you'd like this,' Rob said, placing something in my hand. He'd found me a beautiful, shiny yellow rock for my collection. Without so much as one blade of grass in the entire Rongbuk valley, it was the equivalent of a bunch of wild flowers. I was delighted.

Several hours later we were back at base camp and my throat was continuing to worsen. With the extra effort of breathing and the dry air it was ominously painful. But we were both relieved to have completed our first major walk. With every new height gained, a little of the mystery shrouding Everest would be dispelled.

At 4 am the following morning I sat bolt upright and flicked my head torch on. 'This is just no use Rob, I'm going to move next door.' Rob and I were going to have to split up. We'd been sharing the same tent for many months but it was no longer working. It was the third night of continual disturbances. Whether Rob was snoring or rustling with his pee bottle, or I was blowing my nose, they were all a result of our increased altitude. Although he was able to get back to sleep, every little disturbance kept me awake for hours. Two or three hours' sleep a night was not helping my throat get better. I needed to take action before I got too tired.

'You can't go out now, Bella,' Rob said blearily, squinting towards my head torch.

'I have to, I'm desperate to sleep. See you in the morning.' And with that I crawled out into the freezing night air, dragging my sleeping bag into the empty tent next door. Russell in his wisdom had given everyone a separate tent and now it was time to use it. Outside the sky was lit with thousands of stars, camp was perfectly still and the only sound to be heard was that of my snoring team mates. Snuggling back into my still warm sleeping bag, I tried to get some sleep.

I woke up the following morning in a cold empty tent. It was only three hours since I'd left Rob but crazily I was already missing him. Shuffling back into his tent just before seven, I was caught in the act by a chuckling Chakra and Karsang as they delivered our bed tea. Even though Rob and I had been married for nearly eight years, I suddenly felt guilty as if I'd been caught in the act and giggled back. We loved the mornings and sat with our steaming mugs of tea watching base camp come alive. All that was missing was a sofa, our slippers and a newspaper.

After several days of tough hikes, Russell announced we should move to ABC in the next two days. I needed my throat to settle before pushing higher, so we elected to rest for the next few days. The morning was spent rigging our climbing harnesses, adjusting crampons and enjoying the warm sunshine and calm weather at base camp.

The following day Russell briefed us for our departure. 'It'll take you five or six hours to get to interim camp and then the same to ABC. Follow the Central Rongbuk Glacier and turn left before Mount Changtse. You can't get lost, just follow the yak shit.' He planned to join us in a few days when he moved up with Team Chhiring and his parting words were, 'Rest when you get there and expect to feel terrible.'

Starting out at 8 am the following day I had a spring in my step. It was the first day in over a week that I hadn't woken with a sore throat. It was perfect timing. The whole team was excited to be moving up to ABC. From there we'd be able to see the rest of the route between camps one and four.

As we picked our way around truck-sized boulders in the gully of lateral moraine sandwiched between the glacier and the valley walls, we felt vulnerable. High above us stood loose, heavily eroded cliffs looking like a teetering game of giant Jenga, ready to crash down. Just before I reached the valley corner to turn left onto the East Rongbuk Glacier, Jamie came steaming up behind me and I stepped aside. Passing by, he muttered something about getting to camp in three hours but I didn't hear properly and within seconds he was gone. Perching on a high rock, I took the opportunity to wait for the others and revelled in my surroundings. Everest in her desolate beauty stared down on me, snow pouring from her high ridges. I was mesmerised by the west ridge, its cascade of fantastical ice flutings decorating it like a sacred veil.

Ten minutes later Rob, Cecile, Richard and Graham joined me and we continued our trudge. We moved at a snail's pace along the path and soon a steady trickle of snorting yaks with ringing bells overtook us, making a much better job of getting uphill than we were. Underneath their shaggy matted coats, each animal was equipped with a set of nimble hooves and their footwork was impressively agile. As the line of yaks trundled past, for the first time it became apparent why they were called yak trains – they seemed almost coupled together, their horns seemingly in constant danger of skewering the backside of the yak in front.

As the yaks passed, the local herders temporarily refrained from the barrage of airborne rocks they used to propel them uphill. I wondered if someone yelled and threw rocks at me whether I too would move faster. Both the yaks and their masters seemed completely at home in the rarefied air. While the Tibetans had evolved to cope with the thin air, it was the natural habitat of the yaks. Just as humans cannot live permanently above about 5,500 metres, yaks cannot live at sea level; they eventually become infertile and die from oxygen poisoning. They are endowed with various physiological traits that equip them well for living at altitude – they have twice as many red blood cells as the average cow, plus special enzymes that facilitate oxygen transport, and a few extra ribs to boot. Worryingly, I found myself almost envying the yaks.

As they grunted past us with their thick, fleshy tongues hanging from their steaming mouths, I shouted ahead. 'Rob, uphill side.' On such cliff-edge trails it was imperative to let them pass below. Trails were rarely sufficient for more than one wide load and many people had met untimely deaths in the Himalaya due to an innocent nudge from a yak. The herders scampered past, attentive as sheepdogs,

MAP OF EVEREST

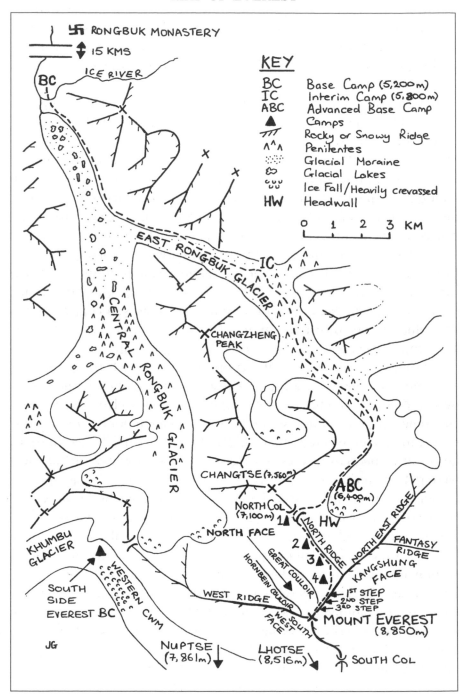

making light of the uphill work. An even more pungent aroma followed in their wake, a distinctive and stomach-turning combination of yak dung smoke and various body odours. With the katabatic wind funnelling down the East Rongbuk in our direction, walking behind them was a little too much for our stomachs, already queasy with the altitude.

Initially, we climbed along the valley sides above the East Rongbuk Glacier. High above us the winds blew hanging waterfalls vertically upwards and iridescent rainbows flickered in their mists. The yak trail followed a crumbling edge of the lateral moraine, which occasionally disintegrated altogether leaving gravelly chutes that plummeted hundreds of metres to the river below. With the start of the spring melt, a torrent of milky, sediment-choked water spewed from the glacier, racing headlong to quench the parched Tibetan plains.

Trudging into interim camp, at 5,800 metres, everyone was weary from the interminable up and down of the glacial moraines. But the surroundings were a fabulous reward for our efforts. Our puny tents were dwarfed in a field of giant ice pinnacles, their sun-cupped white and blue towers thrusting up for 100 feet or more, like massive gleaming sharks' fins.

By the time we'd trailed into camp the yaks were feasting on hay, and smoke was pouring from the herders' tents. All cosy with fires lit inside, their lively chatter and laughter was a welcoming sound. Camping here was both a harsh necessity and a temporary novelty for us, yet for these Tibetan nomads it was their life. Travelling with their family and community, they may have been materially poor but they were rich in spirit.

On our arrival at interim, Jamie was conspicuous by his absence. We all assumed he had arrived hours ago. As the hours passed wild speculation started around the group. He had gone ahead alone and had no radio. He could have fallen and injured himself, been swallowed up by a crevasse or even been hit by rock fall. With night fall fast approaching, search parties were dispatched. Co-ordinating the search by radio, Sherpas agreed to descend from ABC while others set out from interim to scour the route for any signs of him. As darkness fell on Everest, the glaciers that poured from her flanks were no longer a safe place to be. The idle banter in the mess tent had ceased and the atmosphere was tense as we waited by the radio.

Hours later Russell's voice came on the air.

'Jamie has been found, he said, and cheers of relief went up in our tent. 'He's with the Russians at the head of the Central Rongbuk Glacier below the north face.' With this information our cheering stopped abruptly and we stared quizzically at each other. Russell continued, 'He accidentally walked passed the East Rongbuk Glacier and continued up the central. He was very lucky. There aren't normally any camps at the bottom of the north face, but the Russians found him . . .', Russell paused '. . . so the Russians are looking after our boy!' and with that everyone dissolved into relieved laughter.

'How can anyone misunderstand the instruction '*turn left before Changtse*'? It's a 7,500 metre mountain!' Graham joked. Fortunately, with youth and vigour on his side, Jamie coped admirably with the additional 18 kilometres. The greater challenge lay in dealing with the endless ribbing he was to receive from the lads. As a token of appreciation for finding our team member, Russell sent thanks to the Russian team with a bottle of Famous Grouse.

That night, sleeping on the glacier was like camping on a giant behemoth. Millions of tonnes of ice creaked and groaned beneath us as it ground its way down the mountainside. Nothing could stand in the way of these giants as they gave birth to the valleys of tomorrow. My heart periodically missed a beat as the ice shook beneath us, as if an explosion had detonated from deep inside.

Starting our journey to ABC the next morning, we made our way through the giant penitentes that guard the entrance to Everest's inner courts. Ice-encrusted turquoise lakes nestled in hollows between them and rushing streams spilled out of icy chutes like severed arteries. The faint rumblings under our feet only hinted at a massive labyrinthine network of underground rivers deep in the bowels of the glacier.

Every minute had seemed an eternity as we argued with our legs and lungs but after five debilitating hours, ABC finally came into view. At 6,400 metres, it seemed preposterous that our advanced base camp was even higher than the summit of Denali. Even at ABC we had only 45% of the oxygen available at sea level, yet we still had well over two vertical kilometres to the summit.

Our camp was one of about ten sandwiched between the East Rongbuk Glacier and Changtse's huge south-east face, from which most rock avalanches would hopefully miss us. Everest now reared up right in front of us. There was no escape. Beyond camp, the East Rongbuk headwall rose up to the North Col and the intimidating north ridge – the route we'd take.

It was gut-wrenching yet exciting to be able to see so much of our intended route. Camp one would be perched on the North Col, which lies between Changtse and Everest's north ridge, and camps two and three above on the north ridge itself. Our fourth and final camp would be high on Everest's north face, which was now obscured from sight. Rising many kilometres away behind the north ridge, her north-east ridge and summit pyramid were just visible. Everest is so colossal that even up close, it was still impossible to grasp her sheer immensity.

On our arrival, the troops gradually filtered into the mess tent in need of liquid refreshment. But seconds after I entered there was a violent explosion, which startled everyone and left several of us covered in brown powder. I had foolishly opened a new jar of cocoa without engaging my brain. At high altitude the unopened contents were under as much pressure as a shaken bottle of champagne. Thankfully, the human body is a little more adept at accommodating dramatic pressure changes than jars of cocoa.

With everyone feeling a little off-colour from our new altitude, the whole team crashed for an early night. The following morning, instead of feeling refreshed, I woke to the familiar symptoms of the altitude being ratcheted up a notch. Pulling my icy boots on, I went round to Rob's tent to join him for bed tea. From the morning chorus of coughs around camp, it seemed everyone was feeling the worse for wear. Altitude symptoms aside, I was more concerned about the feverish shivers that had been plaguing me all night. I hoped they were no more than a little bodily rebellion from yesterday's hard work. Failing to summon any enthusiasm for breakfast, I retired to decorate my tent with family photos. Their smiling faces were good medicine for my fragile head and queasy stomach.

With Team Chhiring's arrival the next day, we would soon be able to start our acclimatisation climbs again. This time we would be aiming for repeated climbs until we eventually reached camp one at an altitude of 7,100 metres. After several days' rest, we would push all the way to camp two, with a brief foray towards camp three if we were able. We would never fully acclimatise, even to the height of

ABC, but repeated exposure to the thinner air was the only way of stimulating our bodies to adapt as best they could.

Over time the cheerful dispositions of base camp gave way to the physical and mental stresses of our new home. Tempers were frayed on Team Chhiring and even Dale, a friendly Californian, who was always gracious, now felt frustrated at some members' selfish attitudes. We had also just lost the first team member, David, an entrepreneur from the UK on Team Chhiring. He had not been well and without warning had suddenly left the expedition. Even Russell was storming around camp, clearly unimpressed at the morning's events.

'I'm not some free bloody internet service,' he said, having just escorted an unknown Spanish climber from our communications tent. The Spaniard had had the audacity to wander in and help himself to Russell's laptop and sat phone, in order to send photos home. Even members of our own teams had to ask before using any equipment and sending photos was never allowed. The communications equipment was an essential part of Russell's safety artillery and while he willingly used it to help other teams who were in trouble, having it used by stealth incensed him.

With many teams now established at ABC, mountain politics had raised its ugly head and bickering had broken out. Russell called for a meeting of all team leaders to discuss the three M's: manpower, material and money. He wanted to establish a co-ordinated effort and a fair system of contributing to the work of fixing ropes. For teams that were too small to contribute Sherpa manpower, Russell proposed a small fee should be paid, per climber, to a central fund. But with high altitude distorting emotions, tolerance was in short supply and selfish attitudes quickly laid bare. Several leaders happily agreed but a number refused and it ended in stalemate. After the meeting, some members from other teams were mortified to discover how their leaders were operating, and even privately offered Russell a contribution for fixing ropes. To complicate matters further, the situation became international news as mountaineering websites, some run by people who had never climbed Everest, were vilifying Russell's actions from the other side of the world.

The long, cold nights at ABC had started to fill me with dread as I became increasingly deprived of sleep, and struggled with the onset of a heavy cold. Instead of improving, as many of the team were, I seemed to be going downhill fast. Despite repeated steam inhalations my head was permanently congested. My sinuses were still the chink in my armour. Being objective about how you feel at altitude is never easy but I did have two reliable tests – my pulse oximeter and Rob. A pulse oximeter is a small device placed on a finger to measure the percentage saturation of oxygen in arterial blood. It is normal to have between 97 and 99% at sea level but at this altitude low readings were to be expected and largely ignored, as long as we felt OK. When we'd arrived at ABC the saturation of oxygen in our arterial blood had been averaging 70%. But now my sinuses were infected and the oximeter readings confirmed my suspicions. Rob's averaged 79% and he was feeling ready to start climbing again. Mine was averaging 58% and all I felt ready for was my sleeping bag.

At 6,400 metres we were being slowly suffocated. Even the smallest of cuts on our hands stopped healing. At 58% my body simply didn't have the reserves to get better. If I pushed myself higher, I was risking getting worse and possibly dangerously ill.

By the morning of 21 April, Rob and I both knew the time had come for a decision. 'I've thrown everything at it, vitamin C, zinc, garlic and echinachea, the whole lot. But I'm still losing the battle,' I said despondently. Although I'd tried not to burden Russell, we agreed I'd have to discuss my options with him.

Later that morning Russell and I were sitting alone in the cook tent. 'You're gonna feel crap on Everest. I told you it was going to be hard. You need to just get on with it and be more focused,' he reprimanded me. 'I've been concerned about you. You've not been well ever since Kathmandu and I don't know if you are going to get well enough to make it.' He paused. 'You've been different on this trip, you seem anxious, you're not the normal fun Jo.' I recoiled inside at his words, feeling terrible for letting him down, but I knew he was right. From the first day in Kathmandu there had been issues that worried me. Whether it was the difficult team issue that we were assigned to deal with, my health or just the prospect of climbing Everest itself. Somehow, I was going to have to pull myself together, focus and be less anxious. Finishing our conversation, we agreed that I would return to base camp to try and get well.

Returning to Rob's tent I climbed back inside with a long face. He pulled me over and held me in his arms. It was just what I needed, but being too close made me nervous. 'I don't want to give you my cold,' I said pulling away.

I relayed my conversation with Russell. Rob was always good at understanding both sides of the coin.

'Maybe you aren't your normal gregarious self, even I can see that. But everyone is having a hard time up here, leaders included. You're not here to entertain. Just concentrate on getting better and coming back up to ABC. Understood?'

'Yes, understood. But I'm going to miss you. I really don't want to go down,' I said, wishing there was some way to delay my departure. I just wanted to curl up like a hamster in Rob's lap and hope the whole situation would go away.

Underneath, I knew Jo was delicate and had taken Russell's words to heart. Hearing him question her focus and doubt her chances had knocked her for six. If it was me, I would have fought back to prove him wrong – it's probably a male thing. But Jo needed encouragement, especially now. The last thing I wanted to do was say goodbye, but we both knew it was the right decision.

As I started to gather a few items for base camp, the rest of our team were excitedly packing their rucksacks for their second acclimatisation walk to the east Rongbuk headwall. Soul destroying as it was to lose all my hard-earned height so soon, I could only contemplate climbing Everest by going back to the start line and trying again. Sometimes the best way up a mountain is down. Russell had told us all 'Everest is a game of high altitude snakes and ladders, just make sure you don't get on a snake,' but that was exactly what I had done.

Kissing Rob goodbye, I listed all the things he should do while I was away. 'Double check your harness if you're climbing, don't forget your vitamins, get as acclimatised as you can.' Rob kissed me back and I reluctantly pulled away until our hands slipped apart.

'Call me on the radio as soon as you arrive,' he said. I nodded back with the best smile I could muster.

Turning downhill my composure finally cracked and tears

streamed down my cheeks. I was convinced I'd never catch the team up in time. The summit weather window only ever lasted a matter of days, or even hours. Everest wasn't going to wait for me to acclimatise. Dismayed at my performance, I began reproaching myself. Surely there must have been an alternative to dropping off the programme? But whichever way I dissected it, the results were the same. I wasn't going to climb Everest unless I got better. It was as simple as that.

CHAPTER 16

Don't Let Go

'I discovered I always have choices and sometimes it's only a choice of attitude.'

Judith Knowlton

It was late afternoon when I finally returned to base camp. Rows of empty tents rustled in the wind and dust devils whipped around the cairns on Memorial Hill. Less than a week before, the communications tent had been a hive of activity, the control centre. Now it was silent and empty inside. I radioed ABC twice hoping to speak with Rob and waited by the radio for an hour. Occasional interference raised my hopes but nothing came. Giving up, I walked across a shadowy base camp to my tent as the last vestiges of light dissolved into the night sky. I slid into my chilled sleeping bag, and peered through a torch beam of steaming breath to write a letter to Rob, a letter he'd never receive.

Logically, I knew recent events, sleep deprivation, the effects of altitude and even my monthly hormones were all reasonable explanations for feeling depressed. But in spite of this, I just couldn't pull myself together. The next morning I wandered into the kitchen tent. KB and Chakra were the only staff left to monitor base camp and their affectionate smiles and laughter were the perfect therapy.

'Drink, Didi?'

'*Taato paani, dhanyabaad*,' I said, asking for hot water and quickly exhausting my few words of Nepali. We couldn't even discuss the weather but with the gas stove roaring away, the kitchen tent was the warmest place to be and I busied myself stirring noodles or washing up to prolong my stay.

I finally made contact with Rob that morning. He seemed distant and neither of us said much. It was difficult, knowing other teams stayed tuned into Russell's radio frequencies, always hopeful of gleaning information about his next move or weather forecasts. After being together for so long, Rob too was finding our separation strange.

With Jo no longer around, I realised just how much I appreciated her company. Time was our most precious gift and I loved sharing it with her. I hated seeing her leave. Everyone probably thought I was a heel for letting her go alone but we agreed it was the right decision. It always took me longer to acclimatise and if I lost time as well, Everest would be over. But if Jo didn't get better, it was over anyway. No matter what happened, I wouldn't summit without her.

Later that morning we had our own small puja at base camp. Both our puja, and the one at ABC, had been scheduled to coincide with a special day on the lunar Tibetan calendar. As I sat cross-legged on my bed mat with the sun warming my back, Everest looked serene against the deep blue skies. The aroma of burning juniper and joss sticks wafted past me on the morning breeze. Offerings of food, beer and Coca Cola were piled around the high stone cairn. Normally ice axes and crampons would also have been stacked there, smeared and blessed with yak butter, but mine were at ABC. Two monks from the Rongbuk monastery were in full flow with their chants. Their outfits were an eclectic fusion of maroon robes and prayer beads accessorized with yellow fleeces, Casio watches and sunglasses. Their shaved heads rocked hypnotically as they paid respect and homage to Amyolungsoma, the deity that resides on Everest. It was believed she would protect those who were pure of heart and worked hard, but for the arrogant and disrespectful, their time would come.

I sat alone with the monks for most of the ceremony as KB and Chakra came and went. I'd read so much about the Everest puja, not only as a special ceremony but also as a time for the team to bond before their struggle with the mountain commenced. To have my own private puja was intensely lonely, yet strangely wonderful.

Periodically the monks threw rice in the air and I followed suit. Hours later, with the puja complete, it was time to throw the tsampa, barley flour. On Cho Oyu our team had enjoyed throwing it over each other. Its effect of making our hair white was supposed to signify long life and old age but with just two bald monks and no common language, I restrained myself and simply released it on the wind. With the puja concluded, the monks raised the juniper pole, unfurling red, green, yellow, blue and white prayer flags across camp, each colour symbolising one of the elements. Then the senior monk tied a red string around my neck with a special knot for good luck.

Gathering their prayer books, cymbals and beads, the monks bade me farewell. As I sat alone by the stone altar, the valley was peacefully still. Only the flags could be heard in the breeze as I looked beyond them to Everest's north face. It was magical and ethereal, a moment to treasure. Whatever the future held, I would never forget this morning.

I spent the rest of the day waiting for Rob to contact me. I was filled with a mixture of frustration and worry that he hadn't called and started to imagine the worst. Although I was only 22 kilometres away and two days walk, it felt as if he was on the other side of the planet. With no contact by 8 pm, I went to bed feeling utterly cut off.

By the following morning my ribs ached from coughing. There was little to do around camp but I'd noticed Chakra had been religiously watering the moraine soil by our mess tent and I was amazed to see a few blades of grass poking through. Chakra happily relinquished this job and I took it on board with all the seriousness of a Wimbledon grass expert. We even planted plastic flowers and arranged a small rockery. It would be a welcoming sight for the team when they were next down.

Throughout the day I continued to pine for radio contact from Rob, though I didn't want to radio him and be a nuisance on the air waves. With another day of no-one to talk to I felt trapped. One moment I was upbeat, the next hopeless and apathetic. Each night as it got dark, my mood seemed to follow suit. I felt stalked by irrational fears. Quitting would be so easy. All it would take was one radio call.

Burying myself deep in my sleeping bag, I stooped to the lowest form of entertainment and started to read my own diary. In a moment of clarity, I suddenly realised endless comparisons between my situation and the rest of the team were doing me no good. I needed to break the cycle and have a grateful heart. Instead of listening to sad music on my MP3 player, I found songs that lifted my spirit. Instead of letters of doom and gloom to Rob, I wrote a prayer in my diary.

Mallory once said that 'climbing Everest is all about heart' and that night I made a decision. Tomorrow was going to be a different day.

*

After four good nights' rest at base camp, my sinuses were finally on the mend. It was time to return to ABC. Massive rock avalanches had obliterated sections of our previous route and I was glad of Chakra's company for the two-day walk. I was encouraged at my speedy climb to ABC and couldn't help feeling pleased that even Chakra was struggling to keep up. Beating a cook to ABC probably wasn't a reliable yardstick for climbing Everest, but right now it was just the confidence boost I needed.

Tramping excitedly into ABC, I was surprised to find it deathly quiet. Many of the team were away for the night, acclimatising at camp one, and those left behind were recovering from a previous climb. Everyone was worn down and some seemed to have aged years. Things had moved on. I almost felt like a visitor.

Not anticipating my early arrival, Rob was still doing his best to spruce himself up in the wash tent. When I unzipped the door with a great flurry to surprise him, in front of me stood a naked, emaciated Rob. He looked like a vacuum packed bag of skin and bones. In just one week he had been visibly ravaged by the altitude and his head looked oddly oversized on his rake-like body. But his smile was bigger than ever.

'Bella, you're back!' he exclaimed. I zipped the tent up and threw my arms round his bony shoulders.

'Am I happy to see you!' I said and stood back to inspect his body again. 'But look at you! You look like ET! You're wasting away far too fast. You've got to start eating more or there'll be nothing left of you for the summit.'

'You don't exactly look fat yourself!' Rob said as he pulled me back for another hug. I was less worried about my weight though. I'd never lost proportionately as much as Rob, although at 48 kilos that was probably just as well. I'd noticed women always seemed to lose less weight at altitude, probably because the body burns muscle instead of fat. Living at 6,400 metres had also caused a significant increase in Rob's basal metabolic rate. He should have been consuming over 5,000 calories a day but he'd barely been managing

1,000 and it showed. Everest is a war of attrition and a race against time to acclimatise and summit before you become too weak or fall ill.

Over the next few hours Rob updated me on events at ABC. Richard had become ill with a chest infection and was returning to base camp. It seemed history was repeating itself from the Cho Oyu expedition. He was a real loss to the team but it was the only safe thing to do. The rest of the team had been doing well and in my absence they'd been progressively climbing higher. On their third push most of them had finally reached camp one at the North Col and some had even spent a night there. Their progress had left me no option. I would have to catch up by climbing straight to camp one, carrying all my equipment in one big push. It was a daunting task. As I listened, I found it hard not to get disheartened realising how far I'd fallen behind. Rob read my face. 'You shouldn't worry, Bella. Now you're back, there's plenty of time to catch up.' I hoped he was right.

The next day Rob and I left camp before 8 am, hoping to miss the fiercest of the afternoon sun on the glacier. Skirting below Changtse's disintegrating south-east face, we followed the lateral moraine up to a location called crampon point, harnessed up and set off across the glacier. By 10 am I was standing wide-eyed at the foot of the headwall. A colossal wall of ice over half a kilometre high reared up in front of us, forming the beginning of the East Rongbuk Glacier. At the top of this wall thousands of tonnes of snow were dumped, compressed into concrete-like ice and then inexorably pulled down by gravity on the long journey to the glacier's snout over 20 kilometres away.

Everest's first deaths had been on this very headwall. Mallory's second expedition in 1922 suffered a devastating blow when seven Sherpas were swept into a crevasse by a monstrous avalanche. No other slope on Everest has ever claimed as many Sherpas as the North Col headwall did that fateful day. I was grateful that the headwall was free from fresh and avalanche-prone snow but climbing beneath blocks of unstable, hanging ice would keep the threat of collapse constant and unpredictable. If we felt a rumble or air blast, it would probably be too late.

'Let me see you're all fastened up,' Rob said, lifting the rope that attached to my harness. 'If it's too much today, Jo, please don't push it.'

I nodded, but actually I had every intention of pushing it. This was my only opportunity to claw back the lost ground. Russell had told team members they should now be able to get to camp one in five hours. I expected to take longer but I was determined to reach camp one and get back on the team schedule. Today I would have to listen closely to my inner voice, to go right to the edge, but not over. Clipping in, I set my mind in gear and kicked my first steps into the steep ice.

After several hours, trickles of sweat ran down my back. All around us the glacier flowed like a giant waterfall yet fissured like a solid. Tearing apart, it left bottomless chasms and cascading ice cliffs. High above, I could just make out minuscule black dots weaving their way down through the seracs, like a string of ants. It was only seeing how insignificant people were that we could begin to appreciate the headwall's vast proportions. I was barely halfway but my fuel gauge had long since been on empty. My chunky boots swung like lead beneath me and my rucksack dragged me down. I didn't dare look too far ahead now. It had to be one rope section at a time. My mind was in the driving seat, my body had capitulated hours before. Even with the air temperature still below zero, the heat on the glacier was searing. The snow glared like burning white magnesium as the sun reflected off the ice, but in the thin atmosphere stripping off wasn't an option – we'd get burnt to a crisp. I shoved more sun cream up my nostrils to stop them getting burnt from the glacier's reflection. The roof of my mouth was also vulnerable but breathing with my mouth closed or wearing a bandana was too suffocating, making it a harder problem to solve.

Suddenly I fell to my knees, choking on phlegm that had formed a dry plug and wedged itself at the back of my throat. Bracing myself on the snow, I coughed violently trying to clear it. Fearing I was about to cough my lungs out, I suddenly felt a sharp blow to my left side. Darting my eyes upwards, I checked to see if a chunk of ice had hit me, perhaps dislodged by someone above, but there was nothing and the ice fall was eerily quiet. As I attempted to stand up, I crumpled over with a second wave of pain that dug into my rib cage. I felt as if I had barbed wire caught in my lungs. Coughing again until I retched, I finally dislodged the phlegm. I gulped a mouthful of water from my bottle and dragged myself back to my feet. Even the tiniest movement sent excruciating pain through the left side of my chest. I had been lucky though. On a previous expedition, someone had coughed up the entire mucous lining of their larynx.

I started to climb again, every breath and every pull on my ascender was like a red-hot poker in my side, but I had to keep moving. Pain was irrelevant. The clock was ticking and I knew Russell would be watching my performance. Rob had been turning around frequently to monitor my progress. I knew his game, I'd done it myself. He was staying just far enough in front to draw me on but not too far to make me give up hope.

For Jo, this was the crucial test. We would find out if she had fallen too far behind in the most critical step of climbing Everest – acclimatising. She was always last on the team to put her camera away but today I hadn't seen her stop once for photos. She must be taking it hard. To climb from base camp at 5,200 metres through interim and ABC to 7,100 metres in four days was a huge altitude jump, but if anyone could catch up, I felt confident she could.

I could feel Rob willing me on from above. Ignoring my screaming lungs and shaking legs, I squeezed out one more laboured step after another. I wasn't going to let Rob down. Above me I'd become aware of the clanking and chinking of metal, and it was getting louder. I knew what it was, but the effort of lifting my head to look was too much. It was our Sherpas who had been ferrying oxygen supplies up. Without their labours, we wouldn't be able to climb any higher. They were our keepers on this mountain. Seconds later they came barrelling past, whistling and laughing as they moved swiftly down the ropes. 'Strong, Didi. Strong, Didi,' Lhakpa Sherpa called out as he passed. I felt anything but strong but I appreciated his encouragement. Leaning on my axe, I stood dumbfounded and breathless as I watched them glide by. Our feeble efforts were almost laughable in comparison to their strength. They are the true mountain people of this world. We will always be visitors.

Pushing harder than I thought possible, I closed the gap between me and Rob. With my left side in spasm I could no longer use my left arm to pull on the fixed lines. After five and a half gruelling hours of weaving around crevasses, leaping over chasms and climbing imposing vertical ice cliffs, I wobbled into camp. I hadn't just hit the wall, I'd crashed into it at high speed. Though I was hypoglycaemic, the thin air had prevented my body switching its fuel supply to fat, leaving me running on stubborn mindedness alone. I was utterly shattered but overjoyed. I was only half an hour over Russell's estimated time – not only had I done it but I had amazed myself and made good time.

'Welcome home, Honey.' I looked up through my steamed sunglasses to see Bill, one of the guides on Team Chhiring, grinning at me. From his sprightly behaviour, I could see he was reaping the benefit of living at altitude in Colorado. Before I'd even got my sack off, he was back with hot water. It was liquid gold to our parched throats.

The North Col was a deceptively grand name for the location of our first camp. Compared to the better-known South Col, a broad, barren plateau of rock and ice, it was little more than a narrow ridge of snow and ice hanging between Everest and Changtse. Our tents were perched on a sliver of flat ground sandwiched between an overhanging wall of ice and a soaring cliff. At 7,100 metres we were now higher than any other mountain range in the world, but we still had three more camps to go.

As so often happened at altitude, when I stopped working and taking deep breaths my oxygen intake dropped dramatically, leaving my oxygen-starved head to pound like a freight train. Crawling with our last morsels of energy into the tent, we both sat in a drained and silent daze. Time passed, maybe an hour or more before either of us moved. Nearly two hours later we had summoned the will power to climb into our down suits and light the stove to melt snow. We had to get more fluids on board. Whether it's eating, sleeping or any other body function, they are all the bane of climbing.

It was now nearly 4 pm and it had started snowing heavily. I was relieved to have pushed hard while the weather held. Unfortunately not all of our team made it. We heard news on the radio that Barry had felt too weak and turned around. It was his third attempt to reach camp one. He was the only member of our team who hadn't previously climbed above 8,000 metres. He would need to dig deep if he was to have a chance for the summit. It was not all bad news though, and as the daylight started to fade, there were murmurs of exhausted celebration around camp. Paul from Team Chhiring had just made it to camp one. Paul was no ordinary climber; he had lost his right arm to cancer when he was just three weeks old. But he was a fighter. Climbing to the North Col had been an epic struggle and even with the dedicated help of Karsang Sherpa, he was spent. He had shown a resilience of spirit that was truly humbling.

'I'm not fussed about food. I feel sick.' Rob puffed as he finished using his pee bottle.

'Me too, but we've got to eat,' I said, feeling envious that Rob was hydrated enough to use his bottle. After sharing one small pasta boil-in-the-bag, we had reached our limit. At 7,100 metres our bodies struggled to absorb food and the only successful strategy was speed. Glucose and simple carbohydrates were quickly absorbed and the only useful fuel to feed our bodies. Luckily carbohydrates were the one thing we could tolerate and our Antarctic cravings for munching on slabs of butter were nothing but a distant memory. There was also little point in eating protein to try and stem our rapid loss of muscle bulk. Both our protein digestion and muscle protein synthesis were now too sluggish. Our bodies were in a state of permanent anorexia, which would only increase with altitude.

With nothing to do but endure the freezing night, we squeezed into our sleeping bags, still wearing our down suits. As the hours drifted tortuously past, I was unable to sleep and needed distraction from my throbbing head, so I started to monitor my pulse and silently marvelled that it never dipped below 120 beats per minute. Even at complete rest my body was sprinting just to stay alive. The dry air snagged like fish bones in my parched throat and I repeatedly found myself coughing, doubled over with the shooting pain in my ribs. My thoughts raced. *A cracked rib?* Whatever damage I'd done, I was going to put up with it. Acclimatising seemed more than ever to be a crazy game of waiting for some parts of the body to catch up, while desperately trying to stop the rest falling apart.

With the arrival of first light at 5.30 am, I took some more painkillers and finally vomited. I felt wretchedly weak but I would have to find the energy to get back to ABC. Firing up our stove, I used our saucepan to scoop snow from our tent vestibule, being careful to avoid the patches of vomit. Even having to make a cup of tea now felt like too much effort. In the last four days, in order to catch up, I'd pushed my body well in excess of the recommended progression. But we'd got to know our bodies well and we had the added advantage of being a 24-hour mobile monitoring unit for each other. However, there is a fine line at altitude over which no-one can afford to tread. Had we not spent the last year at high altitude, I would have lost confidence and turned around long before now.

I was glad to be leaving my rucksack load at camp one. Struggling to get my gear there would prove a worthwhile investment for future weeks. Just 40 minutes later we'd made enjoyably light work of descending the fixed ropes. Back at 6,500 metres, the air seemed thick, though in reality it was far from it. Nevertheless, my calmer breathing was a relief to my painful ribs. We unclipped and enjoyed the freedom of walking side by side across the flat part of the glacier. I felt positively euphoric knowing we were safely off the fixed lines and that I had done what I set out to do. 'I knew you had it in you,' Rob said, gently patting my bottom.

We arrived back at ABC confused to see the rest of the team packing. Russell saw us and came over. 'There are high winds coming in, so I want all of you out of here today.' As he said the word 'today' my eyebrows shot up. 'Or tomorrow at the latest,' he qualified. 'And make sure you travel light. It's just for a few days. Leave all your books and camera gear.' Russell also instructed us to pack the rest of our gear into our barrels and place them inside our tents to stop them blowing away.

Collapsing in a heap next to Rob in his tent, I was in a state of shock. I'd barely finished running up the mountain all the way from base camp and I was going to have to go back down again. To have to lose all that height gain so soon was hugely demoralising. My body had only just started to do the vital work of acclimatising above ABC. In five days I would have walked 50 kilometres and climbed nearly 2,000 metres, all considerably above the height of Mont Blanc. It was a lot by anyone's standards.

'I know what you must be thinking, Bella,' Rob said, stroking my head.

'And I was feeling so happy that –'

'I know, Bella, I know'. Though Rob tried to comfort me, I was beginning to feel like a high altitude yoyo and suddenly felt on thin ice again. The fact was I had missed repeated trips to higher altitude, with the exception of one climb to 7,100 metres. It seemed inconceivable to go for the summit with such a shaky track record. It was common practice to rest and make gradual acclimatisation climbs at least as high as camp two, before a rest at base camp and then the final big push for the summit. It would be a reduced acclimatisation programme for everyone, but especially for me. Even Russell hadn't done it this way before.

Mulling over my situation, I realised Everest was about to become a case of paralysis by analysis. My perfectionist streak wanted everything to be 100% right before I could move forward but it wasn't going to be like that. It was my choice how I experienced things. I had to decide if the glass was going to be half empty or half full.

As we wandered over to the mess tent for drinks we discovered Roy, a South African on team Chhiring, packing to leave the expedition. He felt too out of shape for the climb but the expedition had still been a success as he'd achieved publicity for his paint and ladder company. Roy's new ladder would replace the rusting 1975 Chinese ladder that spanned a holdless slab of vertical rock on the upper section of the Second Step at 8,600 metres.

On our return to base camp, it was soon was clear that our standards of comfort had been recalibrated once again. Base camp felt like a five-star hotel in comparison to camp one, and by the following morning we were glad of Russell's decision to evacuate. Overnight, ferocious winds had swept in and were wreaking destruction high on the mountain. Teams that hadn't evacuated were now regretting it. Thankfully, none of our higher camps had been fully set up and unlike the previous year when 18 tents were blown off the mountain in high winds, we had only lost two.

It was 30 April when Russell gathered us in the mess tent. 'I'm afraid the winds are here to stay. We won't be going anywhere for several weeks. The high winds are due to be around until at least May 16th. It's not going to be easy to stay here for that long, so you're going to have to be patient.'

We always knew there would be storms on Everest, it was just a question of when and how bad. The critical factor from now on was not how well we could climb but how well we could weather the storm. Somehow we would have to stay strong and not allow it to further deplete our reserves. Rob leaned over and whispered in my ear. 'This is bad news. I've only got one pair of underpants.'

'Me too,' I whispered back. Being the obedient campers that we were we'd left books, clothes, and games at ABC, as had everyone else. We were ill equipped for our life of tent sitting, which was about to begin in earnest.

The next day roaring winds still encased Everest's summit as menacing grey clouds moved in from the west like an advancing army. The snow caking Everest yesterday had been scoured away overnight, leaving the yellow limestone bands high on her north face glowing orange against the darkening sky. With the high winds and clouds of dust, even walking around base camp had become remarkably unpleasant. It was a challenge to stay occupied. Thankfully, with the return of our appetites, eating had become a particularly enjoyable pastime.

After several days at base camp, little routines began to emerge that helped pass the time of day. Every morning I tidied the wash tent, its condition prompting memories of the men's changing rooms at the rugby club. I enjoyed the momentary reward of a shiny wash bowl and a waft of citrus air freshener. Although I'd felt foolish for packing toilet freshener for climbing Everest, a sun-warmed loo tent now made the idea seem pure genius.

With little else to do we congregated in the mess tent. A combination of boredom and stress was eating away at everyone's tolerance. Even team members who were normally patient had become fractious. The frustrations of camp life gradually spilled over to our marital tent.

'Rob, do you have to leave all these snotty tissues on the tent floor?'

'I'll clean up later.'

'You always say that but you still leave them lying around.'

'You never give me a chance to clear them up.'

But within minutes we were arguing about something completely different. Neither of us was listening properly and we began wheeling each other's failings out of the closet while choosing to ignore our own. Suddenly Rob barked at me and my composure cracked. I growled back and we both burst into laughter. Winning the argument had instantly lost its appeal.

'Do you know what,' Rob said, 'I really don't care about the tissues. I'd rather you just pretend they're not there. But I'll promise to try and clear them up anyway.' He kissed me on my eyes and nose. After a sensible chat and with the air cleared we both felt we'd just had a service and oil change at the relationship garage.

Bad news was circulating around camp the next day. Ed, one of the guides on Team Chhiring, had quit. He'd apparently left very quickly that morning, without saying goodbye to his team. Allegedly, he felt he wasn't performing well but whatever his reason, losing a second Western guide had left Russell like a bear with a sore head. Their role was valuable forming an interface between Russell and the teams. They were his eyes and ears.

Our team wasn't the only one losing people though. The BBC Challenge Everest team, who were filming for a documentary, had been thrown into disarray because Tony, an ex-marine and the star of their show, had given up just above ABC feeling unwell. The BBC film crew were allegedly upset but in fairness to Tony, it was his first attempt at an 8,000-metre peak, compared to some teams on their eighth.

Although base camp was becoming a little less hostile, the weather still had the upper hand on Everest. Savage jetstream winds raged above 7,000 metres, producing spectacular streamers of lenticular cloud. Even from 15 kilometres away, convoluted ribbons visibly ripped across Everest's north face, spiralling and contorting as they went.

On our fifth night at base camp, I crawled out of Rob's tent and couldn't believe what I saw. 'Rob, come and look at this,' I whispered.

'Not now Bel, it's too cold,' he said pulling his sleeping bag up higher.

'Forget the cold, you've simply got to come out,' I urged him excitedly.

Rob scrambled out to join me, making it clear he was not impressed – until he looked up. A brilliant full moon hung above us and silvery clouds scudded across the night sky. Everest's north face glowed a phantasmal blue and her plume snaked off into the blackness like a ghostly wraith. It was a night unlike any we'd ever seen.

By the next day we'd been stuck at base camp for a week. We delighted in our small treats. For Rob it was the joy of clean socks and his small travel pillow; for me, wet wipes and my Lancôme SPF 15 face cream; for everyone our weekly ten litres allowance of hot water. Irrespective of these rationed treats, tent fever was taking hold.

After lunch Rob went for a lie down while the rest of our team hung out in the mess tent. Jamie was enthusiastically espousing his mountaineering knowledge while questioning one of our guides on their facts. Everyone else had long since dropped out of the conversation. Jamie was not worth challenging in this mode. Sadly, I had a temporary lapse of sanity and opened my mouth.

'It is possible for a guide to know more than you do, Jamie,' I said, not comprehending the fury I was about to unleash. When the chaps on the team challenged Jamie, he usually simmered down, but when I foolishly made the mistake of challenging him it was like a red rag to a bull.

'And what have you contributed to the team then, Jo? You haven't done any cooking or pulled any teeth out either,' he said venomously. I was completely thrown by his answer. Incomprehensibly, the conversation had flipped from snow stakes to my very existence in the team. Shocked by his outburst, I didn't stop to consider that his first line of defence might have been attack and stupidly answered back.

'But Jamie, no-one on either team has done any cooking or dentistry except you. Russell has employed an army of Sherpa cooks and they're doing a great job . . . And you're a dentist. I'm not. I can't pull teeth out.' But I wasn't going to play a point scoring game. There was a curt exchange of words on both sides and I left the tent before things deteriorated further.

As I stood in a daze outside, Cecile came out and gave me a hug. 'Just ignore him,' she said, but I could feel myself crumbling inside. As I climbed inside Rob's tent, I was already in tears.

'What on earth's wrong, Bella?' he said as he rolled over.

'Just had a barney with Jamie. It started about snow stakes but suddenly got personal and I don't know why.'

Rob sighed and handed me his toilet roll. 'You're a soft target,' he said giving me a cuddle.

'Yes, but he made me so mad I ended up speaking my mind and probably saying things I shouldn't have.'

'I'm so sorry I wasn't there, but it's happened now, so try not to worry about it.'

'All the other lads jibe him so much. Why did he turn on me? What am I supposed to do, just stroke his ego and flutter my eyelids?'

'Yeah, well, I'm not saying you should have done that, but you would have had a quieter life. Anyway, you can't please everyone, so stop trying and concentrate on what you can affect, which is summiting.'

Soon after Russell came to find me. He'd heard about the argument. 'Don't worry about him. You're doing fine,' he said giving me a big hug. I held back the tears, wanting to be brave but still feeling crushed. I knew I should have turned the other cheek and not fought back. We had both wielded the sword of words and been pointlessly hurt. I was left to face the harsh reality of Russell's words about Everest – it won't be fun.

For the next three hours I escaped for a walk with Rob to clear my head. Later that afternoon, Dale, Harry and Paul from team Chhiring paid me a visit. They were fed up of constant bickering and competition on their team and were intrigued by news of disagreements on ours. Playing it down, I felt terrible I'd become a source of interest to break up the tedium of base camp. It seemed boredom and stress had been a touchpaper and caused trouble to break out and now everyone wanted to know the bad news.

As the day went on I realised my reaction to the conflict was colouring everything. It was my choice to enjoy Everest and not allow it to be spoilt. I knew I had to forgive Jamie so that I didn't waste energy and become a prisoner to my own resentment. That evening I still felt subdued but hoped that in time, it would all blow over.

The next day Russell announced he was arranging a party for our team that evening. It was a good plan and would boost everyone's spirits. With Sherpas, yak herders and even other expedition teams it was a cosmopolitan night with a fusion of disco grooving, Tibetan line dancing and plenty of heavy breathing.

The morning after the party, base camp lassitude was heavily afflicting some team members. Headaches, beer consumption and bedtimes were enthusiastically compared. But it was a gorgeous morning and Rob and I set out for a picnic at a secret hollow by the Blue Lakes. Paddling barefoot in the glassy green water we skimmed stones till we stumbled from our numb feet. Planting ourselves among the sun-warmed rocks, we both stripped off. It was divine to feel the sun and warm air on our anaemic skin. The air was still and the only sounds were of the distant rushing snow melt and a warbling Tibetan lark. I wrote poems and repaired my toenails while Rob watched Everest's plume. It was a balmy day and it was hard to believe that hurricane force winds still pummelled her summit.

As our second week got under way, it was disheartening to hear that bad weather was forecast to continue for another fortnight. Many of us drifted further down the valley in search of interesting destinations. The Rongbuk monastery was a favourite, along with a trip to visit a village school. Having learnt about Russell's school building projects on our Cho Oyu expedition, we'd started supporting them ourselves and were using our climb of Everest to raise money for a second school in Pangi. We were excited to discover that we were the first Westerners ever to visit Pangi village. In addition to Pangi, we visited another remote village called Tashidum, where Russell had already built a school. Sharing the day with these incredible village people was an extraordinary honour. In spite of their poverty and harsh subsistence lifestyle, their gratitude and generosity was humbling beyond words.

*

After several weeks at base camp and refreshed from our school trip, we were finally released to go back to ABC. We arrived on May 14th, the date of our our shared birthday, to find that KB had managed to cook us a cake on his gas stove. It was the highest birthday cake we'd ever had, by many miles.

With a day of rest at ABC under our belts, the radios started to buzz with activity and we heard of the first successful south side summits. A mood of nervous excitement pervaded camp. No-one had summited from the north side yet because higher winds always prevented early summits. Everyone gathered for our final briefing and Russell delivered his precise instructions. 'If you haven't climbed with oxygen before, make sure you're absolutely clear about how to operate it. Practise and practise again. You can't afford to have a problem up there.'

Everyone on our teams would be using oxygen, including all the Sherpas. The success rate for climbers who use oxygen is 20%, as opposed to about 8% without. The odds still weren't great but we were all keen to stack them in our favour. For our teams oxygen was just another safety device to be employed alongside climbing equipment, hi-tech boots and down suits.

As Russell continued the briefing he placed a bottle on his lap and patted it affectionately. 'I've had these filled with moisture-free aircraft grade oxygen, so the valves shouldn't freeze.' It was critical that the right type of oxygen was used. Expeditions that had cut corners in this department had paid the highest price – failed summit bids, tragic news and grieving relatives – all to save a few dollars.

Flow rates were another big issue and Russell had precisely calculated how much we could use. 'Make sure you've got things straight in your heads before leaving ABC. You aren't going to be able to calculate anything much up there,' he said. Each bottle held 1,000 litres of oxygen which, compressed to 250 bar, fitted into a four-litre stainless steel and Kevlar bottle weighing just over three kilos. Running at a flow of two litres per minute, this would give us 500 minutes, or just over eight hours per bottle. 'You need to sleep on half a litre per minute and on summit day you'll need to use two litres per minute except for the exit cracks and the Second Step, where you can use four.' Even at ABC my brain felt sluggish and mathematically inept. I wasn't at all sure if I could trust myself to do the right thing when I was over two kilometres higher. We would need to continually double and triple check our own and each other's systems to avoid any costly mistakes.

As Russell started to tackle the next issue a deathly hush fell over the group. 'On summit day, you'll be passing dead bodies. There are about 20 near the route. You won't see them all but there is one you should know about – Green Boots. You'll have to step over his feet to get past.' For a dead person to acquire a name like 'Green Boots' seemed strangely impersonal, yet discussions had already broken out about various other dead climbers we might see, like the Waving Korean and the Unidentified Sleeper. Russell couldn't afford for us to be shocked by the sight of dead bodies. Nearly 200 climbers had died on Everest and about 100 corpses still lay on the mountain, making it the highest graveyard in the world.

The next subject Russell tackled caused as much reaction as the dead bodies. Looks of concern rippled around the group as he started talking about a first and second team. 'I know you're all keen to be on the first team,' he said, 'but I can't have everyone going together. Can I have a show of hands of those of you who'd be willing to go on the second team?'

The group quickly fell silent. Out of 15 climbers only three of us immediately put our hands up. Rob and I had already discussed it. We knew the first team would be bigger, so there was more likelihood of dangerous bottlenecks, forcing people to wait and increase their risk of frostbite and running out of oxygen. We had aesthetic reasons too. The remote beauty of high mountains is part of what makes climbing so special and it seemed ludicrous to climb Everest bumper to bumper.

Seeing the imbalance in team sizes, Russell started to pick out individuals he thought should move to the second team. Being publicly selected to move into team B clearly dented people's pride and although some conceded, a few didn't. But the effects of being in team B were largely psychological. The only practical disadvantage of the second team was that we could be impacted by problems in the team ahead of us. Rob and I had agreed that if we could hold our nerve, we'd be better off in the long run, and on balance our decision felt right.

As I wandered back to my tent Russell called over, 'Jo, let's have a chat.' He signalled me towards the comms tent. Sitting on the rocks he broached the very subject that was troubling me. I had been feeling panicked by the likely timing of our summit attempt as I was due to start my period on 22 May, almost the exact day we were due to summit. Previously at 6,400 metres on Cho Oyu, the very height we were now living at, my period had caused me to become dangerously faint. If my period started on time, my summit chances were over. I would be pushing my body so hard that I would have no margin for lost performance.

'The problem is, I can't let you go up later than the others. Apart from the logistics, the good weather window won't hold . . . I'm hoping that as you get higher, you're body will shut down.' Russell was right, it was my only chance.

Early the next morning a little queue of team members waited patiently by the high-powered telescope, eager to watch the first climbers making their summit bid from the north side. Watching the climbers move was an unnerving experience for all of us. They were now at 8,700 metres on the final snow pyramid. Half an hour had passed and there had been no evidence of movement. Even though we knew the difficulties of moving at altitude, it was hard to believe our eyes. Only being there and knowing how utterly powerless the thin air made us, would bring true understanding. Russell looked through the telescope, studying not only the climbers but also the skies. Not so much as a puff of wind would escape his watchful eye over the next ten days.

The jet stream clipped the upper reaches of Everest for most of the year and typically smashed into her at 200 kph. Even in the calmest month arctic winds of 100 kph are not uncommon. The only opportunity to summit is in the few days when the monsoon pushes up from the Bay of Bengal, shunting the jetstream and associated bad weather further north and before the monsoon snows arrive. An unexpected change in the weather on Everest could snuff out lives like candles in a storm. Russell would make his final weather call from a combination of intuition, experience and accurate forecasts from Meteotest in Switzerland. We trusted his judgement. Everest's plume was not running today but he had decided not to send us up at the first opportunity. He was playing the long game and knew that too many climbers up high was a potential death trap.

After breakfast on 18 May the teams milled around, getting ready for the first departures the next day. Calling a brief meeting, Russell made an unexpected announcement. 'I want the first team to go today. You need to get to camp one tonight. So I will wish you all good luck and remember, you're not successful till you're back here with all your fingers and toes.'

After initial yelps of surprise, the first team leapt into action. We didn't know if Russell had kept his precise battle plan a secret for fear it would leak to other teams, but it no longer mattered. The starting pistol had gone off. We had done all the preparation that we could and now nothing else mattered beyond the next six days of our lives. Within hours the first team were leaving in a cloud of excitement and noise. Making our way around the team, Rob and I hugged and shook hands, wishing them all luck as they filtered out of camp. The next time we would see them was after the summit.

Later that day we also bade farewell to Graham. He was leaving too, but to go home. Time had run out for him, along with the opportunity to look for Irvine's camera. With another aborted search, the question of Mallory and Irvine's success or failure to achieve the summit would remain unanswered for another year, and maybe forever.

ABC was eerily quiet the next day as Rob and I finished our packing together. Every item was agreed and checked – essentials only. Too much weight could make us dangerously slow. Even the toothbrush didn't get sawn in half as some legendary mountaineers had done. Our decision was simpler. It wasn't going.

I kissed Rob goodnight for the last time in separate tents. Despite all we'd done to get to this point, we weren't going to climb Everest on past accomplishments. We had to want with all our heart to stand on top of Everest. She would demand our all, and if our all wasn't enough I prayed we'd have the strength and sense to turn around.

At 2 am I was startled out of my sleep by loud wailing. Sitting up, I strained to listen to the shouting and yelling unable to work out what it was. Had someone just returned? Were they having a party at this time in the morning? Or was something very wrong? I felt troubled by the commotion and wondered if Rob had heard it too. Eventually camp fell quiet again. Flicking my head torch on, I opened my Bible and some words stood out on the page as if they were on fire: '*Be strong and courageous. Do not be terrified; do not be discouraged, for the Lord your God will be with you wherever you go.*' Joshua 1:9.

CHAPTER 17

One More Step

'In the confrontation between the stream and the rock, the stream always wins, though not through strength but by perseverance.'

H. Jackson Brown

EARLY THE NEXT morning, with frost still caking the ground, our small team slipped quietly out of camp. Hours later, as we wove our way up through the frozen headwall cliffs to camp one, panic broke out on the radio. An Italian had gone missing after his summit attempt and his team were now asking Russell for help.

The icefall had moved since our last visit over three weeks ago and crevasses that we'd previously stepped over were now yawning chasms. As we neared camp one, Rob climbed quickly over an aluminium ladder spanning a freshly opened crevasse. I followed behind but as the ground fell away into a glistening blue vault, I was drawn to stop and stare.

'Come on Jo, why are you stopping there?' Rob called in a sharp tone.

'It's amazing. Look at the –'

'Get moving, Jo.' Without saying another word I started moving again.

After four and a half hours, as we passed the first tent perched on a narrow ledge below the North Col, we stopped in our tracks. Two exhausted Sherpas were descending a narrow snow ramp towards us. A climber hung between their shoulders, his head bouncing and legs flailing behind in a drunken stagger. Dropping him into the tent the Sherpas collapsed on the snow. I wondered if he was the missing Italian. He was almost certainly a victim of HACE – high altitude cerebral oedema, the deadliest of high-altitude afflictions. In a desperate attempt to access more oxygen, the brain becomes increasingly engorged with blood but this quickly backfires as the brain swells inside the unyielding skull. Within hours the victim starts suffering from impaired sight, judgement and co-ordination. As pressure builds, hallucinations start and primitive instincts of aggression are deregulated, after which coma and death are swift and sure. The only chance of survival is immediate descent, assuming the victim can still walk. A few more hours may be bought with dexamethosone, a strong steroid that temporarily reduces swelling of the brain. Ironically this was a drug that Rob knew well from his chemotherapy days and hoped he'd never need again.

Safely huddled inside our tent there was little more to do than listen to radio transmissions and hope the hours would pass quickly. We heard that two more of Team Chhiring, Gabi and Joseph, had decided to quit. We also realised the shouting and wailing we'd heard before leaving ABC hadn't been a party at all, but the Korean team leader's cries of despair as he received news that three of his team were dead. High on the north-east summit ridge, their Sherpas had been unable to save them. An American climber had died the same day while summiting from the south side. It wasn't clear from the radio transmissions what had happened to any of them. Chances were no-one would ever really know.

As the radio went dead again, we sat in silence listening to the roar of our stove. We were lost in a maze of unanswered questions. Why had they died? Was it an oxygen problem? Did they have the same system as us? Had their budget not allowed them to climb safely? Did cultural values pressure them into not giving up for fear of losing face? Or was it just an accident? The stark arithmetic is that one out of every ten who summit Everest will die.

Overnight, heavy snows converted camp one into a village of igloos, but their deceptive winter garb gave no hint of the frying pan we were now trapped in. Even the thin veneer of cloud did nothing to diminish the sun's searing radiation. Despite the heat, dressing light was not an option. From now on we had to wear our full down suit. Russell had warned us, 'The weather changes fast up there. You can't afford to get caught out.' With our sleeves rolled up the undiluted sun cooked our bare arms. I longed for the refreshing blasts of icy wind and watched my forearms in detached amazement as exquisite ice crystals grew along every hair.

Forty minutes out of camp we had crossed the col and were climbing the north ridge. The cloud had already thickened, snow was falling and the wind had freshened. We were already grateful for our down suits and stopped to seal ourselves in. As we did, we noticed Ian was alone. Barry, his tent buddy, had disappeared.

'Where's Barry?' Rob called down to Ian.

'Turned around. Said he was feeling too weak,' he shrugged before collapsing back over his axe. To have turned around so soon didn't bode well. Having repeatedly failed to get to camp one, and by turning around again, he had more than likely forfeited his chances. Rob looked at me and even behind his reflective goggles, I sensed his mood. Camp two was still many hours away. We needed to press on.

With each passing hour, the weather continued to deteriorate. By late morning Rob was barely visible, even just metres away. The fixed line was our only guide as it vanished above us into the white void. As I waded up to my thighs, the effort of kicking steps sapped my morale. It was like climbing a mountain of sugar; every step collapsed behind us, cruelly forcing whoever was behind to rebreak the trail. Panting furiously, I leant over my axe and stared between my legs. Rob was just four steps behind me but there was no hurry. Four steps would take him time. He too was motionless, not wasting a single movement as he got ready for his next step. The cold, dry air made me cough, aggravating my rib pain; each time my radio crackled to life from inside my breast pocket, it was a welcome distraction.

This time it was the Mexican team asking for Russell's help. They had lost a climber several days ago, somewhere above high camp. No-one had heard from him since. Every year as the summit weather window arrived, Russell was called upon for assistance and this year was proving no different. His voice came over the radio.

'We will do our best to look for you,' he said.

'But you have so many Sherpas, please, you must send some to look,' they pleaded again.

'My first obligation is to my climbers but I will ask my Sherpas to look.' As we continued stepping up and sliding down, the transmissions of bad news continued. Two more climbers, a Japanese lady and a Bulgarian man, had also gone missing yesterday. Like the Koreans, they were last seen high on the north-east summit ridge.

The howling winds were now driving snow horizontally, blasting it into every crevice. I pulled my hood forwards to shield my face and shut out the radio chatter. With the grim news, it was no longer a helpful distraction. Waves of snow and ice fragments washed over us on the wind, our right sides now caked in a growing mass of rime ice. Every gruelling step felt like my last, yet we hadn't even reached camp two. How was I going to get higher? I could see Rob was fighting too. I longed for a break but I had to keep moving. If either of us stopped, we might give up and turn around.

Hours before in the hazy morning sunshine, camp two had looked no more than a few hours away, but the magnifying effect of the thin air had deceived us. Seven hours later we crawled into camp two at 7,500 metres. We were utterly drained and my exhaustion was compounded by the pain in my ribs. Russell's cautionary words echoed in my mind: 'It will only get worse.' With nearly one and a half vertical kilometres to go, I wondered how much worse. If the weather stayed this bad, attempting the summit would be suicide.

Inspecting the precarious campsite, I realised one idle move would leave us wishing we'd packed our parachutes en route to the East Rongbuk Glacier far below. The tents were barely visible as they nestled in their carved-out ledges, buried under a mountain of fresh snow. All the tents were umbilically linked and we followed the rope to the first empty one. Clambering inside, we crashed in a heap, showering the floor with snow and ice.

After some time I summoned the energy to speak. 'We need to light the stove, Rob,' I said, panting with the effort. There was no reply, only silence. I inhaled deeply again. 'Rob.' I paused, hoping for an answer. There was an affirmative grunt but nothing more. As I lay on the tent floor, uncontrollable bouts of shaking finally prompted me to action. Shivering was a waste of calories I could ill afford.

With our less than perfect acclimatisation, we were relieved that we'd taken Russell's advice to start sleeping on oxygen tonight. In spite of this, some had chosen to wait until the next camp, but that was a gamble we didn't want to take. If we were on the south side it would have been normal to start using oxygen at this altitude, but Russell's teams usually waited until camp three. 'Let's check the oxygen before we light the stove,' Rob said, dragging a cylinder towards him. Playing with fire and compressed oxygen at the same time was not a wise idea, especially with only half our brains functioning. Talking each other through the process of checking our oxygen, we couldn't afford a mistake. Even the smallest amount of sun cream or oil on our hands, if transferred to the regulator thread, could cause an explosion.

The cold night hours limped past. The next day was 22 May, supposedly the start of my next period. I continued to pray my body would stop functioning properly – or at least like that of a woman – for just a few days.

As we left the security of our tent, a strong wind was still blowing. Bill, Andy and Ian had already gone, leaving just Paul, Karsang Sherpa and us. Barry was still at camp one, having aborted the previous morning. However, having spent a day and night on oxygen, Russell had agreed to give him one last chance and extra oxygen from camp one, so he could catch the team up.

Pulling the icy cold rubber of the oxygen mask onto my face, I sealed myself in. The oxygen cylinder weighed me down but without oxygen I'd almost certainly get frostbite. Whether we made it to the top or not, both of us were determined to return with all 20 digits. Within minutes of leaving camp two, a series of rock ledges were staring me in the face. Scrabbling around on the snow-covered rocks, I fought to find purchase. Rob stood patiently beneath me. I felt panicky and distraught to be struggling so soon. I turned to Rob, feeling terrible for making him wait.

'Sorry,' I rasped from behind my mask.

'You can do it!' he called, shaking his fist positively. Staring at the sloping rock slabs I could see they were no more than a hard scramble and yet every move was a battle. I tentatively pulled on the rope for support but with every pull it got longer, as if I was trying to climb a piece of elastic. Scrambling clumsily on all fours, I hauled myself up. *What on earth are you doing, Jo? That's no way to climb. Do it properly, find decent holds.* But as I scanned, there were none. It was like climbing steep icy roof tiles in fancy dress. Clambering to my feet again, I sucked on my oxygen. The trickle of oxygen from my mask was barely 5% of the air my lungs were now consuming, but little as it was, I was grateful for every molecule. I pulled the rope taut and signalled for Rob to come up.

As the strong crosswinds buffeted us from the west, even trying to stay upright was a challenge. Moving slower than a funeral march, I focused on fragments of shale or the next rope anchor and one mind game at a time, I negotiated my body towards camp three.

After several hours the radios were buzzing once more. The Mexican who was missing in action and presumed dead, had been found by Russell's Sherpas. He had collapsed in a tent at high camp. Tragically, the missing Japanese and Bulgarian had not been so lucky. Their deaths were now confirmed. Both of them had perished on the north-east ridge. The Japanese lady now hung from the ropes on the Second Step and the Bulgarian sat hauntingly just above at the top of the Second Step. We numbly listened to Russell instructing our Sherpas to clear the bodies that blocked the route.

The wind that had battered us all morning was now hurling a golden veil of ice crystals that danced and cavorted like a wild animal along the ridge. As I crested onto a rocky outcrop, Ian came into view, but he appeared to be asleep and was reclined on a rock like a floppy rag doll. Knowing Ian had gone snow blind on Cho Oyu, I hoped everything was alright. Turning my radio up, I could hear him talking to Russell. But it wasn't the Ian we knew. He was obsessed with his altimeter watch, repeatedly telling Russell it wasn't working. As we drew alongside him, his face was haggard. We both felt uneasy about how he looked.

'You OK, Ian?' Rob asked.

'Fine, thanks,' he replied. The quintessential Brit and unfailingly polite, Ian always maintained a stiff upper lip, but his face told another story.

'Do you want to suck on my O's for a bit?' I asked, pulling away my mask away and offering it to him.

'No. I'm fine, thank you.'

'Are you sure? It will really help,' I asked, almost begging him to accept.

'No thanks. I'm fine, you go on.'

As we continued up, we both kept turning to see where Ian was. Half an hour later he was moving, but desperately slowly. Just above us we could now see Andy, who was resting on the snow. As we drew near he radioed us. 'I can't go on, guys, I'm finished. Bill's gone ahead.' He sounded extremely upset. It was strange to hear Andy talk like this, he had always been so strong and confident. Rob got straight back on the radio.

'Andy, you can do this.' There was a long silence before Andy spoke again.

'I can't, I'm serious.'

'You can, just get to camp three. You'll feel better on oxygen.' Even on oxygen we both felt wretched but it was giving us what we needed to keep going. The radio fell silent again and Andy stayed where he was. As we came up to him, his face was distraught. We did our best to spur him to go on but there was little else we could do. Our decision to start oxygen at camp two was already paying off. At this altitude, our bodies would not recover from each day's exertions. When we had left ABC, it was as if we'd been allocated a finite number of energy tokens. It was for us to decide when to use them. Our game plan was to save as much as possible and invest everything in our final summit push.

Turning to go on, I was startled by something in my peripheral vision. Thinking I was hallucinating, I stopped to stare, but what I was seeing was real. Just feet away from me, hovering effortlessly on the uplift from the ridge, was a large jet-black mountain chough, a member of the crow family. It tilted its head towards me as if I was a curiosity, its macabre dark eyes watching intently as if waiting for me to make a mistake. Life for the chough was easy up here. Its large heart and custom-designed lungs made the job of flying at nearly eight kilometres nothing more than an idle game. Losing interest, it peeled away, folded its wings back and plummeted like a bullet.

Over the next hour a string of weary climbers from another team staggered down past us. They'd been testing a new lightweight oxygen system but now they were aborting their summit push. As we stopped to exchange short greetings, I noticed their nasal oxygen tubes were clogged with frozen mucus. Cumbersome and uncomfortable as our Russian oxygen system was, at least it was still working. Behind them two Sherpas moved awkwardly down the rocks with something large between them. Drawing near I saw it was a body, crudely strapped to a flat board. I wondered if it was the Mexican who'd been found at camp four. Letting them past, I caught a glimpse of his eyes. They were open but hollow; he seemed alive, but only just. Cerebral oedema had him in its clutches and without the Sherpas' heroic efforts he'd be dead in a matter of hours.

Just like camp two, liveable real estate was in short supply at camp three. Each tent was pitched on a snow platform scarcely bigger than a car bonnet, leaving the downhill edge of the tents precariously hanging in thin air. The wind hadn't abated at all. Camp three was known to be the windiest camp site on Everest and it was now receiving the full force of it. As I saw the tent fabric snapping furiously in the unrelenting wind, I was relieved to see that they had been practically nailed to the mountain. Dainty tent pegs and spindly guy lines had been replaced with giant metal stakes and a basket weave of thick ropes that lashed the tents to the ground. As double insurance, football-sized rocks had been loaded inside.

We were now at 7,900 metres, the height of the highest camp on the south side, but we still had one more camp to go. Much noise has been made in the past about the South Col – the south side's highest camp, being the highest rubbish dump in the world. We'd seen photographs of oxygen canisters and piles of frozen rubbish and were bracing ourselves for similarly disappointing sights on the north. But on our arrival, we were pleasantly surprised to find nothing except the shredded remnants of a few tents. Admittedly fewer people climbed this route, but nevertheless, either rubbish didn't get left or it had simply been blown off the mountain.

As Rob passed a bag of snow to me in the vestibule we saw each other uncovered for the first time all day. Both our faces were puffed up and if we hadn't been so shattered, no doubt humorous quips would have ensued. On further inspection our hands were markedly swollen too. Our decision to remove wedding rings once again had been the right one. Working together, we started the stove to melt snow. The stove was barely audible over the wind as it battered our flimsy nylon home but its quiet purr was comforting. With every new height gain, the water took longer to boil and would never get as hot. Even a simple cup of tea took 45 minutes.

As my fingertips started to warm, they began to throb and felt as if I had cocktail sticks jammed into them. As a result of the intensely cold, dry atmosphere, my nails were peeling off their beds as if they'd somehow lost their stickiness and my only defence was to strap them down with duct tape. 'Can you do mine too,' Rob said holding out his thumbs. They were deeply cracked and had troubled him all expedition. Our bodies were rapidly falling apart. In addition to altitude sickness, we had a growing collection of ailments from ulcers, sore throats and unhealed cuts to haemorrhoids and my damaged ribs.

Although we'd arrived in the middle of the afternoon, it was soon dark and we'd barely completed a few basic tasks. The nights were no longer about sleep, they were just about resting, hydrating and getting ready for the next day. Shuffling together in our sleeping bags, we shared as much warmth as we could. It was too suffocating to zip the tent fully shut, which left us regularly clearing spindrift off our sleeping bags throughout the night.

At 1 am I prodded Rob. 'This is it,' I said.

'What?' Rob answered from the darkness, clearly as awake as I was.

'The other team are leaving now. Shall we turn our radios on to listen?'

'Better not. We need to save our batteries.' Another gust slammed into our tent and I prayed the winds were calmer at camp four. Wind was one of our fiercest enemies, its power could blow us away like rag dolls. Poking our gloved hands out of the top of our sleeping bags we squeezed each other's hands tight. Tomorrow it would be our turn to move up to the start line.

As the first light of morning broke over the horizon we could still hear the wind blasting spindrift against our tent. Pulling my goggles on, I peered through a crack in our tent door and was greeted by a stunning crystal-clear day. Looking to the summit I saw that Everest's familiar plume was no longer running. Russell had been spot on with his forecasting. It was a summit day.

For us, we still had one camp to go, yet even to get there we'd be climbing higher than ever before. As we left camp my sack felt increasingly heavy and even with oxygen our pace was barely a crawl. As we left the north ridge behind and traversed onto the north face the winds finally began to subside. Ascending snow-filled gullies, we worked our way around rocky outcrops onto increasingly broken and slabby ground. Knowing that exactly 80 years ago the great mountaineers George Mallory and Andrew Irvine had climbed here seemed utterly surreal.

By 11 am the radios were buzzing with activity. It was marvellous to hear that the first team had all summited and were now descending. But all was not well and Russell was sounding agitated. 'Tell her she needs to turn around,' he said forcefully over the radio. Watching everyone's movements through the telescope, he had seen a solitary Bulgarian woman still on her way up, moving dangerously slowly. Her Sherpa had apparently refused to climb with her, complaining she was crazy. For safety, 11 am was the turnaround time many teams used, including ours, but she was still hours from the summit.

'She won't turn around, Russ,' said Jamie. He was at the bottom of the second step, trying to reason with her. One by one Russell told each of our team members to try and turn her around as they came past. But as if on a suicide mission, she refused to listen, wanting to continue alone. Exasperated, Russell changed his tone.

'Guys, you've got to tell her, make her listen, she's going to fucking die. Tell her she won't make it, it's too late.' But it was no use, she ignored everyone's pleas. Though the entire first team had tried, no-one could protect her from herself. For most of us, high altitude draws out our most basic instincts of self-preservation. But not for this woman. Five other climbers had been killed on the north-east ridge alone in the last few days, six on the mountain overall. This was only two fewer than died in the infamous Everest disaster of 1996, and by tomorrow seven were likely to be dead. No-one expected to see the Bulgarian woman again. It seemed it was not a question of if, but who and how many would die on the slopes of Everest.

It was midday when we arrived at camp four. Our small cluster of tents was perched high on the north face at 8,300 metres, the highest camp in the world. Beneath us the north face tumbled away and was swallowed up by the towering cumulus clouds that lay far below. At this height, if airline passengers were suddenly exposed to the air outside, they would lapse into a coma within minutes. Starved and suffocating, our bodies would never acclimatise to this altitude but our hopes were pinned on just one more day.

Dropping our sacks, Rob and I hung in each other's arms. After so many weeks, it was hard to believe we were still in the game and finally in position. Although we were both getting weaker, our resolve grew by the day. The continuing news of tragedies no longer scared us but primed our minds before we stepped into the final arena. Climbing into what was Jamie and Dean's tent, we could barely move for the chaotic piles of gear. I felt irrationally frustrated at the mess but suspected we would leave it in an equally bad state when we left for the summit later that night.

One by one the summit team straggled back into high camp over the next few hours. Every one of them was ravaged and in a state of shock. Jamie came back to our tent to collect his gear. We congratulated him, but his face was riddled with fear.

'That's it. I'm through with climbing. It's too bloody scary. I'm out of here.' With that he left Rob and me to ponder his words. Later, Derek and Keik from Team Chhiring returned back. Derek, who had always been so strong and capable, looked empty, as if his soul had been sucked from his body. Keik, a confident and strong-minded individual, staggered like a drunkard and looked a broken man. Russell spoke to them on the radio.

'I want you to try and get to a lower camp. It's not safe for you to stay at camp four, especially not in your state.'

'We can't do it, Russ, we need more oxygen,' Keik said.

Russell appealed to them again. 'I need you to try to get lower.'

'I can't, I'll kill myself. Please, we need more oxygen,' Keik said, now sounding distraught.

'OK. I'll get the Sherpas to bring you extra oxygen, but you must come down at first light tomorrow. Understood?' Russell clicked off.

The last one to arrive back at high camp was Thimo. As the least experienced climber of both teams, he was barely able to walk and looked like the waking dead. He tripped and stumbled past our tent, totally unaware of his surroundings, the only thing holding him on the mountain was a Sherpa who had him by a short, tight rope. He had no idea how lucky he was and maybe he would never know. Seeing so many of our team members in this state was sobering. Not even the strongest had escaped untouched.

For years I'd wondered what it would feel like to be in Everest's death zone. Curiously I wasn't choking or gasping my last breath, but the smallest of movements, the tiniest of efforts sent my heart racing and lungs pumping like bellows. Reaching for my sack I pulled out my one luxury item – my tiny pulse oximeter. I was intrigued to know what our arterial blood oxygen saturations would be at this altitude. Having warmed our fingers on the stove lid in our best attempt to maximise accuracy, Rob's reading was 48%, mine was 49%.

I marvelled in silence that we were still functioning at all. Levels below 75% are known to lead to impaired judgement, emotions and muscular function. At below 50% thinking allegedly cuts off and below 30 to 40% results in unconsciousness and death. The only people I'd ever witnessed with saturations as low as ours were patients just before they died in intensive care. Statistically, things weren't looking too good, but as many high-altitude climbers had proved before us, the body can function under the most extreme circumstances.

In slow motion we completed our few essential maintenance and preparation tasks. Most of the time was spent staring blankly into space or trying to summon the motivation for the next movement. In our hypoxic confusion, even setting our oxygen systems felt complicated. After laboriously triple checking each other's bottles, regulators, hoses and masks, we were finally satisfied. We'd managed a few mouthfuls of noodles before sunset, but on tomorrow's summit push we'd be burning well over 10,000 calories and at best we had just consumed 200. It didn't add up. Our bodies were having their last supper, feasting on themselves.

Seven hours after our arrival, we lay slumped in the dark, frozen world of the death zone. Listening to the fragile roar of the stove, our only security was our canvas home. Propped against my rucksack, I tried to glean some warmth from the stove's small flame. Between us lay two sets of oxygen equipment and radios, both essential sources of life for us now. The cold was penetrating and I felt I was freezing from within. I was in my sleeping bag, wearing everything I had, yet still getting colder. The temperature inside our tent was only −15°C, we'd experienced worse, but my hypoxic body had shut down peripheral circulation in a desperate attempt to save vital organs. From my selfish brain's perspective, my hands and feet were surplus to requirements. But I had to fight the enemy within. Without my feet, my brain wasn't going anywhere.

Clothes only conserve heat produced by the body and in our exhausted, malnourished, dehydrated, sleep-deprived state our heat production was at an all-time low. Our oxygen-starved internal combustion was now failing. For a decrease in body temperature of just 0.6°C, our cerebral metabolism would dip by 5%, leaving our thought processes dangerously sluggish. We couldn't allow ourselves to be numbed into oblivion.

Oxygen was the only solution. My system craved it to burn fuel and generate heat. I fumbled in the dark for my head torch. Clicking it on, I shone its beam at Rob. He was nestled under layers of down, only his eyes and nose visible. Leaning over I slowly manoeuvred the cylinder and mask towards me, even that made my breathing laboured. *How on earth are we supposed to crawl out of this tent just after midnight and scale Everest?* But this was no time for questions, no time to lose my grip. I had to be strong and I had to believe. After 30 seconds of oxygen, warmth flooded my body as if hot water was trickling down inside my arms and legs. Rob shifted his hand towards mine and tapped it gently. 'Better?' he said. I nodded and we exchanged reassuring glances. Together we'd be OK. Clicking my head torch off again, we returned to our private worlds. As we sat in the pitch black, my imagination oscillated from numb vacancy to terror at what we were attempting.

Tonight the radios would stay on all night. We'd placed our spare batteries on the saucepan lid to stop them from freezing. It was 8.30 pm and Bill had just radioed Barry and Ian, asking how they were doing. Listening to Ian was worrying.

'I'm fucked, absolutely fucked', he said. The radio went silent again. We had never heard him speak like this before. We hoped Barry would be able to keep an eye on him throughout the night. Moments later the airwaves were buzzing again, this time with a tense conversation between Bill and Paul.

'I'm sorry, Paul. I just don't think you're up to the summit. You've been dangerously slow getting to every camp. It's not safe for you to go higher.'

'Please, I'm begging you, give me one last chance,' Paul pleaded.

'I'm sorry, Paul,' Bill said and clicked off.

In preparation for our imminent departure, Russell was now manning the radios and had been listening in. Now he came on. 'Paul, I can only let you go up if you promise me you will follow my instructions.'

'I promise, just give me a shot. Please.'

'If I think you're moving too slow and I tell you to turn around, you have to promise me you will,' Russell said sternly.

'I promise, I'll turn around.'

Minutes later the airwaves had fallen silent again. Paul had got his wish and we hoped it was the right decision. Russell had told the entire team that any orders on summit day were to be strictly obeyed. He knew all too well our judgement would be poor.

Rob and I were under no illusions about orders. We had a strict turnaround time of 11 am, even if we were only 100 metres from the summit. Some of the most skilful high-altitude climbers had perished without warning because they'd ignored turnaround times. Time was our enemy and we both accepted tomorrow was the day we might get that call.

When we summited Cho Oyu eight months ago, time had slipped away from us and we had left high camp 20 minutes late. Tonight there was no room for that mistake. With weather that could deteriorate cruelly in minutes, any delay could cause things to spiral out of control. We could not be late. We had double, even triple checked everything: oxygen regulators and cylinders, crampons, harnesses, hand warmers, head torches and radios. No item had been overlooked. Once climbing, speed and efficiency would be vital. Sacrifice them and we might be sacrificing the summit, possibly even our lives.

At 10.30 pm my watch alarm went off. We clicked our head torches on and began our final preparations before leaving the security of the tent for the last time. Two hours later we were ready and ahead of schedule. Suddenly I realised we had forgotten one critical question – what were we going to do if one of us had to turn back? On previous mountains we'd always agreed that both of us would turn around if one of us had to give up. But this was different, this was Everest. Our solution was simple – if one of us was too exhausted to go on, the other would continue, but if there was any problem or injury we'd both come down. Our eyes locked together. The decision to separate under certain circumstances was far from ideal and it felt strange even to be discussing it. Knowing the enormity of the effort we'd made to get this far, it was the only sensible decision, but it was one we hoped we'd never have to make.

Now, with the final summit push ahead of us, it was half past midnight and all our checks were done. Wrestling to keep our minds focused, we crouched in the tent's freezing vestibule. My heart was pounding, adrenalin surging through my veins. Despite all our preparations, we didn't feel ready. I don't suppose we ever would.

Radioing Russell at camp one, I asked if we could leave as soon as possible. We didn't want to blame ourselves for failing at the last hurdle. Just then we heard the crunching and squeaking of crampons and beams of light pierced the darkness. Our Sherpas, Kili Pemba and Nawang Drumdu, were clambering up the slope towards us. We'd only met them for the first time a few hours ago when we'd agreed our departure time. Prior to tonight our different schedules had kept the Sherpa and climbing teams apart on the mountain. We could see just enough of their faces, wrapped up from the stinging night air, to read their expressions. They seemed relaxed but the concentration in their eyes betrayed the magnitude of the task ahead. They had a deep respect for the mountain and understood her moods. Their small frames were not impressive, but their movements were efficient, strong and confident. Our wellbeing and safety was their concern and together we would do all that Everest would allow us. Pemba glanced at Rob and me in turn. 'You ready?' This was it. Vibrating with adrenalin and nerves, we were desperate to get started. The fear of the unknown had us tight in its grip.

CHAPTER 18

In the Death Zone

'It does not matter how slow you go as long as you do not stop.'
Confucius

As we struggled out of the vestibule on hands and knees and clambered to our feet, I tried to convince myself this was just like any alpine start. But this wasn't an alpine start. My left rib stabbed as I twisted and pulled myself up, my lungs felt crushed with the burden of breathing and left me coughing until I retched. Russell had told us we'd be ill on this mountain, and now his stark words were strangely reassuring.

The instant I stood away from our tent, the wind bit into my exposed flesh. With the wind chill it was about −35°C but for our oxygen-depleted bodies, it felt much colder. Snow flakes whirled around in strange eddies, adding to my already disoriented mind. The blackness was a predatory void, waiting for a wrong move: a dropped mitten, a stumble, a careless moment. I wanted to find comfort in the darkness, I was sure there were stars out there, something for me to marvel at. But I saw nothing. By torchlight Rob and I tightened our rucksacks and fitted masks in place. Silently we flicked into automatic, as if we were pilots doing pre-flight checks. Harness – *doubled back*. Oxygen cylinder – *full*. Oxygen gauge – *flowing*. Crampon straps – *tight*. Zippers – *done up*. Skin – *covered*. Our torch beams illuminated each other's faces.

'Ready?' Rob said.

'Yes. You OK?'

'Let's go.' He nodded. In my mittened hand it was hard to grip Rob's thick down-suited arm, so I patted him firmly. He gave the thumbs up. We were ready.

It was 1 am when we moved out of camp. I felt strangely relieved as we took our first steps into the night. At last we were facing our fears.

But with those first steps my breathing had already become laboured, my heart banged in my chest and my legs felt like jelly. In the tiny world illuminated by my headlamp I tried to find an efficient rhythm, no matter how slow, no matter how tedious. As I watched Rob's and Pemba's head torches bob in the blackness ahead of me, my semi-comatose mind crawled through its maddening 'to do' list, never complete, always behind. Pressure breathe, rest step, wiggle toes, de-ice ascender, change anchor, check safety clip, wiggle fingers, pressure breathe.

Thirty minutes later I was jolted out of my private world of pain. Trouble was breaking out on the radio. It was Ian. He sounded distressed and confused. 'My oxygen isn't working and I've been standing outside for 20 minutes. I'm fucking freezing. Is someone going to come and help me?'

My mind changed gear, racing through possibilities. Was he alone? How could his oxygen fail before even leaving camp? Why was he standing outside?

'Ian, you need to get inside your tent and check the regulator,' Russell replied.

'I've checked, it isn't working. I'm fucking freezing.'

'Where is your Sherpa, Ian?'

'He can't help. I need some oxygen that works.' I didn't understand what was happening to Ian and worryingly, it seemed, neither did he. On hearing the problem Rob and I had both stopped. Russell got back on the radio to Bill. Someone had to go back to help. Both Dorje, our senior Sherpa, and Bill were not far behind us. It was agreed that Dorje would return to help Ian. Unanswered questions continued to barrage my spongy mind. Was Ian's problem more sinister than just his oxygen? He didn't sound in control. But the radios had fallen silent again. I prayed Dorje would be quick.

Rob had moved off and I started my tortuously slow steps again. The snow ramp had steepened and a wall of rock flanked me to my left. I had to be near the exit cracks, supposedly a series of easy scrambles that would get us onto the north-east ridge, but it didn't make sense. My light flashed ahead onto a vertical buttress of rock. Swivelling around I shone the beam to the right expecting to see a snow ledge, some kind of platform to get around it. There was nothing. My tiny beam of light was swallowed by emptiness. I glanced further down to the right. A gaping void confronted me. The mountain simply fell away into the night. I felt disoriented by the emptiness beneath, as if I was losing balance. Such a huge obstacle so early in our ascent unnerved me and doubts about what lay ahead flooded my mind. High above I could see Rob's head torch bobbing around. That meant just one thing – it was steepening far more than we'd expected at this stage. To distract myself I called Rob on the radio. Just hearing him would be reassuring. I tried to steady my breathing. 'Rob, this is Jo. Are you going to wait for me?' I panted. There was no answer, maybe he hadn't heard.

He finally replied, sounding reassuring. 'You'll catch me.' Feeling comforted, I returned to the sound of my squeaking crampons and laboured breathing.

Reaching out to explore the first section of rock with my hand it seemed different, as if I were touching some sleeping dinosaur. The colours and marks made me nervous to touch it, as if it had a mind of its own. But there was no way to avoid close contact. The beautiful yellow rock glinted in my torchlight. We had to be on the yellow bands, the huge belt of limestone that slices across Everest's high pyramid. I hauled myself up, every muscle and sinew straining to steady me. Dizzy with effort, I couldn't meet my insatiable demand for oxygen. The last time I'd felt like this was on an operating table after anaesthetic, it was like trying to run in a nightmare. *If these are just the easy exit cracks, how on earth am I going to cope with what's ahead?* I tried to shut down my fear.

Sparks flew into the darkness as my crampons fought for purchase. My breathing was like some parody of Darth Vader, I craved far more oxygen than I could get. The ice-encrusted rubber mask was suffocating and claustrophobic and contorted my face. I convinced myself there was more air outside and ripped the mask away. But there was simply nothing, my breath felt sucked out as if in a vacuum. Gasping harder, I squashed the mask back onto my face. I had to get my breathing under control and fast.

As it settled I allowed myself to examine something I'd chosen to ignore – the frayed and tattered ropes, eaten away by the savage elements. With my whole body weight I'd been hanging on a thin nylon line; when I reached the anchor point, I saw it was no more than a fragile thread. All I could do was clip more than one rope hoping that, in the darkness above, Rob was doing the same.

Feeling for a good hold I reached forward to the rock again, trying to focus my torch on where my feet should go. Suddenly everything went black. My light had flicked off. Like a frightened animal I dared not move. *A wrong step now might result in a slip, a slip might mean a swing on the rope, a swing might mean a knocked head. Stop. Concentrate. Do something!* I was lucky. Nawang scrambled up beneath me, his torch illuminating my feet. Wrenching my mittens off I fumbled with the switch till it came on again. I convinced myself it couldn't be the batteries, they were brand new and should be warm enough beneath my down-filled hood. My mittens flapped in the wind, held by their retaining straps. A lost mitten would mean a frostbitten hand, leaving me unable to climb either up or down. Up here absolutely everything had a consequence.

I started climbing again but my torch flicked off once more. *Damn! This can't be happening.* I wouldn't even dream of doing a simple alpine route without a head torch, yet here I was on the world's highest mountain, touching the edge of space, operating in the dark. Furious, I tore the mittens off, pulling my rucksack forward to retrieve a replacement torch. As I scrabbled around with no light, I hated my predicament. We'd gone through all our kit items in fine detail, ironing out any potential problems. And now this. I knew my anger was wasting valuable energy but why my head torch, and why today of all days?

Rob came on the radio later. 'Rob to Russell. Do you copy?'

'Yes, go ahead, Rob.'

'I'm at the top of the exit cracks, starting along the ridge.'

He'd made it. The first hurdle was behind him, and I'd soon be there as well. It must have been about half past three, but we still had the First, Second and Third Steps to scale and were many hours from the summit.

Just then my second head torch died. 'Crap!' I frantically grabbed my radio. 'Rob, Rob, this is Jo. Wait for me,' I gasped. 'I need a torch.' No sooner did I get Rob's spare torch than it failed as well. *This is unbelievable!* I was desperate. Even Rob couldn't help now – we only had four torches between us. Seeing my exasperation, Nawang shared his torch with me and we took turns to see properly. There was nothing that could be done, but I couldn't afford anything else to go wrong. My repeated fiddling in thin gloves had left my fingers frozen and stiff. I beat them on my thighs but they ricocheted off my legs like clumsy chunks of meat. If I was going to climb the three rock steps, somehow I had to get them warm enough to function.

Lumbering along, I could see the fragile snowy crest beneath my feet. A grey light was now just discernible but it wasn't daylight. I couldn't see far, but my eyes were beginning to pick out shapes – patches of white snow set against dark rocks. It was moonlight. *Why am I only seeing the moonlight now? Has it been hidden behind the north-east ridge?* I didn't care, it was my saviour.

The eerie, unworldly light cast strange patterns and shadows on the landscape. Slowly I realised just what I was seeing. The crest of snow I now traversed was suspended like a high wire between two unimaginable voids. To my right was the north face, to my left a terrifying wall of cascading snow and ice, plummeting into the shadowy abyss below. It was the mighty Kangshung face, heart-stoppingly sheer and frightening. The shapes formed along its top edge had been sculpted by the wind, designs of intricate beauty that could evaporate instantly, blasted into the atmosphere by the jetstream or a storm.

Teetering just two feet from the black emptiness, Rob and I took short, nervous steps over gaping, fragile holes. With no torch, my only indication of their presence were the moonbeams reflecting back off the Kangshung face, sending shafts of light upwards through the holes. A wrong foot placement onto a crumbling hole and it would collapse like a house of cards. A deadly one-way ticket to the chasm below.

In the gloom, I could just detect Rob and Pemba's yellow suits ahead of me. They'd stopped by a rocky outcrop about 20 metres ahead. *Is something wrong or is he just waiting for me?* On the high, exposed ridge the light breeze had gathered momentum and become a bone-numbing and vicious foe. It now screamed in from the north-west, blasting up the north face and hitting us on our right side. We had experienced colder winds, but never so high. Our defenceless bodies had been raped of their ability to combat heat loss. The wind cut like a knife, piercing my down suit, down jacket and thermal layers right through to my sternum. My straining lungs felt stiff with cold. I pulled my hood forward to act as a shield, but my hood was not enough. A tiny triangle of exposed skin between my goggles, balaclava and oxygen mask felt detached. I knew my face was beginning to freeze.

As I joined Rob, I realised his eyelashes were freezing together. But something else troubled him more. He signalled to the top of his head.

'What's wrong?' I asked.

'My head is burning.' Freezing air was tunnelling beneath his down hood, burrowing through his Gore-tex hat and thick balaclava. Though we didn't realise it, he was getting frostnip on his scalp. I tightened his hood Velcro as best I could with my mitts on. I couldn't afford to remove them now. As Rob moved on again, I was relieved to see he had clipped several lines. As always, our instinctive reactions had been the same; neither of us wanted to take chances with the fragile ropes.

Picking our way along the north-east ridge, I traversed between a high rock wall and the sheer north face until I was cornered. Looking up, I glimpsed Rob's and Pemba's lights briefly before they disappeared. This had to be the First Step. Hidden from the moonlight, I was faced with a seemingly impenetrable black wall. I turned to Nawang, who was right behind me. 'I need light,' I said.

Without a word Nawang shuffled up behind me, angling his torch upwards. The ropes ran up into a truncated snowy couloir and vanished over a high rock ledge. Sliding my ascender as high as I could, I hauled my limp body up an inch at a time. Suddenly Nawang's faint pool of illumination had gone, I was in darkness. My numb mind and body stalled. The words 'Nawang, I need light,' slowly formed in my head, but to speak them aloud was one demand too much. I continued to hang. I hoped he'd come soon.

Sometime later, as I reached the brow of the rock step, the first ember of hope burned deep inside me. Progress was being made. The interminable night had finally loosened its grip and a sliver of light was seeping towards us from the eastern horizon. Leaving the ridge crest we started to traverse high across the north face. With each passing anchor the ropes snaked ever higher and loose metal stakes rattled in the rock cracks, seemingly held in place by no more than a snarled ball of ragged cord. It appeared that even the gentlest of horizontal pulls could tweak the stake right out. I had to hold my nerve and my footing. Large tilted slabs now lay ahead, poised to lever off all who dared tread on them. Selecting every step with all the care I could muster, I teetered across.

Suddenly my concentration was broken. Ahead of me and emerging from the twilight was something fluorescent and green. As I drew near, I realised what it was – Green Boots, the dead climber Russell had tried to prepare us for. He lay right where we had to pass. Frozen in his coffin of ice and snow, he was tucked in a foetal position, his luminous green boots protruding from under a rocky overhang. This desolate place had witnessed his last moments. I wondered if he had crawled under here to escape the torment of the wind. As I passed I was glad not to see his face, but death stared out at me and shocked but inquisitive, I stared back.

With every minute the hint of light broadened to infuse the dawn sky. Many kilometres below, a silvery fleece blanketed the land and shadowy giants jutted through like mammoth icebergs. Below those clouds lay another world – a world of people and communities, animals and vegetation, a world of life.

We joined Rob and Pemba beside a strange rock bollard which had acquired the name Mushroom Rock. It was here that we'd planned to rest, change oxygen bottles and savour a few moments of sunrise. But now we were here it was far too cold and windy to stop. In our obsession not to be turned around, we'd pushed ourselves unrelentingly and now, absurdly, we were too early. Pressing on across the awkward and broken rock ledges of the north face, we traversed towards the Second Step. My radio clicked on. It was Russell.

'Rob and Jo, you need to slow down. You're going to miss the summit if you're too early. The winds are still too strong high up.' Bizarre as his words were, we had to take heed. If we carried on even at this agonising pace, we might have to turn around. But desperate as we were for a rest, it was too dangerous to stop here and now. We would have to rest if and when we reached the top of the Second Step.

The sky was constantly changing, brushed with colours from deep blue to grey, lilac and pink. The icy wind raced through my bones. Doubts began to quench my hopes. This was far, far too cold, far too windy, far too difficult. If it stayed like this I doubted we could reach the summit and even if we did, the moment of a lifetime would be reduced to a few snatched seconds on the roof of the world. All this time, all this planning and effort, now quite possibly beyond reach, gone in a matter of seconds. Disappointment flooded through me. But we hadn't been told to turn around. Not yet.

Looking up I was horrified. I was staring at what had to be the infamous Second Step. Obliterating the sky, its dark brooding mass towered above us like the bow of a gigantic ocean liner. This was no ordinary rock outcrop to be circumnavigated as we climbed the ridge. It was the ridge. My heart sank. If I'd had the energy to do anything except put one foot in front of the other I would have shouted to Rob; surely he must also be surprised at the sheer scale of this rock face.

Nawang tugged at my rucksack. 'Oxygen, Didi.' I'd forgotten Russell had told us we could use four litres per minute for this section. We stopped and Nawang turned my regulator up. Summoning the energy to speak I forced a few words out. 'You want more oxygen?'

He shook his head and waved me on. *Has he done his own? Is he going to climb the Second Step on just two litres?* I wanted to care, to make sure he was OK, but executing my thoughts was impossible. He was still moving, he had to be fine. Sherpas are strong.

I craned my head to examine the cliff, searching out the route we would climb. My thoughts were coming slowly now. The words 'Second Step' sound quite harmless – almost innocuous – but perched high on Everest's north-east ridge this cliff was far more intimidating than we'd ever imagined. Rob had forged up and to the right and it was now my turn. I already felt too exhausted to hold my own weight. Yet a ten-foot rock step reared vertically just inches from my mask and this was only the start. I had to do it.

Stepping up onto a sloping rock platform, I tried to steady my balance. The metal points of my crampons clattered and screeched awkwardly across the rock. My next move up forced me backwards till I was leaning away from the rock face, my legs no longer under me. Gravity was dragging me precisely where I didn't want to go – back towards the north face. Tightening my ascender I reached for a good handhold, a contradiction in terms with gloves and mittens. As I looked down to check my next foot placement, it all went horribly wrong. My mask pushed across my eyes, the goggles splaying high on my forehead. I couldn't see and I couldn't breathe. My feet were teetering, waiting for instructions from central control. My fingers weren't gripping, inexorably coming off the rock one by one, as if some invisible force was prizing them away. My legs began to shake, vibrating with fatigue. I knew this was my muscles' last effort, that I had to move before they failed. Panic swept through me. If I didn't go now I'd fall.

Summoning every ounce of energy and power I clawed upwards, agonisingly slowly. Sliding my ascender along the rope for more support I pushed away from the rock, far enough to look down at my feet. I had to choose between oxygen and vision. Yanking the mask away, I simply had to see where to place my feet.

Up two feet, then another. I'd made it, I was climbing the Second Step. Suddenly my rucksack was jerked back. *What's happening, who's pulling me?* Of course there was no-one there, I'd climbed too close into a cleft of rock and it had snagged. I had to lower myself down till I cleared it. Gasping, I wrestled the mask back into position and breathed deeply. I yanked on the rope, hauling myself up a series of rock ledges. It felt wrong to have all my weight on these ropes, but I had no choice. I prayed I'd selected the right one. Just two days ago our Sherpas had cut a dead climber down who was hanging from these very ropes. Swinging left I moved onto a shelving snow ramp, an oasis in the middle of the forbidding sheer wall. Glancing to my right, the north face peeled away, the sheer enormity of the drop making me dizzy. My stomach was clenched tight as a fist. Bracing myself forwards on the snow, I could feel my heart beating in my throat. Giddy from effort and too little oxygen my mind raced out of control. *If I black out now I'll . . . don't even think about it. Calm down, control yourself. Just breathe.*

I turned and looked up to see Rob disappearing. He'd climbed the six-metre vertical section on the ladder and had vanished from sight. I hoped he was safe at the top. As I took my first step onto the ladder it suddenly jolted down and left me almost choking on my racing heart. I knew our Sherpas had put this ladder up just two days ago, alongside the rusting Chinese ladder. I told myself I could trust them, their rope work was good. Slowly, I began to climb, but halfway up the ladder was flush with the rock and I was unable to hook my metal spikes over the rungs. I tried again, and a third time but they refused. With no good footing and a weak mittened grip, my only security was my ascender. *Have I clipped the right rope?* Shaking with exhaustion and fear, I slid my ascender high. Its metal teeth bit into the thin nylon cord. I dragged every molecule of oxygen from my mask but it was still not enough for my crippled body.

At the top of the ladder, an awkward step across to a rock ledge was all that now lay between Rob and me. But this was no ordinary step. As I strained sideways reaching to the ledge, 3,000 metres of thin air was all that hung beneath me. My mind was too traumatised to acknowledge what it saw. All I could do was keep moving.

Minutes later, as if in a drugged trance, I stared ahead at Rob. I didn't dare believe what we'd done. The crux of the north-east ridge was now beneath us. The wind still buffeted my weary body, but we had crossed a threshold. Surely nothing could stop us now, yet we still had over 200 vertical metres to go. The summit was hours away. Falling prey to summit fever, even here, could spell disaster.

Just days before a Bulgarian climber had sat, drained and exhausted, right here at the top of the Second Step. With that one innocent mistake of sitting alone for a rest, he had forfeited his life. He had never moved again and was now sitting right in front of me. Slumped over on a rock, he was still attached to the ropes, his blood frozen in his veins. One of his mittens moved casually in the breeze. With a mixture of fascination and horror, Rob and I moved slowly past. Nothing seemed quite real. I felt I was in a dream, my senses were numb. As if floating above it all, I observed myself, my fear and the mountain.

From the angle of the sun I guessed it was around six in the morning. Rob, Pemba and Nawang were now crouching on a snowy platform. Unclipping from the rope, I joined them just 15 metres from the dead Bulgarian and carefully dug my crampons in. It was here we had to switch bottles and turn our regulators back down to two litres.

Looking around for the first time I noticed the darkness had leached away and the sky was incandescent with the dawn sun, exploding its rays over the horizon, brushing the peaks with orange and pink. Looking west I was dumbstruck as Everest's colossal pyramid cast a vast, immeasurable shadow. Spanning the Himalaya of Tibet and Nepal, it stretched far beyond the horizon into the lightening dawn sky.

Gathering ourselves together, we pressed on. With my heavy eyelids I felt drugged. *If only I could lie down. Some more rest, not for long. NO! Don't be crazy. Stay with it, Jo.* Everywhere I looked was seductively beautiful. Even the terrain was now deceptively easy, a gentle snow ridge running to the Third Step. But this was no time to miss my footing.

At the bottom of the Third Step, I pinned myself into a cleft. Resting my head on the rock, I shielded my face as violent gusts whipped up vortices of snow and hurled them over the Kangshung edge. I tried to convince myself the winds were diminishing but angry snow plumes still screamed from the summit pinnacle. With Rob right behind, we started our laboured scramble up the Third Step. At this height, nothing surrendered without a fight.

Finishing the final step, we had less than 100 vertical metres to go. The ridge narrowed, its corniced edge rolled over the Kangshung face like the crest of a mighty wave. To my left a three-kilometre wall of ice and to my right a three-kilometre wall of rock. I was only capable of following one instruction: left, breathe, breathe, breathe, breathe, right, breathe, breathe, breathe, breathe – the repetition oddly soothing. Each second broke another barrier of exhaustion and pain. Despite my doubts and fears I was inexorably moving up.

Starting up the summit pyramid I kicked one debilitating step after another into knee-deep powder. Great slabs of snow were dislodged with each step, gathering momentum and size as they plummeted down. As we climbed the snowy waterfall, we passed yet another dead climber ensnared in Everest's trap. Inches from where I trod the body lay face down, encased in ice, hard as iron. Days or years old, I could not tell.

We reached the high traverse. This was where, through the telescope, we'd watched other climbers and their almost imperceptible progress. Only now that we were under the spell of the death zone could we fully appreciate why they had seemed so motionless, as if frozen in time. Even here, so near our ambition, every step was a monumental act of will. As I reached the next anchor, I stared distractedly at it – a twisted metal spike erupting with one shredded rope after another. I felt totally disengaged. I clipped my ascender in and moved on. With my left hand against the rock I teetered along the six-inch ledge, ignoring the sheer north face that hung below my feet.

Escaping the airy traverse we climbed into a gully, the last bastion of rock that crowned the summit pyramid. Emerging out of the gully, we arrived on Everest's final ridge, with just 50 vertical metres to go.

Rob came up behind me and we stood side by side. Ahead of us lay the gleaming icy pinnacle of the summit. Swallowing hard, my eyes were watery but I checked myself, this was no time for tears, they would freeze anyway. I had to maintain control. But we both knew that no-one has control up here. We weren't about to conquer this mountain. At best we might be granted safe passage.

Setting out up the final summit ridge, we were on the cusp of moving from dream to reality. I had long since gone beyond what I thought possible. Progress was now agonisingly slow. Mentally I chanted my mantra, *just one more step, just one more step*. Every laboured step was accompanied by weak, frenzied breathing as my lungs raced simply to fuel the next. Staring out from behind my goggles I realised the winds had abated, leaving no more than a light breeze flowing along the summit ridge. As the fluttering summit prayer flags came into focus, the mirage of Everest was finally beginning to dissolve.

I waited for Rob and, linking arms, we took our final steps together onto the rooftop of the world. It was 8.15 am on 24 May 2004; there was nowhere higher on the planet that we could go, the world lay at our feet. Holding each other tightly, we tried to absorb where we were. To be standing here, together, exactly three years since Rob's cancer treatment, was nothing short of a miracle. Standing on top of Everest was more than just climbing a mountain – it was a gift of life. With Pemba and Nawang we crowded together, wrapping our arms around each other. They had been more than Sherpas, they had been our guardian angels.

Standing beside each other, we feasted our eyes. Above us the cerulean sky deepened to an inky black as the remnants of the atmosphere gave way to the depths of space. The mighty Himalaya were now a sparkling relief map spread out before us and garnished with a gleaming lattice work of swirling glaciers. Even Cho Oyu, Lhotse and Makalu, all 8,000-metre giants, were dwarfed. To the east and west, Kanchenjunga and Shishapangma, two more great sentinels of the Himalaya, stood crystal clear over 100 kilometres away. To the north were the burnished plains of Tibet, and to the south the majestic peaks and lush foothills of Nepal. We stood on the crown jewel of the earth, the curved horizon spinning endlessly around us.

With the ground dropping steeply, we manoeuvred carefully on the small summit pinnacle clipping ourselves into a snow stake to sit and rest our legs. We left our oxygen masks and goggles on, as we'd agreed at high camp. To starve our already struggling brains or risk iced-up goggles for the sake of a few recognisable photos would not be wise. We knew death due to snow blindness on the descent was a very real danger.

Digging around inside my rucksack I found my pink Frisbee, along with our flags, a Cancer Research UK poster and a thank-you sign we'd made for Russell. After releasing my Frisbee to sail on the winds from Tibet into Nepal, we took our photos and huddled together to savour our last moments on the roof of the world.

In a state of dreamy disbelief I pressed my masked face into Rob's.

'Can you believe we're really here?' he said, clasping my face in his mittened hand. I beamed incredulously inside my mask and shook my head. To share these moments was an unforgettable and sublime blessing. Even in my altitude-induced stupor, my heart leapt for joy to see the beauty and design of our planet – as if confirming we are not alone, not here by chance. It was utterly breathtaking.

We tried to rest and savour the delights of Chomolungma but this was no place to relax. What preyed on our exhausted minds now were the ghosts of this mountain, the shadows of those climbers who had never returned. The treacherous descent was beckoning. Our lives were still in the balance. After 20 minutes, it was time to go.

I tugged Rob's harness. 'Rob, checks.' We inspected each other's harnesses and ascenders. As we left the summit, I wondered what lay in store. We knew we needed to save at least 25% of our energy for the descent, yet I'd already gone far beyond anything I'd ever known. I had no idea if I was already running on empty.

We passed Andy, his head hung low, just 50 metres from the summit and encouraged him he was nearly there. Starting down I could see growing clouds billowing far below. Innocent as they looked, any change in the weather couldn't be ignored. In 1996, clouds had been the early warning signs, heralding one of the most ferocious and fatal storms ever to strike Everest.

By the time we reached the top of the Second Step, I felt like a stunned animal. My muscles constantly twitched with fatigue. I felt unable to do anything more than survive. Rob had long since vanished over the edge but I'd seen he was moving well and knew he was 'in the zone'. Nawang shook his arm at me but I didn't understand why.

'No, Didi,' he kept saying. Why would he not want me to put my descender device on?

'But I have to,' I pleaded with him for the third time, knowing I was too weak to lower myself on my arms alone. Nawang was becoming impatient and our communications were still misfiring.

'Didi, quick, Didi.' He tugged at my harness. In a confused panic, I took a massive leap of faith. I decided to trust Nawang, even though it made no sense. My whole body quivered with fear as I stepped over the gaping void from the rock ledge towards the ladder. The abyss of the north face was the only thing beneath me. I was terrified. All I could think about was the Japanese woman who just days earlier had caught her crampon in the tangled lines. She had fallen, broken her neck and been left hanging in these very ropes. Although I had no idea at the time, Nawang had been right. Had I simply abseiled down, I would have swung away from the ladder and been left stranded, hanging over the north face.

At the bottom of the Second Step, I tried to regroup my shaking legs for the downward-sloping slabs that lay ahead. Everything within me wanted to lie down, yet a primal instinct to survive was driving me on. I stared blankly below as the tips of my boots came in and out of my vision. The loose unstable rocks tried to tip me off with every step. I stopped in front of a big steep slab that blocked my way. *How did I get up it this morning?*

I placed my crampon on the slab, but the metal spikes were as useless as kitchen knives on paving stones. Screeching off, my reactions were too slow and I fell. With nothing to hold onto, there was just the Rongbuk Glacier waiting to catch me three kilometres below. One thought filled my mind – the frayed ropes, the loose metal stakes. Then, as suddenly as I'd fallen, I stopped, all the wind punched out of me. A second later the ropes jerked down. I dropped another foot. Hanging a few metres from where I'd slipped, I had to get my weight off the ropes, I needed help. *Where is Nawang?* I strained my head to look behind. 'Nawang, why aren't you here?' I whimpered. *Rob, where is Rob?* I swung around and let out a gasp. He was almost out of sight. I was on my own and no-one was coming. I scanned to find the anchors, they were out of sight too. I had to get my weight off the lines. I clawed my way back to the traverse, my heart and lungs ready to explode. Shaking from the effort, my limp arms now hung uselessly by my side. That had been too close for comfort. I had to be more careful, much more careful.

It was just gone midday when we stumbled back into camp four. I had no idea how I'd got there. Whole sections of our descent were a complete blank in my mind. We collapsed into our tent in a dazed exhaustion. I started to talk into the radio but nothing came out. I was agonisingly thirsty. When I pulled my bottle out from inside my suit it was still frozen, but I managed to knock some ice fragments out and passed it to Rob.

'Russ, this is Rob. Jo and I are at camp four.' Rob's voice was faint and husky.

'Well done, you two. Get as low as you can. Try and get to camp two.'

'Will do,' Rob said and clicked off.

Time floated by as we lay in paralysed fatigue. I began to drift off into a pleasant sleep. It felt nice. *A little sleep won't hurt.* But some tiny part of my brain was not fooled. It had spotted the traitor long ago and was already issuing commands. 'Got to go, Rob, got to go,' my barely audible voice wavered. Fear was still running through my veins and it was my fear that would keep me alive. We were well inside the death zone and it still had us by the scruff of the neck. We had to get out. As if rising from the dead, our bodies moved robotically as we packed our remaining gear.

Sometime later Pemba, Nawang, Rob and I lay strewn across the rocks at camp three. No words were spoken, but we all exchanged satisfied and weary smiles. Stirring into action, we looked for our stashed gear. It was nowhere to be seen. Several tents had gone, others were shredded and flapping in the breeze. We concluded our gear must have been blown away with them. Descending towards camp two, my thirst continued to rage. Over the next few hours my brain seesawed between thoughts of Coca-Cola and the radio news of imminently worsening weather.

Reaching camp two, we stopped again, both desperate to get inside a tent and lie down. 'Do you want to keep going, Jo? We can stop here,' Rob asked, but I could tell he wanted to carry on and I did too, as long as our legs would carry us.

With our camp two gear packed, we descended into thick cloud and heavy snow. It seemed there was as much fog inside my head as out. For the entire hour I thought I saw people beside me but it was just a mark on my goggles, confusing my peripheral vision. I felt as if I'd been drugged with sleeping pills and then weakened with flu.

With a deep sense of relief we stumbled into camp one just before six o'clock. Before Rob or I even spoke we had both independently made a decision. Now we'd made it to camp one, we wanted to get all the way back to ABC. The weather was worsening and my obsessive desire for a can of Coke was undiminished. I knew there was a small stash of them at ABC reserved for special events.

I radioed Russell. 'Russ, this is Jo. We're coming all the way to ABC. Leaving North Col now.'

'OK, Jo. I'll send Sherpas to meet you at the bottom of the headwall with tea.' My mind momentarily drifted away at the sound of the word 'tea'. I tried to imagine what the warm wet liquid would feel like on my swollen tongue and parched throat. What a fitting end to a day in the hills – a cup of tea!

'Ready, Jo?' Rob called, jolting me back to reality. I stared down the now darkening headwall from the North Col. It would require one final, mammoth push for us to beat sundown.

Forty-five minutes later, we should have been off the fixed lines but we were still only halfway down and daylight was fading fast. Rob sat motionless in the snow. My parched throat had left me almost unable to speak and even the effort of talking sucked too much air from my exhausted lungs. Sounding like a record being played at the wrong speed, I spelt out my words one laboured syllable at a time.

'Rob . . . I . . . have . . . only . . . the . . . energy . . . to . . . say . . . this . . . once . . . please . . . please . . . listen . . .' I paused to gather the energy to finish. 'You . . . must . . . get . . . on . . . your . . . feet.' That was it. I didn't have the strength to utter one more word. I rocked from side to side, no longer able to steady myself as my loaded sack swayed high above my head. I studied Rob intently, willing him to make a move. My will was the only weapon I had left in my armoury and it was all Rob had left too. As I waited for him to stir, I tried to lick my cracked and bleeding lips but my tongue, swollen and furry, stuck to the inside of my mouth. Leaning into the slope I chipped more snow away with my axe and fed it in past my desiccated lips. Moments later I was relieved to see Rob moving. He looked like a zombie but that didn't matter. He was on his feet.

It was 8 pm when we finally unclipped from the headwall ropes and the last trace of light vanished from the sky. As we started our walk off the glacier the snow under our feet glowed a dim grey in the dark, just enough to find our way.

'Keep going, Rob, we're nearly there,' I said, talking as much to myself as to him. As we stumbled like two battle-weary soldiers a wonderful sight began to emerge from the gloom. True to his word, Russell had sent two Sherpas to greet us. We stopped for what I had imagined would be the most divine cup of tea but my weary stomach couldn't cope. All I managed was a few sips.

As we left the glacier and returned to the rocky moraine, I finally knew we were safe and Rob would be fine. Drunk with tiredness, I repeatedly lurched forwards onto the rocks, like a blind man looking for a chair. My fingers rubbed over the cold rock and my body sank to the ground. A voice chided me inside my head. *Keep going. Don't sit. Focus.* I pulled myself upright. My eyes continually drifted shut until I stumbled and collapsed onto my hands again. The voice pestered me. *Get up. Keep going. Nearly there.*

It was 9 pm when I finally entered camp. It was eerily quiet and dark, save one small light in the cook tent. With barely enough strength to push the canvas door open I staggered inside, squinting at the bright light.

'Welcome, Didi. Hot lemon?' It was a beaming and very excited Chakra.

'Coke, please,' I said, mustering my best smile, and slumped onto the bench. Fifteen minutes later Rob arrived, so shattered he didn't even recognise Russell, who was now sitting beside me. After five long days we were home and we were safe. The hard labour was done and the battle was over. Everest had briefly smiled on us and allowed us to tread in her throne room.

As I walked towards my tent, Chakra's voice came out of the blackness behind me. 'Help, Didi?' I pointed him towards Rob's tent. I knew he wouldn't manage his boots. Seconds later I fell prostrate into my tent and didn't move again.

An icy breeze wafted over me. I came around. *Where am I? Have I fallen asleep on the summit ridge and now it's dark?* My heart raced. *I'm going to die if I stay here. I've got to move.* Slowly I began to wake. Sliding my arm out I didn't understand what I was feeling.

But the ground is soft. Where am I? I could feel a foam mat, a ground sheet, a sleeping bag . . . and then I remembered. I was in a tent and safely back at ABC. Heaving a sigh of relief, I remained motionless, but as time passed I began to shiver. *Got to move. Got to take boots off. Got to get inside.* Hauling myself upright I removed my boots and with a final burst of effort I slid into my sleeping bag and I was gone.

I woke to the warm red glow of sunshine pouring through my tent walls. Looking at my watch, I was stunned. *This is ridiculous. It can't be 6 am!* After days without sleep, how could I possibly be awake so soon? Not only was I awake, but confusingly I was also bursting with energy. I was always excited after summiting, but this seemed deranged. Feeling my veins pumping with a rush of adrenalin, there was only thing I could do – get busy. In a frenzy of tent cleaning, packing and diary writing, I restrained myself from erupting into Rob's tent for celebratory cuddles. He would definitely be comatose and not want to be disturbed.

Stepping outside to enjoy the early morning sunshine, camp was deathly quiet. Even those who'd summited the day before us were fast asleep. It was only now, trying to stand up, that I realised the impact of the last few days. It seemed my stressed, hypoxic brain had protected itself from pain signals. Now every ligament, muscle and joint was painfully making itself known.

As I stood beside my tent, the crisp, dawn air had a strange tinge to it . . . of excrement. Suddenly I felt flushed with a terrible thought. *Is it me?* Checks were done. The smells coming from inside my down suit after five days' continuous wear were not pleasant, but with great relief I discovered it wasn't me. Further hunting revealed it was our little sack of poo outside, still strapped to my rucksack. Untying it, I tripped and swayed my way to the toilet barrel to deposit our wares. I felt a deep sense of satisfaction, not only had we succeeded in summiting but we had respected the mountain.

After three hours of restraint, I weakened and found myself stealthily unzipping Rob's tent.

'I'm awake, Bella,' he said in a deep gravelly voice.

'Sorry, I couldn't wait any longer. I just wanted to see you,' I said.

'Come here my precious angel, let me hug you,' Rob answered, stretching his arms out with a big sleepy smile. I shuffled closer and lay across his chest. 'Ow, that's too sore. Perhaps just lie beside me.' We didn't say another word, it was wonderful just to be. No fears, not a care in the world.

Later that morning, Jamie padded over to us as we packed our barrels. 'Hey guys, congratulations.'

'You too, Jamie,' I said smiling at him.

'I heard you two got all the way back to ABC last night. That's incredible. Do you realise you're the only ones to have done that on either team? Only the Sherpas managed to get that far.'

'Yeah well, there would have been hell to pay if we didn't. Jo was going nutty for a can of Coke,' Rob laughed.

Derek joined in. 'Big effort, you two. Awesome job to get back to ABC last night.' Having so often been the ones at the back, it felt strange to have everyone complimenting us on our summit-day performance. Our game plan of rigorously pacing ourselves had finally paid off. I thanked Derek but quickly tried to change the subject as I could see Ian hobbling into camp. Things hadn't gone so well for him yesterday, nor had they for Paul. Instead of being dizzy with celebration, the mood around camp was subdued. There were also those wrestling with their deep disappointment at having to turn around. Gabi and Joseph had spent the last few days coming to terms with failing to make the summit, but for Ian and Paul, it was still painfully fresh.

It turned out that when Dorje had got back to Ian on our summit morning, he was not only alone and outside but his regulator wasn't fully opened. With his oxygen system sorted he set off, albeit behind his tent mate and team. But just half an hour without oxygen had left him with frostbitten hands and feet and by the time he'd reached Mushroom Rock, he had lost his peripheral vision too. To have got so far was a testament to his tenacity, but his failing eyesight and uncharacteristic behaviour indicated he was probably experiencing the early stages of cerebral oedema. Had Dorje not returned to help, his condition might have deteriorated fast. As it was, in agreement with Russell, he'd turned around before the Second Step, a move that probably saved his life. People who have lost their sight high on Everest's summit ridge have rarely lived to see again. Ian had been lucky. Similarly, Paul, despite a heroic effort to climb the exit cracks, was unable to go any further and turned back at the bottom of the First

Step. But no matter what the disappointment, no-one could ever be criticised for leaving the Himalaya alive.

*

The next day Rob and I left to walk to base camp together. Prancing from one rock to another, we struck silly poses as we danced our way down the moraines. Stopping for a final rest to savour the moment, I stared dreamily towards Everest's distant summit. 'Can you believe that just three years ago, you struggled to even climb the stairs?' I mused.

No-one could have prepared us for the experience of Everest, for the pain intermingled with joy. Venturing so near to the thin veneer that separates life from death, I felt more alive than ever before. Standing on the roof of the world had been like tasting forbidden fruit. Yet, even now, it felt like a dream. Only the glow of contentment deep inside told me it had been real.

I reflected on all that had happened in the last few years, the adventures we'd had with each other, with friends and with God – it was too much to absorb. The words we had been given from Psalm 121 before we first set out had become a source of continual reassurance, through both the good times and the bad: *'The Lord will watch over your coming and going both now and forever more'*. And even though I had wrestled with these words 18 months ago in Nepal, through all that had happened, God had never wavered.

With every passing hour of our descent, the air became sweet and tangibly thicker. We felt our bodies flood with energy and there was a spring in our step that we hadn't had for weeks. After just one day of relaxing and packing at base camp, amnesia was striking us all. This is the mystery of high altitude – as soon as you descend, all recollection of how bad you felt seems to vanish.

Though Everest is a graveyard, littered with bodies, there was no post mortem to be done. We were no longer lured into the trap of moralising and philosophising about events in the death zone. How can anyone be held accountable for their actions when they are severely hypoxic, exhausted, dehydrated, and sleep deprived? People are human. Even at the best of times, with a plentiful supply of oxygen, we make mistakes. How much harder is it when every system in our bodies is shutting down and our brain is hell bent on just one thing – survival. From the comforts of our chairs at base camp, we no longer tried to find simple answers to complex events. We no longer asked 'why can't those bodies be brought down?' We now understood.

No-one can ever be fully in control in the death zone. But how much control do we have in life anyway? We can neither choose to live, nor die and life itself is beyond our understanding. Yet amidst this mystery, we have been given the greatest gift of all – the blank canvas of our lives on which to paint as we choose.

*

Days later, as we neared the end of the Rongbuk valley in our jeeps, we said our farewells to Chomolungma for the last time. Rob read my mind.

'We'll have to come back one day, Jo,' he said. I smiled and nodded.

'Yes, I'd like to. I'd like that very much.' In our hearts we both felt a twinge of sadness as we left the mountains behind. We were saying goodbye to so much more. I prayed that the trappings and complexities of the life that awaited us far below would never extinguish our precious summit memories.

Several days afterwards, after a nail-biting ride down the Bhote Kosi Gorge, and seeing our Sherpas held at gunpoint and beaten by a power-crazy military officer, we finally arrived safe in Kathmandu. At only 1,300 metres, we felt supercharged from the effects of our extra red blood cells and took delight in dashing up four flights of stairs to our hotel room without so much as a single deep breath.

As we relaxed, sipping G&Ts in the warm, humid garden of Hotel Tibet, I turned to Rob.

'So what's next, Honey?' I asked with a questioning smile

'What do you say we finish the Seven Summits?' Rob replied, his left eyebrow cocked. Having climbed Everest our confidence had soared and for the first time we dared to believe that the Seven Summits was within our grasp. Elbrus, the highest mountain in Europe and the last of our Seven Summits, would be a fitting finish to our year of high adventure.

CHAPTER 19

Dare to Believe

'One of the best things to hold onto in life is each other.'
Audrey Hepburn

IN THEORY, EVEREST had been the ideal slimmer's vacation. We'd lost 14 kilos between us, though whether protruding ribs and pelvic bones are really attractive is debatable. More than that though, Everest had been the ultimate extreme make over. We might not have removed wrinkles, plumped lips, buffoned hair, fixed up wardrobes or even our house. In fact, I had more wrinkles plus blistered lips, matted hair and smelly clothes but this had been a make over with a difference, a detox of our souls.

Six weeks after Everest we'd eaten for Queen and country to regain weight, finalised our arrangements for Elbrus and progressed our fund raising for Cancer Research UK and the Tibetan school. Though our bodies still thought they were entitled to rest, our minds had ratcheted up a gear.

'You'll be careful in Russia, won't you?' Mum said, as she poured another cup of tea for us. This time our parents were as concerned about the region we were going to as they were about the actual climbing. We were heading out to the Caucasus mountains, which lie between the Black and Caspian seas, forming the border between Russia and Georgia as well as Europe and Asia. In the Caucasus, we would be less than 100 kilometres from the civil unrest in Chechnya. Local contacts had satisfied us that the risk was low, although that was before we'd factored in Russian public transport.

On 9 July we landed in St Petersburg, the Venice of Russia. Luis was leading the climb, and in just jeans and a tee-shirt he was barely recognisable since our last rendezvous in a wild Antarctic storm. Our team had a strong Antipodean flavour this time and included Cheryl and Nikki, a dynamic mother-and-daughter team who boosted the female contingent to an unusually high 25%. Chris, who was another Aussie, had previously been to 7,000 metres, and John, a Californian, had recently climbed Everest. For the rest of the team, Elbrus would be a personal altitude best.

Trying to reach the Caucasus in the first place was to prove trickier than anticipated. Even getting into the airport required a $200 bribe to 'allow' our minibus to drop us off. Having boarded the plane, we were a little concerned to find we were taxiing down the runway to a cacophony of ringing mobile phones, and once airborne we preferred to ignore a catalogue of glaring safety issues. But we were to be luckier than some. Several weeks later a plane just like ours crashed, killing everyone on board.

We were relieved to land in one piece at Mineral Vody Airport and start our drive to the small mountain village of Terskol. Thankfully, the service in our Terskol hotel was an improvement on that of the mean and surly flight attendants, even though the women at reception were preoccupied with surfing the internet for a husband. Seeing this, I decided it would be prudent to keep tabs on Rob. Having my husband snatched would be an exceptionally poor outcome for a climbing trip.

Though we were living in relative comfort compared with previous trips, after several days of acclimatisation hikes the novelty of returning to our hotel at night began to wear thin. We concluded that one possible reason for the vast national consumption of vodka was to swill down the traditional culinary delicacy of boiled cabbage with gherkins. Thankfully our local Russian guide, Eugene, came to the rescue and introduced us to shashlyk kebabs, an instant hit with the team. Eugene was a highly intelligent doctor but unable to make ends meet on his $75 a week medic's wage, so he sensibly made his living from dollar-paying Westerners like us.

Our acclimatisation hikes were the antithesis of those we had so recently done on Everest. The Caucasus was a scaled-up but deserted version of the west European Alps, with cool pine forests and picturesque alpine meadows, brimming with flowers. Admittedly, the theoretical risk of being shot at by a Chechyn rebel was a little off-putting and probably kept numbers down, but in our idyllic surroundings, such misfortune seemed extremely remote.

After acclimatising around the Baskan valley, we relocated

ourselves to the Garabashi Barrels. Stationed on a ridge of lava flow between two glaciers on the southern flanks of Elbrus, these were merely disused oil tanks deposited on the mountain after the Priut mountain hut burnt down in 1998. We planned to live in these rusty tanks while acclimatising and waiting for a summit weather window. After days of balmy conditions, it was hard to imagine the weather being anything other than benign. But the highest mountain in any region is liable to sudden and violent changes of weather and we suspected Elbrus might be no different.

Days later, on another of our climbs, our suspicions were confirmed as we all hid from the ferocious westerly winds behind the Pastukhova rocks, at 4,690 metres. Despite being amidst the impressive Caucasus, the atrocious visibility and driving snow gave us views good enough to compete with any grisly Scottish day. As the days rolled past we had not only lost time but also several team members. After an unrelenting fight with the altitude, they'd wisely decided to try another year.

In spite of the weather, compared to Everest, Elbrus was turning out to be a relaxing climb. Jo and I loved the novelty of how we felt about Elbrus. Its wasn't about feeling invincible or even complacent. It was just incredible to feel that the mountain was perfectly within our grasp. For the first time, we were daring to believe in ourselves.

With more days passing, our visas would soon expire and Elbrus was still in the angry clutches of the elements. After our earlier optimism, we both felt deflated to be facing failure at the last hurdle and we reluctantly started packing to descend. It appeared to be game, set and match to the weather. 'Looks like we'll have to settle for the six summits after all!' Rob said.

On the last night before we returned to the valley to head home, Cheryl and I continued to scamper outside, ever hopeful that the skies might clear. By 2 am I was outside our barrel once again, shivering in my thermals with the freezing wind. I stared up in disbelief. Above me, the clouds were rolling back like a parting sea. The curtain had been opened for the final act and this was our chance for the summit.

It was nearly 5 am by the time we reached the Pastukhova Rocks and the first signs of dawn were breaking across the eastern sky. I treasured the moments of predawn gloom, the sense of anticipation and promise, as if a new world is being born every time. By 10 am we'd passed through the saddle that lay between the two glassy domes of Elbrus' twin peaks. In perfect rhythm Rob and I kicked our feet in, steadily climbing the final western summit ridge. Our crampons and axes bit satisfyingly into the snow and I lost myself in the moment. As we reached the ridge, the vista opened out across an ocean of dazzling cloud. A snowy crest stretched in front of us and our goal was within sight. At 11.30 am on 20 July 2004, we took our last steps together to the summit.

As we soaked up the views, we were suddenly grabbed from behind. 'Congratulations on the Seven Summits, guys! You did it!' Luis shouted as he excitedly lavished us with bear hugs. Caught up in the marvel of the summit moment, we'd momentarily forgotten about the Seven Summits. Thoughts raced through my mind. *Us? The Seven Summits? Surely not?* To be standing on top of Europe was one thing but to have stood on top of every continent on the planet was simply overwhelming. Elbrus was not even the seventh summit, it was our twelfth, and all in just over a year. But even more than that, it was a victory over cancer. We'd been blessed and Rob had been able to fight back. It hadn't terrorised our lives.

Buoyed up with the excitement of the day, instead of an exhausting descent, we just seemed to float down. It had been wonderful to share the last of the Seven Summits with the team; and though our time on top of Elbrus had been fleeting, like so many other mountains, the summit moments would last for ever.

*

Just one week later, we were back in London and meeting with friends. 'Can't be anything left to do,' they said. Though we understood their sentiments, the truth was we'd seen barely a fraction of the incredible world we live in. But from a smoky pub in west London, the view is never as clear.

Over the coming months, we had some unfinished business and found ourselves back in the Himalaya. We were attempting two peaks, Island Peak and Ama Dablam. Island peak, together with Mera Peak, were the two summits we had been attempting to climb on our ill-fated first Himalayan expedition. Ama Dablam was a mountain we had dreamt of for seven years. We had first seen this soaring pinnacle of rock and ice on a tatty poster in a Swiss mountain hut and from that moment on, the seed had been planted.

On 18 October, it was a strange and wonderful moment when we stood at 6,189 metres on the summit of Island Peak. It was two years to the day since Rob had been flown into Heathrow and delivered to hospital for bowel surgery. Life with all its twists and turns had, with uncanny precision, brought us back to exactly where it all started.

Over the following weeks, having acclimatised on Island Peak, we were ready to climb Ama Dablam, a breathtaking spire that soars to nearly 7,000 metres. Known as the jewel and the Matterhorn of the Himalaya, she is the mountain that Edmund Hillary once declared 'unclimbable'. Ama Dablam, like so many mountains, is worthy of her own book and to cram her in, as if some afterthought, would be a grave injustice. Suffice to say, she is perhaps the most beautiful mountain we have ever climbed.

*

By the spring of 2005, it was the beginning of the end of our travels. Since Ama Dablam, we'd climbed in Kenya and South Africa, before raising sponsorship and training for our ski to the North Pole. In early April we landed at the remote Norwegian outpost of Longyearben on the island of Spitzbergen. The town is little more than a single street lined with brightly painted wooden houses. Everything is raised on stilts, including a network of giant heating pipes, to prevent the permafrost melting. Mothers chatted casually while pushing their prams through the snow and a herd of short-legged arctic reindeer wandered through town, seemingly unperturbed by the snowmobiles that buzzed past them.

It was nearly midnight as we wandered to the frozen shoreline of the Advent Fjord to watch one of the last sunsets of the Arctic spring. For a few hours the sun crept below the mountainous horizon leaving a faintly glowing sky. This gift of light is a welcome relief for the locals after the perpetual darkness that reigns from late October to mid February every year.

The next day we met the rest of our team, which was half Norwegian and half British, with Rob as the token Australian. Our Norwegian contingent were all accomplished cross-country skiers, several were ex-military and one a national ski medallist. The rest of us simply had large helpings of enthusiasm and hopefully enough training to get us to the North Pole. Our leader, Borge Ousland, was not only ex-Norwegian SAS and a national hero but arguably the most accomplished polar explorer alive, with an impressive array of firsts on his expedition CV.

Days later, although our final preparations and briefing were otherwise complete, I had been unable to solve my boot problem. The boots I'd ordered had arrived with Borge one size too big. It was a seemingly insignificant problem, but one that I'd later pay for dearly.

We were due to fly to the ice sheet that night but rumours about polar bear sightings had us all racing off on snowmobiles behind a suitably armed local. Our briefing was short and to the point: 'Don't turn your engines off and remember to point your scooter away from the polar bears. They can run at up to 40 kilometres per hour.' To our delight we found the bears. But to my horror, just as we spotted them my snowmobile stalled and refused to restart, at which point I quickly decided wildlife holidays, at least with carnivores, weren't for me.

It was midnight when we touched down on the 800-metre ice runway at the floating Russian Ice Station 'Barneo'. The reverse thrusters of our short-runway Antonov 74 jet screamed as we lurched forwards into our frayed and rusty seatbelts. With no windows, we were blissfully unaware that while countering the strong crosswinds we had landed at 45° to the runway and clipped our right wing tip on the ice. Stopping was not just a nicety; collision with the giant piles of ice rubble just ahead would have been considerably worse than ploughing into a field of parked cars.

Although we'd planned to arrive before the warmer summer temperatures that would break the ice sheet up, none of us had grasped the impact of the extremely high Arctic humidity. The temperature was only −17°C but it had a vicious bite. As we off-loaded our gear from the rear ramp, the pilots kept the engines running. There was a real and present danger that the ice sheet could open up at any moment and the plane would sink. It had happened before.

Waiting to greet us on the runway were three stocky, bearded Russians, buried under fur hats that were big enough to be a whole nesting animal. Judging by their behaviour, the size of their hats was also closely correlated to rank. We were due to fly by helicopter that night to our start point for the last degree at 89° north. After a brief discussion between Borge and the chief of the hat brigade, it transpired that the pilot's vodka consumption had been excessive. The night flight was cancelled.

The next day we loaded our sleds into the Mi18 Russian helicopter. However, I wasn't sure that we were in a better position as far as safety was concerned, given the vodka bottles on the dashboard, the unsecured garden chairs in the cockpit and the wooden school bench in the main hold. As we took off I leant against a small window which popped open and left me hoping their engine maintenance had been a little more rigorous.

The flight to our drop-off point provided spectacular views with the ice beneath us stretching to every horizon like a giant ocean of crazy paving. Colossal pressures within the ice sheet had broken and crushed it together, creating huge pressure ridges of ice rubble. In other places it had been ripped apart leaving menacing black gashes – vast swathes of open water otherwise known as leads.

With a hasty drop off, we shuddered from the freezing temperatures and rotor downwash. Minutes later, we were alone, surrounded by nearly seven million square kilometres of Arctic ice cap, bigger than the entire United States – a strange yet curiously delightful feeling. In contrast to the vast open expanses of Antarctica, we were surprised to feel hemmed in by a ring of rubble ridges beyond which we couldn't see. In the overcast weather it seemed as if we'd just been deposited in an icy graveyard of fallen tombstones.

'OK, let's go. Stick together. I only have one gun,' Borge shouted, giving his harness a final yank. After our recent polar bear encounter, his comments made us nervous, but we calmly waited our turn as everyone pulled away in single file. Being on the home turf of the largest carnivore in the world, the only animal known to actively stalk humans, was somewhat unnerving. Although the polar bear's eyesight is allegedly no better than ours, it can smell ringed seals at up to three kilometres away. We hoped their favourite dish was in good supply.

Apart from the complication of being stalked, life had just become wonderfully simple again – go north – and we resumed our polar plod as if we'd never stopped. The hypnotic rhythm and swishing of our skis was comfortingly familiar. Not long after, however, the team had come to a grinding halt. It was time to negotiate our first pressure ridge. In front of us lay a wall of ice blocks ranging in size from a shoe box to a small truck and we had to get over them to continue. Minutes later, seeing a string of our accomplished Norwegian skier friends lying sprawled across the ice blocks gave me pause for thought. Had we been completely mad? Was this just one expedition too far? Should we have stuck to what we knew – mountains? When my turn came, it felt like climbing a pile of precariously stacked office furniture, while wearing planks and simultaneously hauling, lifting or throwing an obstinate filing cabinet. The penalties for wrong footings were many: twisted knees, ankles and wrists, bashed elbows, heads and shoulders, and the worst fate of all – entering the liquid abyss. Lurking beneath the giant, wedged ice cubes were dark holes, at the bottom of which was the freezing black ocean itself.

Soon afterwards, satisfied to have survived my first pressure ridge intact, I foolishly let my skis run on a small incline at the base of the ridge. In an instant my sled jammed on an ice block, yanked my harness and stopped me dead. My legs flew out from under me and I slammed to the ground, jolting my sled from its position. Seconds later a rushing sound was followed by a dull thump and a yelp – the sound of my sled running me over. I had learned pressure ridge lesson number one: never, ever take your eye off your sled.

For the next big pressure ridge we sensibly decided to remove skis and formed a human chain to pass sleds, skis and poles across. Having nearly completed the ridge unharmed, it was time for pressure ridge lesson number two: never walk in snow drifts near ice rubble. Why? Because there is a strong likelihood you will pop straight through into the Arctic Ocean, as I had just done. Looking deceptively like normal snow, it turned out to have the consistency of quicksand. With its salt content, sea water freezes at −1.8°C, allowing snow to settle on top. I might have fared better on skis but my feet had just punched through as if the ice were no more than a sheet of tissue paper. I reacted with lightning speed, but even so had soggy, slush covered boots which quickly started to freeze. Bashing them frantically to clear the worst, I was grateful for the many layers on my feet. The tightly woven canvas and woollen felt inners of my boots along with my vapour barrier liners and thick woolly socks had proved an excellent barrier to the icy water.

By the end of day one, we'd skied 11 kilometres and had just over 100 kilometres left to the Pole, although detours due to the awkward terrain and drift due to the floating ice sheet would ultimately determine that. As I sat shivering in our freezing tent, picking ice out of my frozen hair, I reflected on how privileged we were to be there. The Arctic ice cap is rapidly shrinking and by 2060 it might have disappeared altogether, leaving skiing to the North Pole nothing more than a historic curiosity. According to scientists, not only are things warming up but perhaps more critically they are speeding up. Who knows what irreversible disruption we will bring to our planet's climate during this century?

Having lain awake listening to the dulcet tones of snoring tent mates until 4 am, by the time my alarm went off at 6.30 I was the only one still fast asleep. Bleary eyed, I shuffled over to get the stove going, driven from my toasty sleeping bag by my overwhelming desire for a cup of tea. Our tent soon resembled a Turkish steam room, albeit a rather chilly one. Two hours later I'd boiled enough water for our porridge and flasks with enough for hot drinks and breakfast all round. The ice we melted for our tea wasn't remotely salty due to a cunning process of separation. As the sea freezes, the salts are excluded from the developing ice crystals and gather in tiny brine pockets which, having a lower freezing point and higher density than the surrounding freshwater ice, migrate back into the sea leaving us the delicious salt-free ice for our cup of tea.

As we crawled outside we were awestruck by what we saw. While we slept, the world we inhabited had been transformed. No longer overcast, for 360° we were enveloped in a dazzling blue light. The frozen graveyard of yesterday was now a kingdom of glittering white sands and sparkling turquoise ice sculptures. Although the clear skies had brought much colder temperatures, they were welcomed, giving us beautiful weather and increasing the likelihood of leads freezing.

Borge emerged from his tent, casually strapping his leather holster in place. He carried a Magnum 45, one of the most powerful handguns and an essential deterrent for hungry polar bears. He nonchalantly announced, 'We drifted two kilometres east overnight. Not so bad.' Easterly drift was indeed 'not so bad'. What we really feared was drifting south. It was possible to drift up to 20 kilometres in one night and if that happened, we might never get to the Pole.

By 9 am, skis on and sleds attached, we set off with our possessions in tow. Rob gave me the nod to go in front. After our experiences enroute to the South Pole, he liked to keep an eye on how I was doing. We couldn't have been happier. We were together, being self-sufficient, in one of the planet's most spectacular locations. With our rhythmical movements and the empty page of the day ahead, we had ten whole hours to indulge in the treats of polar travel – the endless skies, the overwhelming sense of space and the sun rolling inexorably around the sky.

Twenty minutes later our easy gliding and my wandering thoughts came to an abrupt end. Clambering to the top of a pressure ridge, I saw we were in for a hard day. A dense maze of closely packed pressure ridges stretched to the horizon. It was like stumbling on the ice-encased ruins of an ancient civilisation. Seducing us with its mystery to go and explore, it was ready to ensnare even the wiliest of travellers. I turned to check Borge's face. He was shaking his head. It wasn't good news.

Irrespective of the ever changing, floating obstacle course, our system of navigation was still the sun. However, navigation was complicated by our constant backtracking and detours, and especially drift. As we drifted east or west, our longitude and therefore our local time changed relative to GMT. Knowing that at midnight local time the sun would be due north, we simply calculated the hourly sun angles from that.

In contrast to our ski to the South Pole, we skied through the local night with the sun tracking in front to keep our hands and faces warmer. Although at midnight navigation became easy, route finding was always at its hardest. With the low sun directly ahead, the shadows of the pressure ridges made even the smallest pile of rubble appear impassable. With everyone keen to take turns leading and route-finding, Borge often skied near the back. Fun as this was, we occasionally got into trouble, sometimes deep, wet trouble. As Thorlief, one of our younger team members, disappeared off into the midnight sun, team concentration began to wane. Borge, Rob and I were deeply engrossed in taking photos at the back and it wasn't until we summited the next pressure ridge that we discovered the carnage ahead. Skis, sledges and kit were strewn everywhere and Jeremy was sitting nursing his legs on the far side of a big depression. Panic had broken out and all I could hear were people shouting 'Borge!'

Scanning the scene I was alarmed to see Petter had disappeared beneath the ice, leaving little more than his head and thrashing arms poking through. Suddenly, at the speed of a bullet, Borge shot past me. Seconds later, after first taking photos of Petter, he helped him crawl out. Petter was shaken up, soaked through and covered in slush, and we had to act fast. At –30°C the slush was already freezing like armour plating. All of us nearby set to work to strip, dry and dress Petter before his core temperature started to plummet. Rummaging around, I found him some hand warmers. 'Here, Petter, get those down your pants. They'll warm you up,' I said, hoping to bring a smile to his face.

Forty-five minutes later, Petter was dressed and Jeremy, who'd also taken a dip, had changed his soggy footwear. As we carefully manoeuvred around the scene of the crime, the nature of the deception was immediately apparent. A large area of innocent-looking snow had been little more than a floating three-inch veneer.

By late in our designated 'afternoon', the team had spread out again with Borge, Thorlief, Rob and I trundling along at the back. Suddenly the ground shuddered and we stopped in our tracks.

'Did you feel that, Jo?' Rob asked. Before I'd even answered, loud pistol cracks and reverberating thumps passed under our feet, confirming what we'd suspected. The ice was breaking up. The only questions in my mind were, *Where will it break?* and *Is the whole team on the same side of it?*

'Rob, Jo, quick – leave your sleds. Come over here!' Borge shouted. Unclipping, we threw our traces to the ground and raced after him. As we did so, I realised why he was calling us over. Instead of running away, we were charging over to get front row seats for the birth of a pressure ridge. A frightening cacophony of noises built up as the ice started to bulge, flex and twist. Creaking and grinding gave way to loud hammering and pounding. Then, as if a depth charge had gone off, there was a deafening boom and glistening, wet slabs of frozen blue ocean were thrust into the air. We were transfixed with its movement, as if watching a dinosaur awake. As the ridge advanced, we steadily retreated. It was like being in a giant geology lab and witnessing plate tectonics in action. Borge shouted and waved to the rest of the group to come back, but seeing us dash madly toward the rending and colliding ice, they decided to stay put.

With a sound like a scrap metal yard at full bore, one block after another was forced up with the accompaniment of spine-tingling squeaking, as if giant styrofoam blocks were being ripped apart. In a dramatic ear-piercing crescendo, the ridge made its last moves towards the sky. Then as suddenly as it had started, the great leviathan that we stood on lay at rest once more. All that remained was the rushing sound of many waterfalls as the water drained back to the ocean. Awestruck, we returned to our sleds.

Later that day and after ten hours of hard work at sea level, I'd been caught out. Unlike when labouring at altitude, I had perspired and my goose down vest had acted like a sponge. It was now freezing into the equivalent of a wine cooler jacket around my body. There was nothing for it but a religious drying crusade. Feeling tired, cold, hungry and thirsty while sitting half naked in a tent at −10°C wasn't my idea of a good Friday night, but I had to get dry. With the stove blasting away, we set to work. Rob and I took to our kit with a penknife, cutting the globules of ice off our masks and balaclavas before stuffing them down our fronts, along with damp socks and gloves, to dry off. Every available source of heat was utilised to dry clothes: my freshly filled pee bag was shoved down my front, I wrapped my socks around my boil-in-the-bag casserole and my down vest around my hot water bottle. Everything was steaming nicely, including us.

The following morning there was much gnashing of teeth when we discovered we'd drifted several kilometres south overnight. But by way of compensation, we had a fine start to the day, with an abundance of frozen leads, many leading north. On the smooth, flat ice, we sped along with well-disciplined sleds. In contrast to the abundance of pressure ridges on previous days, we were all grateful to be in an apparent expansion zone, wrinkle free, but requiring more vigilance than ever. On the horizon, thankfully to the east of our intended track, we could already see opaque black clouds of 'frost smoke'. Signalling open water, they formed as the relatively warm water vapour rose from a freshly opened lead and froze on contact with the super-cooled air, which today was about −25°C. Borge's route-finding skills were intriguing. He told me, with great confidence, 'I can smell water.' At first I assumed he was bluffing, but days later I was amazed when I too smelt open water before even seeing it. It seemed that, like any animal under threat, we were becoming attuned to our predator.

Each time we reached a freshly frozen lead, we tested it by giving three sharp blows with the tip of a pole. Punching through even on the third blow made it marginal, leaving us no option but to continue hunting for better ice. Sea ice starts its life when single crystals grow together into what is known as frazil ice, eventually thickening into a soupy accumulation known as grease or slush ice. Wave action can herd this ice into what is known as pancake ice, which looks pretty but is lethal to tread on. Ideally, with cold calm conditions nilas ice will form, giving a crust of anything up to ten centimetres thick. This can also be known as rubber ice because of its ability to bend on waves or swell under pressure. But we had to find the right sort of nilas. Light nilas was usually safe to ski on but dark nilas, just a few centimetres thick and with the black ocean still visible beneath, was not. Of course, the thicker the ice the better and in just one season, ice can grow up to two metres thick from congelation growth as water molecules stick to the bottom of the ice sheet. However, from my perspective, watching Borge, who was nearly twice my weight, ski across it was always by far the best test.

By the end of the day, wispy high clouds obscured the sky and the watery sun provided little more than decoration. A chill wind had sprung up and a golden veil of spindrift hissed as it swept across the pack ice. Ethereal as it was, it didn't bode well for tomorrow.

As predicted, the next day turned out to be a beast of a day before we had even moved. We woke to discover we had drifted two kilometres south overnight. Borge's assurance that this was 'really unusual' was little consolation for us. The wind, which normally blew from the east, was now blowing from the north at 50 kph and it was this that would have a greater effect on pack ice movement than ocean currents. By the time we'd dismantled our tents, several tent poles had snapped in the wind like brittle twigs, necessitating speedy repairs before our departure.

Although it was only a ground storm reaching a mere 30 metres or so above the ice, it filled our entire world. Freezing temperatures, raging winds and poor visibility, along with vast swathes of rotten ice and unusable leads, made our navigation and progress slow. As I pulled up alongside Borge for our first break, he shouted over the wind at me, 'It's at least 40 below with the windchill so watch out for frostbite today.' As Rob and I checked each other over, he confirmed my suspicions.

'Your right cheek is white and waxy, Jo. Hold still, I'll try and cover it up for you.' Somehow, despite being ultra vigilant, I'd missed a tiny crack in my mask. I found myself envious of Rob's facial hair. There are many reasons for the preponderance of male explorers and I concluded that being able to grow a warm, cosy beard was one of them.

By 8 pm we were safely parcelled away in our tents out of the ravages of the wind. I investigated my ankles, which had become increasingly sore and discovered that my Achilles tendons were swollen into angry red golf balls. The effect of twisting my ankles well over 400 times every day, while my laces were lashed around each ankle to hold my outsized sloppy boots in place, had been like taking a cheese grater to my tendons. I now had a nasty case of Achilles tendonitis, and in a perfect world I would have prescribed ice, rest and anti-inflammatories and definitely not skiing to the North Pole.

The next day we woke to sunshine and large snowdrifts piled around our tent. Thankfully we had only been blown a mere kilometre south overnight, but as I took my first steps outside our tent, I was thrown into a blind panic. My ankles burned with pain and had seized up. As I set off with stilted movements, I was grateful for the distraction of a young pressure ridge that we tracked alongside. Free from drifted snow, its un-weathered and freshly broken edges were like massive sheets of piled-up broken glass. As the ice absorbed red and yellow light, reflecting only blue, a turquoise light seemed to emanate from its very core, as if the colours of a thousand tropical oceans were trapped inside.

Despite being near to tears with the pain from my ankles, it was a magnificent polar day. As we gathered on a recently frozen lead while Borge scouted the route ahead, I was captivated by what I saw. Translucent ice with the black sea beneath bore intricate white swirling patterns, as if the ice had somehow been exquisitely decorated from underneath with liquid icing sugar. Even more remarkable were the salt crystals or 'ice flowers' that dotted the surface like a winter garden in full bloom. Some looked like chrysanthemums and others like feathers, each of their delicate forms perfect and mesmerising.

Forty-five minutes later, we had advanced less than 100 metres. Rob hurtled down a ramp a metre and a half high and landed on his back. Seeing his sled was about to follow, I yelled. 'Mind your sled, it's . . .' I was too late. Rob's sled had careered into his head, leaving him dazed. Our next challenge equalled that of a military assault course and had us balancing on knife-edge blocks, crawling across our sleds and jumping watery chasms. After making repeated chains to pass, haul or throw equipment to each other we miraculously emerged on the other side without any icy baptisms.

The next day we were immersed once more in a furious ground storm with a vicious wind chill below −50°C. The wind felt like a hundred knives on bare flesh and exposure for more than a minute left us in serious danger of frostbite. Breaks were spent with our backs to the wind, buried beneath layers of masks and huddled in a tight group. Even with my goggles on my eyelids were swollen and awkward globules of ice hung from my eyelashes. Everyone was struggling. The cold had us in its grip.

Being too cold to take our usual break of ten minutes did have its advantages. We made good progress, covering more than 20 kilometres, though we also lost over two kilometres due to the continued southerly drift.

'This has been the worst weather in the five trips I've done like this,' Borge announced to us as we set up the tents.

'Just our bloody luck,' Jeremy said, but in a strange way I was rather pleased that we'd seen such grisly weather. After all, we had come to sample the extreme north, so we hadn't been disappointed. If we had wanted a beach holiday, we'd picked the wrong ocean.

Inside our tent, we began to investigate the day's wounds. Despite our conscientious efforts to stay covered up and warm, we had a selection of waxy white fingertips, toes, cheeks and noses. After patching Rob up, I set to work on my right cheek. It looked as if it had suffered a first degree burn and was raw, pink and oozing. But the cold burn on my tongue was by far the most unpleasant. Tunnelling through the small holes in my mask, the wind had blistered my tongue as if I'd scalded it on hot soup. By the end of the day, none of us were a pretty sight.

The peace and quiet of the next morning was shattered by a string of Norwegian expletives. Scrambling outside to investigate the commotion, we discovered the ice had opened up right beneath Thorlief and Petter's tent. The fissure was only six inches wide but it was a metre deep and the ocean was swilling around at the bottom of it. Running straight through camp, it was disconcertingly just feet from where our heads had been that night and we'd never even noticed. Despite camping on thick multiyear ice and right next to a pressure ridge, we'd been caught out. Moreover, although we'd gone to bed just 16 kilometres from the North Pole, we'd woken up 18 kilometres away.

Setting off, I skied at the back so that I could fiddle with my boots and take photos without disturbing the team's pace. Before long we were making our way through a field of old, wind-eroded ice rubble as though it were a museum of magnificent exhibits. In-filled and weathered from multiple seasons, a host of fantastical and ghostly ice shapes lay around. Whether elegant pillars, transparent cubes or luminous blue caves crowded with chandelier-like icicles, each one was a unique work of art. Underfoot lay a carpet of icy blue nodules, which made for awkward skiing. Our skis incorporated the latest technology and instead of using detachable synthetic fur skins to grip the snow, they had a unidirectional fish-scale effect carved into the ski itself. Yet in spite of having the latest kit, we still came a very poor second to local wildlife. Polar bears were far better equipped to traipse across the Arctic wastes, with tiny bumps and cavities on the soles of their feet that acted like suction cups.

As we sat for a break just four kilometres from the Pole, excitement was mounting. In 1894 Edward Whimper had called Everest the third Pole and within a matter of hours, Rob and I would be standing together on top of our third and final pole. By late afternoon we were finally within metres of the North Pole. But with no station, no flag pole or 'X' to mark the spot, we not only had to provide our own marker pole but we first had to find the North Pole. In the middle of a frozen ocean, our small team became the scene of a frenzied treasure hunt. Every minute that we didn't find it, we were drifting further away. Borge and Thorlief ran around holding out the GPS units as if they were metal detectors in search of gold. I hobbled excitedly behind them, clutching my camera ready for the brief moment that the GPS would read 89°59'·999 north. Suddenly Thorlief and Borge stopped dead.

'This is it! We're here!' Thorlief shouted ecstatically. It was 6.45 pm on 20 April 2005. We had arrived and were finally standing at the Geographic North Pole. The team erupted into celebration. For a few precious moments, this time unencumbered by oxygen masks, Rob and I stood and kissed in each other's arms on top of the world. As we stood together on the axis of the planet, it was a unique and unforgettable moment.

Being at the North Pole was not just about standing on top of the world, it was the final page of an incredible chapter in our lives. Even in our wildest dreams the Seven Summits hadn't seemed possible, and now, to have stood at both poles as well was sublime. We leant in silence against each other's puffy down-clad chests and pressed our cold noses together. Closing my eyes and with a smile on my lips, I was deeply grateful. God had not only watched over us every step of the way, he had brought us from the deepest valleys to the very highest summits – and so much more.

Epilogue

'You are never too old to set another goal or to dream a new dream.'

C. S. Lewis

WHEN WE ARRIVED at the North Pole we naively thought that was the end. But by the following morning we had drifted six kilometres while our helicopter was due to land at the North Pole. So it was back on with our skis and off to the North Pole again. Despite my sore ankles I was rather pleased at this turn of events – two North Pole visits for the price of one seemed like remarkably good value. We even stumbled on fresh polar bear tracks – though thankfully without the bear, as our armed guide had raced on ahead.

Within a matter of weeks of returning home, we had forgotten the freezing hostility of the arctic wastes and the North Pole was nothing more than a warm and satisfying glow in our memories. Having been on the road for several years with all our belongings in storage, it was finally time to settle. New challenges lay ahead. Rob started to look for work and I had a book to write. In our tiny rented flat in West London, a warm, comfortable bed, clean running water and a toilet with a seat were sensory heaven and even now have retained their novelty. One of the best things about returning to the UK after all our travels was that one particular person didn't want to see us – Dr Phillips. Rob had been downgraded to annual check-ups, a pleasurable demotion, and we are continually grateful for his clean bill of health.

Looking back over the last few years, there is so much we've been privileged to see and learn from our travels, not to mention the wonderful friends we've made along the way. The beauty and power of nature has constantly amazed us. The world has felt small, not just because of the ease of international travel but because despite the many cultural differences, people's basic struggles, hopes and fears link us all together.

After all our expeditions, coming home has been both a bewildering and wonderful experience. While our bodies have relished the creature comforts, the contrast between frugal mountain lifestyles and Western society has been stark and hard to adjust to. The pressures of consumerism seem to be homogenising us, playing on our herd instincts and attempting to set our internal compasses. Our society isn't an easy environment in which to discover who we really are, to fulfil our potential or follow our dreams. However, living in a democracy, having people that love and support us, being able to make a good living and take the opportunities life throws at us are all gifts we will never take for granted.

Since our return we have faced a barrage of questions from family, friends and media. Our families have asked us if we are really settling down and at times it has been hard to convince either them or ourselves. Especially when months after returning to London, the opportunity to climb Carstensz Pyramid, which had been closed to tourists for years, opened up. Located in West Papua, Indonesia, Carstensz Pyramid is not only a stunning rock climb but as a later addition to the Seven Summits, is sometimes known as the eighth summit.

Now eight months after Carstensz Pyramid, Rob has returned to work as a fund manager, while I am working on my second book, a photographic journal, and planning a return to physiotherapy. Looking back, it's still impossible to absorb all that has happened. We have gone from the darkest times when all we could do was pray, to the most sublime moments when it was intoxicating just to be alive.

We have often been asked 'How will you cope with London life?' The truth is, we don't know and are still finding out. Even after a year, we feel that we are still acclimatising to London. Maybe it's a bit like the death zone and we will never fully acclimatise ... that's probably a good thing! Others have asked 'Would you do it all again?' and without pause for breath we both answer 'Yes!' We may not want to climb the same mountains but we would definitely take time out. Taking a sabbatical has enabled us to experience a more balanced life, while having a profound effect on our relationship and wellbeing.

'So what's next, then?' has always been swift to follow. Perhaps unsurprisingly, we have no shortage of ideas for different projects, jobs and adventures but there is simply not enough time for them all. So in the end, like everyone else, we will need to prioritise and make choices. Our most important dream now is to start a family, and we are past the three-year mark after Rob's chemotherapy.

Of course, as potential parents we're not starting from the ideal position and we aren't spring chickens any more. But neither were we in an ideal position when we started our expeditions. Very few people ever get to pursue dreams from the perfect start point. For most of us there are obstacles, real or perceived, that stand in the way – the time is never right. The most difficult thing will always be deciding what to do and then doing it, almost irrespective of how the odds are stacked. It can be hard not to be put off by the messages surrounding us in the valleys of our routine lives. Right at the beginning, some people told us we were crazy to be attempting such difficult mountains after all we'd been through. Occasionally we wondered if they were right but sensing more than ever that life isn't a rehearsal, we felt we'd be crazy not to try.

Having a family will be our next Everest – we still have no idea if it's even possible. Perhaps just as coping with cancer was good training for climbing big mountains, so our expeditions may prove to be good preparation for parenting. Hopefully, God willing, we will have the opportunity to find out.

As we have reintegrated into 'normal' life once again, we have felt more conscious than ever of the pressures that surround us all. Society leads us to believe that we need to be young, beautiful and talented to succeed but there is rarely success without plain hard work . . . and what is success anyway? Maybe in the end it is just a matter of perspective.

We are sometimes asked how we have achieved everything, as if there is something different about us. It seems to us that we are ordinary people who were living ordinary lives, were faced with some difficult events and made a series of decisions. So if anything makes us different, maybe it's just the choices we made.

Someone recently said to us, 'But you were lucky, you had a reason to take a break.' In many respects they were right, cancer did bring us to a cross road. Of course, we would never have wished for cancer – no-one would – but as it has happened, we are glad for all we have learnt, the experiences we have had and for the way our relationship has been enriched. Surviving this difficulty has been a blessing in disguise and has helped us focus on what is really important.

Stepping out of the rat race was one of the hardest things we chose to do. At times it seemed easier to just keep running. But leaving good careers and the confinement of our 'comfort zones' to embrace fears of the unknown turned out to be the most exhilarating and liberating thing we have ever done. If we had over-insulated ourselves from risk, we might have lost all the reward. Ultimately, our greatest reward has not been the Poles or even the mountains – it has been our journey together. Along the way we have learnt to communicate more effectively and our love and appreciation for each other has deepened. But we will never stop learning and like any relationship, ours isn't a bed of roses but rather a garden in need of constant maintenance and loving care. Above all, to have spent this quality time with my husband, soul mate and best friend has been immeasurably precious.

Looking ahead, good health can never be taken for granted. No doubt we shall continue to seek mountaintop experiences, physical or otherwise, they help to keep our daily valley lives in perspective. From the summits, our horizons always expand, we see a bigger picture and seek different things. Perhaps, in the strangest of ways, occasionally having our heads in the clouds will help keep our feet on the ground.

SPONSORS

Rob and Jo would like to express their thanks to the following companies for their support and sponsorship of their North Pole expedition.

BLUE DIAMOND	www.bluediamond.com
HAMPSHIRE FLAG CO.	www.hampshireflag.co.uk
HIGH FIVE	www.highfive.co.uk
HEAT MAX	www.heatmax.com
K2	www.k2-uk.co.uk
MARMOT	www.marmot.com
MOUNTAIN EQUIPMENT	www.mountain-equipment.co.uk
NALGENE	www.nalgene-outdoor.com
NAVMAN	www.navman.com
NIGEL BRAGGINS DESIGN	braggins@globalnet.co.uk
PADDY POWER	www.paddypower.com
PETER GAFFNEY	www.creativematch.com
PEGLERS	www.peglers.co.uk
RAB	www.rab.uk.com
SNOW AND ROCK	www.snowandrock.com
SOFT PRESS	www.softpress.com
TILLAMOOK	www.tcsjerky.com
WEST MERIA	www.westmeria.com

CANCER RESEARCH UK

THE FACTS . . .

- More than one in three people in the UK will develop cancer during their lifetime.
- More people in this country survive cancer now than ever before, thanks to earlier detection and better treatments.
- Cancer Research UK is the world's leading independent organisation dedicated to cancer research.
- They support research into all aspects of cancer through the work of more than 3,000 scientists, doctors and nurses.
- In 2004–05 their total scientific spend was £217 million.
- Cancer Research UK is almost entirely funded by donations from the public.

Please, if you feel able, join Rob and Jo and support Cancer Research UK. Every donation will enable them to better continue with their vital and life saving work.

To make a donation:

Visit: http://www.cancerresearchuk.org/donate/
Call: 01865 716 655 and quote reference: RE304974077
Mail: Cheques made payable to 'Cancer Research UK'
With the reference: RE304974077 on the back to:

Cancer Research UK, Unit 7400, The Quorum,
Oxford Business Park North, Garsington Road, Cowley,
Oxford, OX4 2JZ

Thank you for your support.

For more information about cancer visit: www.cancerhelp.org.uk

For information about the early signs of cancer and the healthy choices that could reduce your risk visit:
www.cancerresearch uk.org/health

Index

LIFE AND LIMB
Jamie Andrew

0 7499 5052 8

Jamie Andrew's survival and rescue after five nights trapped by a ferocious storm in 1999 has passed into Alpine legend. It was a miracle that he survived; but Jamie had to come to terms not only with the death of his close friend, Jamie Fisher, who died beside him – but also with the loss of all his limbs to frostbite.

Since the accident, Jamie has struggled painfully and successfully to overcome his disabilities; not only has he learnt to walk (and run) on his prosthetic legs, but also to ski, snowboard, paraglide – and even take up his beloved mountaineering again.

His courage, determination and sense of humour shine through the words of this remarkable book ... *Life and Limb* is a genuinely life-enhancing read.

Scottish Mountaineer

Like Joe Simpson, Andrew has discovered a latent talent for writing that only a mountaineering epic seems to have allowed him to uncover. And like *Touching the Void*, *Life and Limb* is brilliantly written and utterly un-put-down-able. If ever a tale evokes the phrase 'life affirming' then this is it.

On the Edge magazine

Jamie Andrew, born in 1969, was brought up near Glasgow; in his teens he became an active mountaineer and rock climber, making many successful climbs on severe routes in the Alps, Dolomites, and in Yosemite Valley, California. After Edinburgh University he took up a career as an industrial rope access technician, carrying out maintenance and construction projects on high buildings, oil rigs and bridges by means of abseil.

Since Jamie's accident in 1999, he has participated in many sporting activities, including running in the London Marathon, skiing, snowboarding, paragliding and caving – as well as returning to rock climbing and mountaineering.

In 2002, Jamie Andrew was the overall winner of the Lloyds TSB/*Sunday Mail* Great Scot Award. In 2004 *Life and Limb* was shortlisted for the Boardman Tasker Prize and won the Banff Mountain Book Festival Prize for Mountain Literature. Jamie lives in Edinburgh with his wife Anna and three children, Iris, Alex and Liam. A documentary reconstruction of Jamie Andrew's story was shown on *Survivors* on ITV.